# PRESSURE GROUPS
# &
# POLITICS
# IN
# ANTEBELLUM TARIFFS

JONATHAN J. PINCUS

# Pressure Groups

# &

# Politics

# in

# Antebellum Tariffs

COLUMBIA UNIVERSITY PRESS

NEW YORK

1977

JONATHAN J. PINCUS

*is*

*a fellow in economic history*

*at*

*the Australian National University,*
*Canberra.*

*This book received*
*the Columbia University Prize*
*in American Economic History*
*in Honor of*
*Allan Nevins.*

*HF*
*1754*
*.P62*

**Library of Congress Cataloging in Publication Data**

PINCUS, JONATHAN J   1939–

PRESSURE GROUPS AND POLITICS IN ANTEBELLUM TARIFFS.

BASED ON THE AUTHOR'S THESIS, STANFORD UNIVERSITY, 1972.

BIBLIOGRAPHY: P.

INCLUDES INDEX.

1. TARIFF—UNITED STATES—HISTORY.
2. PRESSURE GROUPS—UNITED STATES—HISTORY.   I. TITLE.

HF 1754.P62       382.7'0973       76-51733

ISBN 0-231-03963-8

Columbia University Press
New York and Guildford, Surrey
Copyright © 1977 Columbia University Press.
All rights reserved.
Printed in the United States of America

*For Daniel*

# *Foreword*

---

WHETHER gauged by the number and diversity of the branches of industry it affected, or by the public revenues it generated, or by the intensity of the political passions it aroused, the tariff constituted the most important economic policy instrument deployed by the United States' government during the nineteenth century. Although the tariff question was once a central subject in textbooks on American economic history, curiously, it has been slow to regain a corresponding place of prominence in the literature of the "new economic history." Still more surprisingly, no economist or economic historian has seriously studied the positive side of the political economy of American tariff legislation—certainly not since F. W. Taussig's 1931 revision of his *Tariff History of the United States.* Insofar as the general subject has been studied recently, it is the normative aspect that has preoccupied economists. Following the main line of analytical concern in Taussig's own writings, they have focussed on the *consequences* of import taxes. They have tried to determine whether America's indulgence in "protectionism" was justified or not—whether tariffs led to net gains or losses of economic welfare when compared with other relevant (and in some case historically irrelevant) policy alternatives. Except for a few political scientists' forays into more recent episodes of tariff-making, the question of how and why specific pieces of tariff legislation took their actual shapes has remained sorely neglected.

The publication of Jonathan Pincus's work therefore marks not only the concerted resumption of a long and esteemed line of scholarly research on a subject of obvious importance to students of American economic history, but also a most welcome redirection of the inquiry, one well aimed at securing a deeper understanding of the interdependence of economic and political processes. For this book enlists the methods of quantitative economic history in a dual theoretical and historical mission. On the one hand, the author has taken up the task of developing a general conceptual framework for positive economic analyses of the historical formation of public policies. On the other hand, he has sought, by applying it, to explain the concrete details of America's first piece of thorough-going protectionist legislation—the Tariff Act of 1824.

In recent years proponents of "the new institutional economics" have argued that it is possible to make substantial headway in understanding the evolving forms of collective action (of which tariff legislation is one instance) by concentrating attention on the implications of such action for the efficiency of resource allocation. This approach seeks to put normative economic analysis to positive uses, by proceeding on the hypothesis that where private market action cannot exhaust all opportunities to make some members of the society better off without harming others, efforts will ensue to achieve the Pareto optimum through one social device or another. Its adherents therefore eschew close inquiry into the extent to which collective action may be motivated by purely redistributive objectives, and accord the detailed workings of established (political) institutions at most a transient influence upon the pattern of resource allocation.

Pincus, however, has taken a quite different tack. He argues that faith in the relevance of the Coase theorem is vitiated by the existence of significant transactions and bargaining costs in both the political and the economic sphere. The historical context of the early American economy, in particular, affords no real basis for supposing that individuals pursuing their narrow economic interest must have forced collective decisions that were socially efficient, in the sense of maximizing aggregate income or wealth. Quite the contrary. There are cogent reasons to expect that collections of economic agents do not behave (collectively) as though they were a single individual faced with a problem of choice within the same set of aggregate opportunities. Pincus suggests that existing legal institutions, technological conditions affecting access to information, and norms of social and political behavior, all created *biases* in the prevailing structure of bargaining and transactions costs. Such differential costs affect the voluntary formation of collective action groups within societies—favoring particular political pressure groups and legislative coalitions which may utilize the machinery of representative government to pursue their members' narrow ends largely by redistributive means, and quite possibly at the sacrifice of social efficiency. As his work amply demonstrates, this is a far more fruitful conceptual framework within which to re-examine the economic history of American tariff politics.

The essence of the political problem posed by the enactment of protective tariff legislation lies in the formation of redistributive coalitions. That tariffs tax consumers for the benefit of producers is transparent, and that prohibitive duties which reduce the general level of imports are an implicit tax upon export producers is only slightly less obvious. More generally, effective protection against the competition of foreign producers is equally protection against domestic producers who compete for the same economic resources. Inasmuch as the benefits of effective protection cannot be distributed to all domestic producers, to enact a tariff bill it is necessary to form a politically viable coalition among some subset of domestic producer-interests. But herein lies a second problem. While there may exist many subsets of interests that could constitute such mutually beneficial coalitions, it is not clearly advantageous for all the parties whose interests would be thus advanced to contribute the resources required to secure those gains in the political arena. Even for producers in a particular branch of industry, an effective tariff rate constitutes a form of "public good." The benefits will accrue to all similar members of the industry, whether or not they have borne the cost of obtaining them.

These basic insights have been skillfully elaborated by Pincus, who draws upon a sophisticated knowledge of international trade theory to identify (and ultimately to quantify) structural characteristics of early American industries which would have affected the distribution of the potential economic rents that a tariff bill could supply. From modern public goods theory he has drawn insights into other structural characteristics of industries which promoted fuller revelation of their members' demands for tariff benefits, through their contribution to pressure-group activities. And to round out the picture, Pincus shows how locational characteristics of the industries involved interacted with the geographical basis of Congressional representation to influence the degree of success of translating pressure-group efforts into formation of effective legislative coalitions.

When put to the ultimate empirical test of accounting for the pattern of nominal tariffs enacted in 1824, Pincus's focus upon the explanatory power of industries' structural characteristics proves gratifyingly illuminating. But, along the way to this econometric dénouement, he also provides many fascinating, more general historical insights. Among them are those concerning the features of so-called infant industries which raised their chances of obtaining tariff protection, even from legislators unenlightened by the logic of economists' normative infant-industry arguments; and the pragmatic strategy of Congressional coalition-building that underlay the rhetoric of Henry Clay's American System.

Thus, at both the broad conceptual level and the level of substantive historical detail, Jonathan Pincus here furnishes a new foundation for the resumption of research into the political economy of American tariff policy in the ensuing era of sectional conflicts, and beyond. His findings leave us eager to discover whether the structural characteristics of industries that he has identified continued to exert a powerful influence on the levels of import duties. Perhaps, despite entanglement with other issues of sectional and partisan conflict, and despite entrapment in the complex machinery of Congressional log-rolling on disparate bills, American protectionist legislation may yet be found to have retained the largely coherent form that characterized the initial Act of 1824.

Paul A. David
*Stanford, California*

# Acknowledgments

T H I S book developed from my 1972 Stanford University doctoral dissertation, which was completed while I was teaching at Simon Fraser University. Extensions and revisions were made from 1973 to 1975 when I was Research Fellow and, later, Fellow in Economic History at the Institute of Advanced Studies, Australian National University, and during study-leave at Stanford early in 1976. Along the way I received enormous assistance, which it is now my privilege to acknowledge.

My debt to Paul A. David is massive, for his generous and enthusiastic encouragement. His was the suggestion to begin a reassessment of tariff history using recent ideas about the voluntary supply of public goods and the modern theory of international trade. He has a mind both creative and critical, and the instinct to know when the plants he tends need gentle, and when vigorous, pruning. By radiating excitement in discovering which of the many interesting ideas generated each day will work, he helped me over the first step from theory to economic history and he did much more. To Paul goes credit, but no blame.

Stuart W. Bruchey, Allan Nevins Professor of American Economic History at Columbia University, undertook the dreadful task, not only of reading the manuscript with scrupulous care, but of guiding me on its structure and presentation. The final product is far better for his many suggestions. In its various versions, the whole was read by Noel G. Butlin, Neville Cain, and Soren T. Nielsen, and greatly improved. Noel Butlin in addition made available to me the time necessary for its revision. I had extremely valuable discussions with William Brock, Robert Gregory, and Edward Sieper, and benefited from the friendship and advice of Donald Keesing.

It would be nearly impossible to mention all those who have assisted me in different ways, but I would like to thank Joseph Bisignano, Don DeVoretz, Robert Gallman, Herbert Grubel, Peter Lindert, Edwin Lipinski, Steven Magee, Gae Pincus, Michael Porter, Ken Tucker, Graham Tucker, and Gavin Wright. Thanks are also extended to the 1970–71 Abramovitz-David-Milward Seminar at Stanford, the 1971 Cliometrics Conference and audiences at Canberra, Chapel Hill, Davis, LaTrobe, Monash, Rochester, and Simon Fraser universities. Financial assistance was provided by Stanford University, the Canada Council, and the Australian-American Education Foundation. Publication was assisted by a grant from the Allan Nevins' Fund.

J J P

# Contents

# PRESSURE GROUPS
## &
## POLITICS
### IN
## ANTEBELLUM TARIFFS

CHAPTER ONE

# *Introduction*

---

T H E term "Free trade," like "Virginity," refers to one condition only, whereas "Protection" covers a multitude, as does "Sin." This book is an investigation into the morphology of the sin of Protection, not into the conditions of a fall from Grace.

The tariff was of major importance in nineteenth-century U.S. economic policy and figured prominently in contemporary discussions, both scholarly and popular.[1] With the spread of Listian ideas, it had become national policy (a component of Clay's American System, providing the rationale and revenue for internal improvements), and a subject of international conflict and negotiation.[2] Clearly, a correct understanding of it is vital to the interpretation of antebellum political economy.

The United States' duties were not devised by a dictator, or even by an economist with a social welfare function to maximize: a theory of political decision making is needed to analyze the composition of tariff acts. Since the tariff was a major element of antebellum economic policy, we must apply to it an economic theory of political decisions—not psychological or sociological theories—when explaining which products received an import duty, and at what rates. More than twenty years ago Kindleberger (1951) drew attention to the importance of group decisions in resource allocation. In the neoclassical theory of markets, individuals act only as such, and so Kindleberger went searching in sociology for a theory of collective decision-making. This lead was not widely followed, but rather the faith of economists—that models of individual behavior are apposite to the analysis of all economic behavior—has prevailed, recently to be confirmed by work on property

[1] The other main policy questions were banking regulation, land sales and internal improvements.

[2] Since export taxes were unconstitutional, the main sources of federal revenues were tariffs, internal taxes and fees.

rights and institutions. This book accepts the economist's viewpoint while questioning the uncritical use of economic ideas.

Economic historians, like other applied economists, have succumbed to the power and persuasion of Pareto efficiency, believing, along with Arrow, that "if an opportunity for a Pareto improvement exists, then there will be an effort to achieve it through some social device or other." [3] The implication is that Pareto improvements, because they create more than enough to compensate losers, are especially easy to bring about. But, we do not invariably see all opportunities taken to improve efficiency, although we might if we waited long enough: Arrow's prediction is timeless. More importantly, most policy changes seem to leave someone worse off: failure to compensate losers does not seem enough to block movements toward Pareto efficiency. Indeed, many changes seem *inefficient*—the gainers benefit by less than the costs they cause others. Therefore, it is neither necessary nor sufficient that a change improve efficiency, let alone leave no one worse off. [4] Similar objections can be raised against the use made of Coase's (1960) analysis of social cost (examples cited in chapter 5). The unfortunate tendency has been to misuse Coase-like arguments to justify a preoccupation with efficiency and to deduce behavior on the essentially teleological ground that it advances efficiency, rather than to infer efficiency from behavior.

The central argument of this book is as follows. An import duty aided directly domestic factors of production employed in the import-competing industry. Each factor had a common but not identical interest in obtaining the particular industry's protective duty. Because each import competitor benefited from protection regardless of his effort to achieve it, a duty took on aspects of a "public good" to the interested producers: so far as some (or any one) of them succeeded through their own efforts in obtaining a favorable duty, they could not exclude the rest from enjoyment of the fruits of their labor and therefore each would have liked to "free ride," and to leave the lobbying for others. [5]

---

[3] Arrow (1974), p. 8.

[4] Weitzman (1974) has shown under quite general conditions that to limit access to resources by charging efficient rents will make the mobile factor no better off, despite the improvement in efficiency.

[5] Public goods theory, particularly Olson's (1968) contribution, has been the economic historians' other main borrowing from the economics of social choice. The two ingre-

The free-rider problem would disappear if, for example, the domestic import-competing industry were in the hands of a monopoly based on ownership of a specific, nontraded resource. The monopolist would then be able to appropriate all the benefits from any impost.

Therefore, the size of the aggregate economic interests of a group is a poor guide to the strength of its action. Few tariffs have caused more economic good than harm, so there is a presumption that the strength of opposition would have exceeded support if there had been no costs of action and no free-rider problem in lobbies.[6] In particular, consumers had more to lose in 1824 than producers to gain, yet producers exerted more pressure in Congress.

From the analysis in chapter 5 I draw two postulates about the ratio of collective effort to collective benefit. First, that the fewer the individuals who enjoy the benefits and, for any group size, the more concentrated the benefits, then the larger the ratio of group effort to effect; second, that the intensity of pressure-group activity depends on the geographical dispersion of the individuals, because the costs of obtaining information about the actions of others and of coordinating and monitoring efforts can be expected to rise with distance, especially in periods such as the 1820s in which communications were slow and costly.

These theoretical conclusions about lobbies considered as voluntary associations are supported to some extent by the record of public petitions ("memorials") around 1824. A number of large but widespread industries were virtually silent on protection, whereas memorials were received from small, local industries. Manufacturers in the cities were active, although it was rare to find on one memorial producers of the same product from different locations. More common were petitions covering a variety of goods produced in one city, especially Philadelphia. Opposition tended to come from groups organized for other purposes, such as agricultural societies, state legislatures, and chambers of commerce.

In common with most economic decisions, the tariff altered the division of the pie as well as its size, so we need an economic analysis

---

dients—the definition of efficiency and the supply theory of public goods—are mixed in the work on institutional change of Davis and North (1971), and produce, quite unnoticed, a cyclical pattern of action and counteraction (see chapter 5).

[6] Assuming also no asymmetries in knowledge of the likely effects of import duties.

of the distribution of benefits and costs. Recent economic theory of the
effects of tariffs has concentrated on statements about social welfare, or
about the income of broadly defined factors of production.[7] It is ironic
that a suitable starting point for the analysis of the cause of tariffs—a
formula with which to measure the effects of a change in tariffs on
value-added or rent in the various industries—was available from at
least the 1860s, namely, the compensatory tariff, or the net tariff (now
better known as the numerator of the effective protection formula).
Theorists' concentration on the effects of tariffs to the exclusion of the
causes of tariffs has meant that no systematic use has been made of either
the net tariff or effective protection in explaining the process of
tariff formation.[8] An analysis of the consequences of tariffs, both foreseen
and unforeseen, is a major element in the explanation of tariff formation,
but what is also needed is an explicit theory about how the expected
consequences were translated into decisions.[9]

Taussig suggests that the votes in Congress on the tariff bills of the
1820s were a broad reflection of sectional economic interests. The balance
in New England, for example, swung toward protectionism as the
New England economy switched from commerce and agriculture to
manufacturing. Although the concern of this book is not Congressional
voting patterns, Taussig's theory provides a starting point for a theory
of tariff formation.

It was in Congress that bargains were made and compromises
reached. Just as the anticipated aggregate pressure exerted by a group
was not simply in proportion to the aggregate gains motivating the

[7] Histories of the tariff reflect prevailing economic theory, and the emphasis in historical
writing on the triumph of protection over free trade is a manifestation of the decidedly
normative orientation of trade theory, an orientation which indeed persists. The "infant
industry" argument, now called "second best," had a widespread acceptance in the last
century as a justification for some tariffs; to those writers who, like Taussig, regarded it as
the *only* valid argument, all other tariffs were bad, and did not invite extensive theoretical
analysis, let alone empirical investigation.

[8] See, however, Ray (1974).

[9] Examination of the *economic* content of the legislative debates on the passage of tariffs
in the Congresses of the last century has failed to establish any links between the economic
arguments and what was passed or defeated in the bills. See the discussion by
Edwards (1970) of the debates of 1824 and 1894. For a very different reading of the
debates of 1923–24, selecting not economic-theoretic but less refined stuff like bargaining,
see chapter 3.

pressure, so also the effectiveness of the pressure in Congress was not simply in proportion to the total pressure on Congress. Tariff items were debated seriatim, and the opposition case was that each duty benefited the few at the expense of the many exporters and consumers. Proponents, of course, claimed national advantages for protection. The pushing of narrow economic interests in Congress was made difficult, and the promoters of the tariff bill in 1824 therefore contracted it to ensure its passage. Some industries for which substantial increases had been proposed in the defeated bill of 1820 and in the bill of 1824 as introduced, had to be content with more modest increases or none at all. The bill's managers steered the narrow course between losing support through concessions, and having the bill defeated for attempting too much.

Thus cohesiveness of industry lobby made for more pressure, but narrowness for more Congressional resistance. In chapter 6 these conflicting forces are sorted out as well as the data allow, and it is found that larger duties were obtained in 1824 by industries located in numerous states (and so having many sympathetic senators) but with geographically or industrially concentrated production units. In addition, industries with low proprietorial income (high tariff leverage), and those faced with high input duties, received favorable consideration.[10]

The work on American tariffs closest to this in question and method is Schattschneider's *Politics, Pressures and the Tariff* (1935), which examined the tariff revision of 1929–30 as a political process resolving the multiplicity of conflicting pressures from interested groups. Schattschneider's main sources were the public hearings on the Hawley-Smoot bill, which he used to examine the behavior of groups and the legislature (especially the uses made of the evidence collected by the committees). A detailed consideration of the tens of thousands of tariff items in the bill was too great a task to be undertaken by the Congressional committees, so that although the Hawley-Smoot tariff appears complex, it is in fact simple, having three principles: equality, consistency, and precedent. The tariff attempted to protect everyone, and at fairly uniform rates.[11] In Schattschneider's discussion of pressure

---

[10] The chief source of the data, or rather *capta*, is the *Digest of Manufactures* (1820).

[11] P. Desai (1970) skillfully criticized the Indian Tariff Commission for its lack of consistent economic principles.

groups (p. 104), the central question (which I take up in chapters 4 and 5) is whether "the agitation of any group [is] roughly proportional to its stake in the policy." He generally found that there was little opposition to tariffs unless they threatened the existence of some economic group. The most vigorous activity in favor of protective duties came from groups directly and positively affected, namely, the manufacturers of the product concerned. The lack of opposition on the part of other manufacturing industries is explained by a number of factors, the most important of which is that opponents found it expedient to accept protection in practice and seek tariffs of their own.[12] Schattschneider also notes that when those harmed sought compensation instead of attempting opposition, there were usually fewer duties to influence.

There is an important difference between the revisions of 1929–30 and of 1824: in Lowi's (1964) terms, the former was "distributive," that is, a process of handing out individual favors in such a manner that losers and recipients never come into direct confrontation;[13] the 1824 tariff was "redistributive," that is, it involved conflict between winning and losing social groups. Southern planters and Northern merchants fought against protectionism, attempting to lower duties harmful to their interests (and most were considered harmful). This difference, however, does not greatly alter the nature of the case study in chapter 6, because within the redistributive setting, the *pattern* of the tariff still has to be explained.

In some ways, therefore, this book extends Schattschneider's work and attempts to answer similar questions about the intensity and success of pressure group activity. I do not duplicate the range and diversity of his study, but concentrate on the development of a more rigorous theory to derive testable hypotheses about collective action on the tariff of 1824. The considerable economic literature on collective decisions allows a range of outcomes: no unique result can be predicted. Investigation of particular decisions may help narrow the range, and highlight some outcomes as being more likely. Not only is a thorough

[12] In another context, by the end of the 1920s the Australian tariff was criticized for its "protection all round." "Clearly we must reach the stage where government would be promoting each industry by taxing all the others; and the end, in effect, would be a perverted, expensive and very unstable 'Free Trade,'" Brigden et al. (1929), pp. 27, 28.

[13] Lowi (1964), p. 690.

understanding of collective decisions important for the historian, it is also essential to those who want to influence policy. The economist as adviser may wish to tailor his advice to what is politically possible, and (to borrow from tariff theory) recommend second-best policies if the advocacy of first-best precludes the possibility of his having *any* influence at all.

The methodology used in this book is at variance with that proposed by Davis and North (1971). The difference can be briefly characterized: the Davis and North model, in discussing "institutional changes," concentrates on increases in efficiency—action is likely if it improves allocation; this book focuses on distribution—action is likely if it benefits a small cohesive group.[14] The latter viewpoint is useful, for example, in providing an alternative explanation of the historical tendency, apparently satisfactory from the normative point of view, that tariffs do seem to be levied on the products of "infant industries." The model, rather than assuming wisdom on the part of the tariff makers or a political "invisible hand," points to the bases of the tariff power of the infants, especially to the appropriability of the gains or losses from tariffs which were manifested as changes in rents or quasi-rents of essential factors of production like knowledge or natural resources, held in relatively few hands, and in fairly inelastic inward or outward supply.[15]

The plan of the rest of the book is as follows. A brief tariff history makes up the remainder of this chapter. Chapter 2 reviews the economic history of the United States to 1824, with emphasis on the external and manufacturing sectors, and provides details of rates of protection to that date. The third chapter is about visible lobbying (mostly memorials) and the tactics and debates in Congress in the early 1820s.

---

[14] In their section on tariffs, Davis and North (1971) argue that pressure over the tariffs from voluntary associations varied according to the comparative disadvantage of the industry, the size of the group, and whether the group was a formal one with primary functions other than tariff lobbying. The Seventeenth Amendment in 1913 required the direct election of Senators and reduced the effectiveness of tariff lobbies (pp. 178–82). None of these conclusions are at great variance with this chapter. However, they are not supported by the formal model developed by Davis and North. On the contrary, it is possible to argue that a proper consideration of the distributional consequences of what Davis and North call "institutional changes" greatly reduces the range of application of their model. See Pincus (1972), pp. 18–42; Olmstead and Goldberg (1975).

[15] Johnson (1970) restates the normative case for infant industry tariffs.

The theoretical and empirical effects of tariffs are outlined in chapter 4. The basic theoretical ideas about lobbying behavior are developed in chapter 5, which also includes some elementary notions about committee decisions. There follows an empirical investigation of the Tariff of 1824, treated as a "local issue," [16] that is, the rates of duty were the result of pressure from affected economic groups operating in a representative democracy. In particular, the pattern of tariffs in 1824 is seen mostly as the result of efforts by producers to increase their rents or quasi-rents (government revenues being then ignored, but given a role in the dynamics of tariff history sketched in chapter 7). The appendices contain details and more data on the effects of tariffs.

## BRIEF TARIFF HISTORY [17]

The ratio of duty collected to dutiable imports (table 1.1) suffers from several defects as a measure of the "height" of protection, not the least being that prohibitive duties yield no revenue.[18] Rather better, if available, would be the average of duties weighted by domestic production or the sum of production and import. Tariff history from 1789 to 1909 can be divided into five periods.[19]

*1789 to 1815.* The first tariff was passed under pressure of urgent revenue needs. It imposed a general 5 percent levy, higher ad valorem rates on some luxuries, and specific duties on hemp, cordage, nails, manufactured iron, and glass. Progressively, the tariff was raised and extended to provide revenue; by 1804 the usual rate was 17.5 percent. Duties were doubled during the War of 1812.

> For nearly twenty years after the formation of the Union other subjects so absorbed the attention of public men that no distinct opinion appears in their utterances for or against protective duties. . . . Both Federalists and Republicans were influenced in their attitudes to the

[16] The phrase is Stanwood's (1903), whose work is essential reading for students of the politics of nineteenth-century tariffs.

[17] See Dewey (1903), Ratner (1972), Stanwood (1903), and Taussig (1931).

[18] The comparison between the average rate on all imports and the average on dutiable imports, however, gives some guide to the relative importance of the free list: the ratio of the two figures is equal to the ratio of dutiable imports to all imports.

[19] See chapter 2 for a fuller discussion of the first two periods.

TABLE 1.1

*Ratio of Duty Collected to Imports, Selected Years,*
*1789–1909*
(PERCENT)

| DATES | DUTIES/ DUTIABLE IMPORTS | DUTIES/ ALL IMPORTS |
|---|---|---|
| 1789 | — | 8.5 |
| 1794 | — | 14 |
| 1821 | 36 | — |
| 1824 | 38 | — |
| 1830 | 49 | 45 |
| 1840 | 30 | 15 |
| 1842–46 | 32 | — |
| 1846–57 | 26 | 23 |
| 1857–61 | 20 | 16 |
| 1862–65 | 35 | — |
| 1873–75 | 39 | 28 |
| 1876–83 | 43 | 30 |
| 1884–90 | 45 | 30 |
| 1890–92 | 49 | 22 |
| 1894–97 | 41 | 21 |
| 1897–1909 | 46 | 26 |

*Sources:* D. R. Dewey (1903), p. 83; S. Ratner (1972), passim.
*Note:* Until 1821, no separation was made between dutiable and
free imports.

question of protection most of all by its bearing on the other more prominent questions on which parties began to be divided.[20]

Although revenue, national defense, and independence were cited as
the justification, the early pattern of protection reflected the desire,
especially of Massachusetts and Pennsylvania, for a continuation of the
aid they had given to some manufactures. The sectional interest
theory, usually applied to the next period, can be pushed back in time:
some states had more to gain from tariffs on manufactures than others.
And clearly, the industrial pattern of duties was not merely a matter of
defense.

[20] Taussig (1931), p. 13. These other questions involved foreign policy toward the
French and English. Stanwood emphasizes revenue as cause of tariff changes: Stanwood
(1903), I, p. 111.

*1816 to 1832.* This was a time of rising tariffs and sectional tension. The Act of 1816 authorized substantial increases over previous peace-time rates, and can be considered the first in which "protection was adopted as a fundamental basis of the fiscal system and revenue was subordinated to industrial needs," [21] namely, to the manufacturing of cottons, iron (including nails), paper, and glass. The Tariff of 1824, a major revision not made when the Treasury was bare or overflowing, aroused violent sectional opposition because of the degree to which it extended the sectional principle.

The woolen industry, which had not been generously treated in 1824 and which had suffered from the combined effects of the English crisis of 1825–26 and removal of English raw wool duties, failed by one Senate vote to secure additional protection in 1827. Further agitation after the Harrisburg convention by a broader coalition succeeded in 1828, but not exactly in the manner expected. The anti-Adams forces wished both to embarrass Adams's men and to defeat a tariff which some Jacksonians could not oppose openly. The "odious" features of this act were high duties on wool and woolens and on iron, hemp, mo-lasses, and other raw materials, especially those used by New Eng-land's commerce and distilleries.

This "Tariff of Abominations" was soon amended by reductions on molasses, tea, coffee, and salt in 1830 (thereby reducing the Treasury surplus) and on some raw and intermediate inputs in 1832, leaving a tariff like that of 1824, with revenue which was largely collected from duties on protected manufactures, but with no system of minimum val-uations. It was the Act of 1832 that sparked South Carolina's nullifica-tion.

*1833 to 1860.* Apart from a brief reversal in 1842, this was a time of relatively low and falling rates. While insisting on the Force Act against South Carolina, Jackson called for reduction of protection, as did Trea-sury Secretary McLane. The leader of the protectionists and champion

---

[21] Dewey (1902), p. 162. Taylor (1951) disagrees, calling 1816 "mildly protective:" the higher textile duties were to be temporary, and the minimum valuations had unforeseen consequences (p. 360), whereas Taussig (1931) attributes (p. 18) the Act of 1816 not to a strong public feeling for a permanent policy of protection, but to "a knot of young men of the rising generation, who had brought about the war and felt in a measure responsible for its results."

of the American System, Henry Clay, arranged a Compromise whereby duties were progressively reduced to a uniform 20 percent by 1842. In the early years of the operation of the Compromise, the Treasury was in surplus, for the debt was almost paid and land sales were buoyant. Because protectionists preferred the burden of taxation to fall on imports, Clay had proposed the distribution of the surplus to the states, a doubtful procedure which he sought to make constitutionally respectable as "deposits." The panic of 1837 combined with falling rates of duty eliminated the surplus. In 1842, Tyler vetoed two tariff bills with riders on distribution, but, needing revenue, signed into law heavy duties on molasses, nails, refined sugar, and glass.[22]

The opposition was too strong, however, and a new, simplified tariff of nine schedules was enacted, following suggestions by Secretary Walker, with ad valorem rates ranging from 100 percent (spirits, etc.) down to 5 percent (materials or semimanufactures). The free list included tea and coffee. The majority of manufactures obtained a rate of 20 to 30 percent.[23]

Although the national debt increased during the Mexican War, surpluses reappeared after 1851, inflated by land sales.[24] In 1857, reductions were made to the "Walker" rates, some products were added to the free list (including drugs, silk, tin, and wood), and others were shifted between schedules. This was the closest approach in the century to free trade.

*1861 to 1881.* The tariff had barely come into force before the crisis of 1857 brought a series of deficits and revived protectionist forces, a phenomenon which could occur simply because tariffs were rarely pushed above revenue-maximizing levels. The Republican majority proposed a new tariff of specific rates, and higher ones at that. This

---

[22] The Distribution Act of 1841 provided that return of excess land-sale revenues to the States be suspended if the tariff rates were raised above their Compromise levels. The bills vetoed in 1842 rendered this provision inoperative. Tyler had been a free trader in the 1820s, and his views had not been seriously considered when he was placed on Harrison's Whig ticket. By 1842, Western enthusiasm for protection had waned.

[23] Passage was delayed until word of the repeal of English corn laws was received.

[24] There was not the difficulty in financing the Mexican War that had been experienced during the War of 1812. Attention after 1846 was diverted from questions of protection by the slavery debates, 1847–50, and the Kansas-Nebraska Bill. The economy between 1846 and 1857 was very prosperous.

formed the basis of the 1861 Morrill Act, passed after withdrawal of some southern Senators, which made important changes in duties on iron and wool.

The Civil War was financed by heavy external and internal taxes, the former being justified by the latter. There were specific taxes on the production of iron and steel, paper and leather, besides a general ad valorem tax on manufacturing.[25] Both Stanwood and Taussig remark that pressure groups took advantage of the emergency to further their interests, with lasting effect because the war duties became the bases of postwar rates of protection. Although the internal taxes were mostly repealed by 1872, thereby removing the justification for the high "compensatory" tariffs, protection was increased rather than reduced on woolens (1867), copper (1869), nickel, and marble (1870).[26]

Despite reductions in "revenue" duties (tea, coffee, molasses, etc.) in 1870, large surpluses made some tariff revision inevitable. But the Act of 1872 barely touched the principle of protection—most important items were subject to a mere 10 percent reduction, while materials and "revenue" items were reduced further. This horizontal reduction was reversed in 1875, revenue having fallen after the panic of 1873.

*1882 to 1909.* This was a period of great political fluctuations when protection was at center stage and became the chief issue in the presidential election of 1888. Although committed to tariff reform and having House majorities in most of the years from 1875 to 1888, the Democrats failed to make a decisive dent in protection, partly due to the rise in the mid-1880s of a minority protectionist wing.[27]

Huge Treasury surpluses after 1880 were again the occasion for a new act. The Republican-controlled Congress appointed a largely pro-

[25] An income tax and license fees were also imposed.

[26] The Senate had attempted in 1867 to reduce raw materials rates. Taussig (1931) remarked how post–Civil War tariffs illustrate the ability of a single district to win protection (for example nickel and marble), and how the "exploded errors of a small school of economists . . . became the foundation of the policy of a great people" (pp. 174, 224–28). Taussig's attitude was shaped by his feeling that protection before 1842, even though not necessary for growth (as it turned out), was a justifiable attempt to stimulate a nascent industrial sector. But after the Civil War, he could find little "economic" justification, and so his discussion of tariff changes has a tone of distinct disapproval.

[27] Terrill (1973) is criticized by Anderson (1975) for not explaining why the positions on the tariff of the political parties in the 1880s and 1890s did not converge.

tectionist Tariff Commission in 1882 which recommended reductions in the duties on raw materials rather than on manufactures, and on items of general consumption like sugar and molasses.[28] After some congressional maneuvers, a bill was passed in 1883 with decreased duties on raw wool, cheap cottons, pig iron, steel rails, copper, nickel and marble (duties on these last three having been increased from 1867 to 1870). But the duties on iron ore, steel manufactures, fine cottons, and woolens were raised.

The election of 1888, fought over the tariff, resulted in Republican victories in both houses and the presidency. The McKinley Tariff of 1890 was considered the pinnacle of protectionism.[29] For the first time, agricultural goods were extensively "protected," along with fine fabrics, cutlery, and tin plate (this last was anticipatory protection). Raw sugar was put on the free list, but the Trust received a bounty in return.

During his first presidency (1885–89), Cleveland was unable to bring about tariff reductions, despite a strong message to Congress in 1887 and popular support. In his second term (1893–97), silver shattered his party's cohesion. The Gorman bill of 1894 became law without Cleveland's signature. Reductions were made in duties on raw wool (which was put on the free list), iron ore and coal, pig iron, steel rails, chinaware, and tinplate; sugar was taken off the free list, given an ad valorem duty and the bounty was removed. An income tax, later declared unconstitutional, was attached to aid the revenue.

The election of 1896 turned on the silver question, and brought McKinley to the White House. The Treasury ran deficits from 1893 to 1897 as a result of the fall in economic activity. The Dingley Tariff of 1897 generally reversed the changes of the Gorman Act while making concessions to the farming interests by reimposing the wool duty and taxing hides for the first time since 1872.

By the end of the century, the rankings of important manufacturing industries by nominal and effective protection were highly correlated.

[28] Some increases were recommended "according to the amount of labor entering into the production," Stanwood (1903), II, 206.

[29] Hawke (1975) shows that among manufactures there were marked changes in the ranking of effective protection, although not as great as the increase in the general level would lead one to expect.

More than 100 percent effective rates applied in 1899 to zinc smelting, wool and silk manufacturers, leather gloves, butter, tobacco, cottons, blackplate, hosiery, leather, glass, steel works; all except leather and zinc had nominal rates in excess of 35 percent.[30]

[30] Hawke (1975), p. 91, table 2. The 1904 list of products with effective rates exceeding 100 percent is virtually identical.

# Manufacturing Background and Tariff Rates

## THE AMERICAN ECONOMY OF THE EARLY NINETEENTH CENTURY [1]

I N 1824 the United States consisted of the thirteen original colonies, the eleven states admitted after 1790, and the sparsely settled territories beyond, including the vast Louisiana Purchase of 1803.[2] The new nation contested and was eventually to extinguish the land claims of Europeans and Indians; Spain conceded access to the Mississippi ports; France sold its recently acquired territories, and after a struggle, the British yielded maritime rights, and the Ohio Indians sovereignty over the western lands.

We may consider the country as falling roughly into four sections: New England, the Middle Atlantic, the South Atlantic, and the West. The boundaries did not coincide with those of the states because the economic interests and social structure of the transmontane area differed from those of the older, more settled seaboard communities from New Hampshire to Virginia, there being no solid South, but rather a rising and united West. The great migration westward between 1800 and 1825 occasioned a corresponding redistribution of political power to regions less oriented toward the international economy.

Natural increase was rapid and the rate of immigration low; the 9.6 million persons enumerated in the 1820 census were largely native-

---

[1] The following discussion of the economy and manufacturing in 1820 draws heavily on Nettels (1962), Taylor (1931), North (1966), and Clark (1929).

[2] The thirteen were Delaware, New Jersey, Pennsylvania, Georgia, Connecticut, Massachusetts, Maryland, South Carolina, New Hampshire, New York, Virginia, North Carolina, and Rhode Island. The states admitted after 1790 were: Vermont, 1791; Kentucky, 1792; Tennessee, 1796; Ohio, 1803; Louisiana, 1812; Indiana, 1816; Mississippi, 1817; Illinois, 1818; Alabama, 1819; Maine, 1820; Missouri, 1821.

born.[3] Four-fifths of the 1820 labor force of 3.1 million (which included 950,000 slaves) were engaged in agriculture; the remainder were craftsmen—blacksmiths, coopers—or employees—domestic servants, sailors, miners, textile wage workers.[4] The cities, chief among them New York, Philadelphia, Baltimore and Boston, were centers of commerce rather than of manufacturing, and contained less than one-twentieth of the population.[5]

By contemporary standards, per capita income was quite high, but the average hid a considerable degree of inequality.[6] There are not many data with which to assess the growth of income before 1840, let alone 1820. Per capita income must have increased during the period of neutral trade—shipping earnings reached about $7 per capita in 1807, when total income could not have been much above $75 (in prices of 1840).[7] But this source of income disappeared after 1812. Gallman has estimated a $20 increase in per capita income between 1805 and 1840, of which $2 was due to the regional shifts and $9 to the sectoral shifts of the labor force; and most of the $11 increase must have occurred after 1820.[8] The other quantifiable source of income growth, increases in supplies of productive factors per capita, is difficult to apportion between the periods before and after 1820. Although there is some risk of exaggerating the impact of well-recorded foreign events on a predominantly rural society, external conditions do seem to have influenced disproportionately both secular and cyclical change between 1790 and 1820. It is to foreign trade and commerce we now turn (table 2.1).

In 1792 Britain was still the chief source of imports and market for exports. Subsequently a re-export trade grew when France was forced

[3] Congress prohibited the importation of slaves into the United States on and after January 1, 1808.

[4] Lebergott (1964), p. 510. He has suggested that probably less than one-tenth of the labor force before 1860 was engaged in growing and distributing United States farm exports: Lebergott in Davis et al. (1972), p. 188, *n.* 8.

[5] Cities had populations of 8,000 or more. Urban centers with populations of more than 2,500 accounted for about 7.2 percent of the population; see Taylor (1951), p. 7.

[6] See chapters 1 and 2 in Davis et al. (1972).

[7] Gallman in Davis et al. (1972), pp. 21 ff.

[8] The percentages of the labor force in agriculture in 1810, 1820, and 1840 were 80.9, 78.8, and 61.3; Lebergott in Davis et al. (1972), p. 187.

TABLE 2.1

## Merchandise Trade of the United States, 1790–1819
(MILLIONS OF DOLLARS)

|      | EXPORTS | IMPORTS |      | EXPORTS | IMPORTS |
| ---- | ------- | ------- | ---- | ------- | ------- |
| 1790 | 20 | 24 | 1805 | 96 | 126 |
| 1791 | 19 | 31 | 1806 | 102 | 137 |
| 1792 | 21 | 33 | 1807 | 108 | 145 |
| 1793 | 26 | 33 | 1808 | 22 | 58 |
| 1794 | 33 | 36 | 1809 | 52 | 61 |
| 1795 | 48 | 71 | 1810 | 67 | 89 |
| 1796 | 67 | 83 | 1811 | 61 | 58 |
| 1797 | 57 | 77 | 1812 | 39 | 79 |
| 1798 | 62 | 71 | 1813 | 28 | 22 |
| 1799 | 79 | 81 | 1814 | 7 | 13 |
| 1800 | 71 | 93 | 1815 | 53 | 85 |
| 1801 | 94 | 113 | 1816 | 82 | 151 |
| 1802 | 73 | 78 | 1817 | 88 | 102 |
| 1803 | 56 | 67 | 1818 | 93 | 127 |
| 1804 | 78 | 87 | 1819 | 70 | 94 |

Source: D. C. North, "The United States Balance of Payments, 1790–1860," in *Trends in the American Economy in the Nineteenth Century* (1960), p. 577. Copyright © 1960 National Bureau of Economic Research and reprinted with permission of the Bureau and D. C. North.
Note: Fiscal year from October 1 to September 30.

by British naval power to leave to the United States the carrying of tropical and semitropical goods between its colonies and France itself via U.S. ports.[9] After 1805 the belligerents imposed reciprocal blockades and so disrupted neutral trade that Jefferson, fearing war, had the Embargo Act passed in late 1807.[10] In response to pressures from maritime interests, Macon's Bill No. 2 invited a mutual reduction of restrictions with either of the powers; Madison accepted some French promises and a nonintercourse ban applied to Britain alone after March 1811.

[9] The British acceptance of the re-export trade was confirmed in the case of the ship *Polly* (1800), which permitted re-export to France of goods from its colonies after unloading in the United States and payment of duties there. The *Essex* decision in 1805 required proof that it had not been the original intention to re-export the goods.
[10] Replaced in March 1809 by the Nonintercourse Act.

The northeast enjoyed a boom in shipping and shipbuilding during the period of neutral trade, net freight earnings reaching a peak in 1805.[11] In these times of extraordinary commercial prosperity, the northeast became more urbanized, expanding the market for imported goods and hinterland foodstuffs. The re-export trade fell away greatly after the Berlin Decree of 1806 and the Orders in Council of late 1807. During the interruption of foreign trade, manufacturing was given a premature stimulus as local producers sought to replace imported supplies, but naturally these new enterprises were to encounter difficulties with the resumption of foreign competition after 1815. The War of 1812 seriously disrupted both foreign and coastal trade, and recorded exports and imports dwindled. The United States placed a complete embargo, repealed in April 1814, on coastal and foreign trade when the British blockaded her ports and, until neutrals began to carry it to Britain, American cotton piled up in southern ports. As in the earlier embargo, northeastern merchants resorted to privateering.

The agricultural sections of the economy must have experienced fair prosperity between 1790 and 1810 on the evidence of the tenfold increase in the population of the western states and territories, and the growth of coastal shipping.[12] The foreign demand for staples was generally high, with food grains enjoying occasional booms after European harvest failures. Land sales in the South and West reached levels in years around 1818 that were exceeded only in the 1830s, a reflection of buoyant wheat and cotton markets. Immigration, which had picked up after 1810, probably increased substantially after the peace.[13] From 1818, however, prices fell dramatically; those of western produce in Cincinnati more than halved during 1819 and 1820, the terms of trade moving sharply against the West. The collapse of cotton prices after November 1818 was due to a fall in foreign demand.

The immediate postwar years were trying ones for the Northeast. American commerce still found itself restricted by navigation acts, and freight rates fell.[14] The flood of British manufactures, much of it auc-

---

[11] North (1960) p. 595. Despite a fall in volume, freight earnings in 1810–11 almost matched those of 1805.

[12] Johnson et al. (1915), table 12; North (1966), p. 250.

[13] North and Thomas (1968), p. 225, citing the *Preliminary Census Report* (1860).

[14] However, North's index of shipping utilization generally rose 1815–19. See North (1966).

tioned in New York, threatened local production born of war, although the Tariff of 1816 provided some protection.[15] Manufacturing prices fell earlier and less than agricultural prices and the shake-out was less violent, but even so, conditions in 1819 were bad, with widespread bankruptcies and rising unemployment.[16]

Recovery in the early 1820s occurred despite a continuing decline in the general price level. The crisis of 1819 had been monetary, an exaggerated response to the European trade cycle in the relatively small foreign trade sector. The operations of the Second Bank of the United States had not prevented a very rapid increase in western bank notes during the boom and so the final collapse was dramatic. However, the effects on real output were not as severe.[17]

### Economic Policy

After the adoption of the Constitution, the Federalists consolidated the basis of a commercial economy. Their program was laid out in the 1790s in a series of reports by Hamilton on the securing of public credit (by the assumption at par of the depreciated debts of the state governments as well as the debt of the Confederation government), the establishment of the First Bank of the United States and the Mint, and the protection of manufactures (the tariffs before 1824 are discussed in the next section). Hamilton believed that American manufacturing lacked up-to-date machinery and scientific equipment, and imports of these were to be paid for by exporting securities rather than by goods. Internal taxes were used to boost the revenue. Shipping was assisted by discriminatory duties against foreign vessels and the goods they carried, and by naval protection. The wars of the French Revolution further stimulated shipbuilding and the carrying trade, but ended an early

[15] The minimum valuation applied under the Tariff of 1816 resulted in the virtual exclusion of cheap cottons after prices fell, and the industry survived, even prospered, in New England.

[16] Taylor (1951), p. 362 regards this as the earliest instance of American industrial unemployment. On the connection between volcanic dust and trade conditions, 1815–20, see Post (1974).

[17] The economy was less monetized then than now, and the debt structure was less extensive. What occurred was largely a fall in absolute prices, which could be accommodated with less real adjustment than if it had been accompanied by more substantial relative commodity price changes. It may be assumed that the western bank failures caused an unrequited transfer of real resources to the West, to offset somewhat the hardships of the drastic fall in prices.

burst of interest in manufacturing by diverting capital and talent into commerce.[18]

Immediately following 1801 the Republicans, although constrained by the Federalist Bank and debt legacy, did inherit a large Treasury surplus for the reduction of the latter. Yet the hatred of debt did not prevent Jefferson from financing the Louisiana Purchase in 1803 largely in this way. Defense expenditures, stimulated by the quasi-war with France during 1799 and 1800, were pared until war with Tripoli, begun in 1801, forced up naval outlays in 1804. These were financed by temporary increases in ad valorem duties and a 10 percent surcharge on imports carried in foreign vessels. The Treasury surplus vanished after 1809 as the embargo reduced customs revenue. During the War of 1812 fiscal stringency resulted in a doubling of tariffs and the reintroduction of internal taxes. Because Congress was tardy in imposing sufficient additional taxes, the Treasury issued substantial amounts of bonds and Treasury notes. Earlier, Treasury Secretary Gallatin had proposed that wars be financed by debt, and now Congress found it easy to agree with him. Because the conflict was not popular in New England, and because the West lacked ready capital, the debt was taken up mainly in the Middle Atlantic states.[19]

After the refusal of Congress in 1811 to recharter the First Bank of the United States, the number of state banks had risen swiftly. Since most states outside New England suspended specie convertibility in 1814 but not banking operations, the volume of bank notes rose along with prices. Treasury operations were complicated by the discounts on bank notes outside New England. Large deficits incurred from 1812 to 1815 were difficult to cover by borrowings, and the debt was actually

[18] Imports of manufactures were encouraged by the saleability of debt abroad, and by the large foreign exchange earnings in neutral trade. Debt holders were paid in coin collected as customs revenue, and so benefited from the increased imports. Although designed primarily for revenue, the tariff also protected manufacturers, but less than the other Federalist policies harmed them; see Nettels (1962), chapter VI.

[19] Some representatives from New England and the Middle Atlantic states had voted in favor of a war to end British harrassment and restrictions of shipping and commerce. In the northwest, the British had aided the fight by the Ohio Indians against the United States, partly to preserve a buffer between Americans and the Great Lakes fur trade. Once Spanish allegiance to France was weakened, the way was open for the Jeffersonians to seize the Floridas. The benefits of the war accrued chiefly to the West and the hardships were borne chiefly by the coastal regions.

TABLE 2.2

*Federal Receipts and Expenditures, 1816–25*
(MILLIONS OF DOLLARS)

| | RECEIPTS | | | | EXPENDITURES | | | |
|---|---|---|---|---|---|---|---|---|
| | CUSTOMS | PUBLIC LENDING | MISC. | TOTAL | MILITARY | INTEREST | MISC. | TOTAL |
| 1816 | 36.3 | 1.7 | 9.7 | 47.7 | 19.9 | 7.8 | 3.4 | 31.2 |
| 1817 | 26.3 | 2.0 | 5.8 | 33.1 | 11.3 | 4.5 | 4.1 | 20.0 |
| 1818 | 17.2 | 2.6 | 1.8 | 21.6 | 7.6 | 6.2 | 5.2 | 20.0 |
| 1819 | 20.3 | 3.3 | 1.1 | 24.6 | 9.4 | 5.2 | 5.9 | 21.5 |
| 1820 | 15.0 | 1.6 | 1.0 | 17.8 | 6.9 | 5.2 | 6.1 | 18.3 |
| 1821 | 13.0 | 1.2 | .2 | 14.6 | 7.8 | 5.1 | 2.9 | 15.8 |
| 1822 | 17.6 | 1.8 | .8 | 20.2 | 5.3 | 5.2 | 4.5 | 15.0 |
| 1823 | 19.1 | .9 | .5 | 20.5 | 5.6 | 4.9 | 4.2 | 14.7 |
| 1824 | 17.9 | 1.0 | .5 | 19.4 | 6.2 | 4.9 | 9.4 | 20.3 |
| 1825 | 20.1 | 1.2 | .5 | 21.8 | 6.7 | 4.4 | 4.8 | 15.9 |

*Source:* D. R. Dewey (1903), pp. 168, 169.

higher in 1815 than in 1801.[20] Such experiences partly explain the support Madison and Gallatin gave to the chartering of the Second Bank in 1816. And thus the Jeffersonian vision of a society of prosperous small farmers eschewing banks and debt, ruled by the gentry, with no internal taxes and low federal expenditure, was clouded by war.[21]

The three issues that dominated the discussion of economic policy for fifteen years after the War of 1812 were protection, internal improvements, and land sales. Although all were included in Clay's attempt to forge a coalition behind his American System, the tariff was central: by protecting manufacturing, the tariff would stimulate the demand for western foodstuffs and materials, yet without recourse to higher land prices would still provide sufficient revenue for surveys, roads, and postal services. Table 2.2 shows the overwhelming importance of customs as a revenue source, as well as its volatility.

The Tariff of 1816 received fairly general assent, passing the House 88 to 54, and the Senate 54 to 48. Amendments were passed in 1818. By 1820, protection had become a divisive issue, and the bill of that

[20] In only three years between 1816 and 1836 were there deficits.
[21] And ambition? Vidal (1974). See also Bruchey (1965).

year was narrowly defeated in the Senate. Yet the tariff was not a party issue. The elevation of Adams to the presidency in 1824 followed an election that had aroused little public interest and had been decided in the House of Representatives. All the leading candidates (Adams, Jackson, Clay, and Crawford) professed allegiance to the old Republican Party. By 1828, the outlines of the second American party system could be seen in the rival candidacies of Adams and Jackson, but the full development of national parties had to wait the temporary resolution of the tariff issue under the Compromise of 1833.[22]

## Manufacturing in 1820

Every farm and household 150 years ago was engaged in some manufacturing. The frontier farmer was quite self-sufficient in food and drink, lighting and fuel, clothes, and furniture. In the older, more established regions, homespun cloth of flax, wool, and later cotton was preferred to the woodsman's leather shirt and breeches. The War of 1812 greatly stimulated household spinning and weaving, which remained important activities for some decades. Most output was for domestic use, but putting-out occurred in textiles and hat-making. Food preservation—salting or smoking meats, drying fruits, distilling grain and fruits, making butter and cheese—remained a significant occupation until the invention of satisfactory methods of canning and refrigeration. In 1824 most counties boasted a number of small enterprises that shaped and repaired tools and implements, or processed local grain, lumber, and leather. Smaller communities purchased many of their needs from peddlers or itinerant craftsmen, while in larger settlements craftsmen set up small shops to fill local orders. A community's boots and shoes, hats, clothes, saddles, tools and implements, wagons, barrels, nails, building materials and furniture were largely manufactured locally from local materials. Most grist and sawmills were small, although some merchant mills with access to water transport catered to distant (including foreign) markets, as did southern cotton gins, Louisiana sugar mills, and whiskey and rum distilleries that used imported molasses. Manufacturing was small scale and dispersed, and only in the New England textile industry had the factory system taken

[22] Cf. McCormick (1966). Voting on the 1820 and 1824 bills is analyzed in chapter 3.

T A B L E  2.3

*Estimated Ranking of Industries by Total*
*Manufacturing Output, 1809–49*

| INDUSTRY | 1809 | 1839 | 1849 |
|---|---|---|---|
| Hides and leather | 1 | 2 | 3 |
| Food and spirits | 2 | 3 | 2 |
| Metal and ordnance | 3 | 4 | 4 |
| Transportation equipment | 4 | 6 | 7 |
| Textiles and apparel | 5 | 1 | 1 |
| Building and paper | 6 | 5 | 5 |
| Miscellaneous | 7 | 11 | 6 |
| Chemicals and drugs | 8 | 7 | 8 |
| House furnishing | 9 | 9 | 9 |
| Tobacco | 10 | 10 | 11 |
| Fuel and lighting | 11 | 8 | 10 |

*Source:* B. W. Poulson (1969), p. 522. Reprinted with permission of
the *Journal of Economic History* and B. W. Poulson.

hold. If the United States had embarked on a long transformation from
agriculture and external commerce to manufacturing and internal commerce, in 1820 the journey had barely begun.

Poulson has estimated the rank ordering of manufacturing industries
(table 2.3). There are fairly large errors of estimation in the early data,
but the stability of the rankings (excluding textiles and miscellaneous)
lends credence to them. The rise of textiles to the first position by 1839
is not to be disputed. Even by 1824 it must have risen above rank 5
because cotton textiles rode out the postwar flood of imports and the
crisis of 1819, and expanded quickly during 1820–24.[23]

Manufacturing's share of the labor force rose from 3.2 percent in
1810 to 8.8 percent in 1840, but this exaggerates the change because of
the greater weight of persons only partly so occupied at the earlier
date; it may, perhaps, be more usefully regarded as evidence of increasing specialization. In 1820 there were about 10,000 cotton textile
and 5,000 primary iron and steel wage earners (compared with an agri-

[23] The gross output of cotton cloth in 1820 was almost equal that of hides and leather.
See appendix table B.1. By 1839, cotton textiles employed about 1.4 percent of persons
engaged in manufacturing. Lebergott in Davis et al. (1972), p. 187.

cultural labor force, ten years and older, of 2,470,000).[24] From the earliest times children had been found suitable for tending textile machinery and in 1820 were 45 percent of those employed in Massachusetts textile mills and 55 percent in Rhode Island.[25] Mills patterned after the one at Lowell employed young girls recruited from rural districts, and housed them in respectable boarding houses.[26] There is some evidence of attempts to limit competition for labor. In Rhode Island the decline in foreign trade and slaving provided a reservoir of labor for earlier efforts at diversification into manufacturing.[27] Subsequently, manufacturers there followed Samuel Slater's lead in recruiting whole families to the mill towns. Despite British attempts to prevent it, some skilled labor was recruited from Britain, but few operatives arrived before 1840.[28] Elsewhere and in other industries, manufacturing still remained a part-time employment for farmers. The domestic putting-out system in boots and shoes, straw and palm-leaf hats, and weaving, and to a lesser extent in buttons, carriage trimmings, whips, and suspenders, employed an extensive, dispersed labor force that could not have been attracted to a few concentrated towns.[29]

The cities of New York, Boston, Philadelphia, and Baltimore and their immediate environs were minor centers of manufacturing. Pred (1966) argues that manufacturing arose there out of commerce: through processing traded goods or supplying goods and services to traders or the local, commercial population. Manufacturing had no dynamic of its own, and what little growth in manufacturing these cities experienced between 1800 and 1840 was stimulated by the prior growth of commerce.[30] Pred, in effect, has a staple theory of growth, except that the

[24] Lebergott in Davis et al. (1972), p. 187.

[25] Ware (1931), p. 210; Taylor (1951), p. 271.

[26] Hamilton had pointed to recent "improvements in the construction and application of Machines" and to the availability of women and children "in the populous parts of the country" as evidence that the "dearness of labour" was a less formidable obstacle to the success of manufactures than previously believed: "Prospectus of the Society for Establishing Useful Manufactures," August 1791. Alexander Hamilton, *The Papers of Alexander Hamilton*, ed. Harold C. Syrett (New York and London: Columbia University Press, 1965), IX, 145.

[27] Coleman (1963), pp. 49, 73.    [28] Taylor (1951), p. 272.    [29] *Ibid.*, pp. 215–20.

[30] Dorothy Brady estimates that cities, accounting for 11 percent of the population in 1830, made 27 percent of the national expenditure on food, 16 percent on clothing and 24 percent on home furnishings. Davis et al. (1972), p. 62. Population in places with 2,500 or

staple is commerce. In discussing manufacturing growth, Pred barely mentions import competition, yet because these four cities were seaports, their manufacturing was exposed to foreign competition. Inland manufacturers enjoyed the natural protection of distance from the seaboard, the extent of which is to be discussed later.

The transfer of manufacturing from household to factory proceeded at different rates in different products and regions. Broadly speaking, the closer the settlement to navigable water and the more populous the county, the lower the level of household manufacture.[31] Families were relieved of the more arduous tasks like grinding as soon as the settlement was large enough to support a mill, suitable water power being almost everywhere readily available, whereas the manufacture and repair of farm implements, household utensils, and furniture passed somewhat later into the hands of craftsmen as the community consolidated. Last to be displaced were clothing and textiles, luminants, food and drink. The displacement of homespun was complete by about 1830. As for handicraft activities, family manufacture largely for its own consumption was soon supplemented by itinerant craftsmen as dressmakers, tailors, weavers, and shoemakers came into the home, and as fulling mills, carding machines, and dyeing and bleaching establishments took over some household tasks. Then came shops in which craftsmen worked up local materials for sale or barter in the surrounding area, sometimes involving households by putting out semifinished goods for working up in the home. There followed the stage of the small mill-factory (especially yarn mills), and finally the factory proper (which became typical only after 1850).[32] Prior to that, manufactures for sale were chiefly the output of small shops or the domestic putting-out system.

Given the low level of technology and the influence of transport costs on location, manufacturing establishments were inevitably nu-

---

more residents possibly grew no faster than the population of the country as a whole, 1806–40. Pred (1966), p. 104.

[31] Tryon (1917), p. 168 ff., has an analysis of the 1810 data on household manufactures prepared by Tench Coxe. See also Cole (1926), I, 181.

[32] Except in Philadelphia, carpet manufacturing did not pass through the stages intermediate between household and factory. Cole and Williamson (1941), p. 22. Cole (1965), pp. 220–2, sees need for emendation of Tryon's stages.

merous and small, and apart from a few corporations in the cotton textiles, firms were typically sole proprietorships or partnerships, operating a mill or shop. Clark has stressed the commercial origins of manufacturers by calling them "shop-keeping industrialists," and has described the antebellum period as "a time when manufactures were integrating out of commerce." [33] There was neither separation of ownership from control nor any great pooling or spreading of risk. In short, the manufacturing enterprise resembled more a family farm than a modern factory.

The origins of manufacturing corporations lay in trading and land corporations like the East India Company, and in the charters given for local government, religious, and charity organizations. The colonies and states gave special charters to banks and for the building of turnpikes, bridges, and canals in the public interest: of the 300 business charters granted by states up to 1800, two-thirds were for these purposes. With the interruptions of trade during the Embargo and the War of 1812, manufacturing incorporations became more frequent, there being 165 in New York between 1808 and 1815. [34] The costs and delays of securing special charters led to the passage of general incorporation laws for business in New York (1811), New Jersey (enacted in 1816, repealed in 1819), and Massachusetts (1809). However, most incorporations before 1860 were by special (more liberal) statute. [35] Rhode Island and Pennsylvania did not then allow incorporation. The advantage of incorporation was that the sale by one owner did not require dissolution of the business entity. [36] Limited liability followed in Massachusetts in 1830, New Jersey in 1837, and Rhode Island in 1847. [37]

---

[33] Clark (1929), I, 442; see also pp. 333, 451 and 464 ff. The theme that manufacturing depended on commerce until 1840 is developed in Pred (1966).

[34] Bruchey (1965), pp. 128 ff.

[35] Taylor (1951), p. 241. Even after the passage of the 1811 general incorporation laws in New York, most manufacturers still incorporated under special statute. That forms of organization alone did not dictate manufacturing location is illustrated by the extent of manufacturing in Pennsylvania. Clark (1929), I, 266, 268.

[36] In the 1840s the great New England textile companies remained substantially in the hands of a few families.

[37] Ware (1931), pp. 147 ff. Nettels (1962), p. 294, mentions double liability; see Heath (1954), p. 316.

*Technology and location.* Except in cotton textiles, technology was primitive. Steam power had been installed in mills as early as 1801; yet by 1812 only 10 high-pressure engines (made by Oliver Evans) were in use.[38] The 1820 census records steam engines in five flour mills, three sawmills, two each in iron works, textile mills, and paper mills, one in a rice mill, and one in marble works. They were scattered through Kentucky (four), Ohio (three), western Pennsylvania (three), Virginia (two), and one each in Tennessee, Georgia, Maryland, and New York City.[39] As suitable streams abounded, the predominant power source was water (supplemented by horsepower in the West), but until 1840 water was harnessed inefficiently.[40] Energy transmission was also in an early stage of development.

Important advances had been made in textile machinery,[41] especially in spinning, which had helped cottons to displace linens in household weaving.[42] In iron, no great changes had occurred for thirty years; although puddling and rolling had been introduced around 1817, the inferior quality of the product and British competition retarded their widespread adoption until after 1830.[43] The use of coal in blast furnaces was adopted only slowly.[44] Nail- and cord-making machinery had been developed around 1790. The first papermaking machine in the United States was developed in 1817, and a relatively large producer in Ohio in 1820 used a steam engine.[45] The flour milling tech-

[38] Clark (1929), I, 403, 409.

[39] Depew (1895), pp. xix ff., also mentions steam power for cabinetware (1815) and printing (in Albany, 1823), but neither appears in the *Digest*.

[40] Clark (1929), I, 406. The wooden pitchback wheel turned toward the streams, and so the water hit the wheel close to the top of its fall.

[41] Ginning (Whitney, 1793); carding (circa 1807); spinning by power (after the War of 1812); power looms (Lowell, 1814; Scotch loom, 1817). Clark (1929), I, 422–37.

[42] The word *homespun* was then a misnomer. The 1810 census shows households produced more yards of flaxen than cotton cloths. See Tryon (1917), pp. 268, 275 for a discussion of the effects of machinery on homespun; Zevin, in Fogel and Engerman (1971), pp. 122–37, has an analysis of the growth of demand for factory output. Almy and Brown had to market their yarns aggressively, so that cotton's initial success was no easy matter. Ware (1931), pp. 161 ff.

[43] Temin (1964), chapter 5. The discrimination against the import of rolled bars in favor of hammered did not appreciably hasten development in the United States. Berglund and Wright (1929), pp. 105–6.

[44] Clark (1929), I, 420; see also Temin (1964).

[45] Taylor (1951), p. 221; Depew (1895), p. 304.

niques of Oliver Evans had not been much improved upon for forty years and were not to be for another fifty.[46] The only changes in glass-making was the introduction of coal as a fuel.[47] The "first revolution in shoemaking"—the use of wooden shoe pegs—came into general use in 1815, but only in the 1850s was machinery developed.[48] In woodworking, however, there was considerable progress, including the invention of a machine that automatically turned out gun stocks to a pattern.[49] The products requiring the highest installed capital per unit of gross output in 1820 were primary iron, glass, cotton yarn, castings, muskets, and plow irons (see appendix table B.1). Making no allowance for idle capacity, and including water rights, stands of trees, and ore bodies, besides buildings and equipment, their capital coefficients ranged from 3.4 to 2.0.

Water greatly influenced the location of industry, directly as a source of power and means of transport, and indirectly through the pattern of settlement and markets for outputs and inputs. Shipbuilding was the first industry in which the United States loomed large in the world, and its scattering along the northeastern seaboard reflected the abundance of suitable timber and streams. It brought with it, too, the business of fitting, provisioning, and repairing vessels. Until the days of steam, water power limited the geographical concentration of the New England cotton textile industry. Industries using imported materials—fine furniture, distillation of rum, spermaceti candles—were located near ports. The early primary iron industry used charcoal to smelt bog ores (both inputs were widely available, the latter supplemented and eventually displaced by magnetic ores).[50] By 1810, moving slowly up the rivers, the primary iron industry established itself in the Lehigh Valley. The water power required in smelting furnaces, forges, and slitting mills, to drive bellows, trip hammers, rollers, and cutters was available all over the country.[51] Within the wide limits set by materials and power, demand was able to influence the location of the iron in-

[46] Ibid., pp. 266 ff.    [47] Ibid., p. 276.    [48] Ibid., p. 567.    [49] Clark (1929), I, 421.
[50] Iron was made in all states except Georgia before the close of the Revolution. The magnetic ores extended from the Berkshires in Massachusetts and the Salisbury district in Connecticut, through Orange County, New York into Morris County, New Jersey. Ibid., pp. 496, 497.
[51] Until after 1825, a prejudice existed in favor of castings directly from ore, but the assembling of thin castings into stoves was done by merchants. Later the complete manufacture was centralized at the distribution points. Ibid., pp. 502,503.

dustry. Thus several industries—lumber, milling, tanning, grain milling and distilling, food preparation—situated themselves according to materials rather than markets. A product had to be, like whiskey, imperishable and valuable relative to volume, to bear the cost of transport for any great distance overland; and so the outlet for much western produce was the great waterway of the Mississippi.[52] The transportation revolution was just beginning. Steam navigation was attempted on the Mississippi in the mid-1810s, but its domination of the river was decades away. The Erie Canal (linking the Hudson to Lake Erie) was completed in 1825. Only after the 1830s did the railroads compete with canals (although not with coastwise shipping) for freight and passengers. All in all, in the 1820s population density and manufacturing location were dictated mostly by transport costs.[53]

Offending the general locational pattern were two industries in particular: footwear and cotton textiles. The former's concentration in Massachusetts towns began before the Revolution; by 1760, for example, Lynn was already specializing in women's and children's shoes and leaving men's boots and shoes to custom work. Access to the large tanneries near Boston was a localizing influence, but no simple explanation of the growth of this manufacture can be given.[54] The rise of the New England textiles has been investigated extensively. Humidity was high, which helped spinning; streams were available for power and bleaching; coastwise shipping put major markets in New York and Philadelphia within reach; and declining agricultural opportunities provided an unorganized if unskilled labor force. Boston's capitalists, like Rhode Island's, had to seek new outlets after the deterioration of foreign trade, and both New York and Philadelphia competed strongly for internal commerce. And all this is aside from the spirit of Yankee enterprise.[55]

---

[52] Yet there was commodity flow east to west that had to be paid for somehow: as early as 1808, Almy and Brown were shipping yarn to the West via Philadelphia. Ware (1931), pp. 48, 55.

[53] The most widely dispersed industries (in terms of output by state) in 1820 were leather, flour, paper, hats, wood products, and distilleries. The most commonly reported outputs were spirits (more than 1,000 distilleries), leather, flour, cotton and wool yarns and cloths, wood and wood products, and boots and shoes; see appendix table B.1; flour milling was not fully tabulated, and so is excluded from the table.

[54] Hazard (1921), p. 39; Clark (1929), p. 186.

[55] Ware (1931), pp. 14 ff.; Porter and Livesay (1971), pp. 65–8.

To read the list of American disadvantages in, say, Clark (or in Hamilton's *Report,* for that matter), would make one despair for the survival of manufacturing in this early period. Capital and labor (especially skilled labor) were scarce, but land was abundant. The work force in 1820 looked to agriculture for its chief employment. The lure of cheap, fertile land has often been given as the explanation of the high-priced, inelastic supply of labor in manufacturing; thus the success of the Waltham system lay partly in tapping a source of underemployed labor, namely, young woman. For working capital (a more pressing need than fixed capital), manufacturing had to compete with the demands of commerce for the financing of exports and imports.[56] The embryonic banking system was not geared to manufacturing,[57] and, in any case, was subject to periodic crisis. Yet colonial America exported to England and Europe a variety of manufactures including lumber, ships, naval stores (tar, pitch, etc.) and iron, and to the West Indies whale oil, soap and candles, pot and pearl ashes, bread and flour and rum, along with lesser items like cider, beer, pottery, hats, leather, shoes, furniture, and vehicles.[58] By the mid-1820s American cotton textiles were being exported in small quantities, but were the exception to the rule.[59]


## IMPORTS AND TARIFFS TO 1824

Local producers, especially those near water transport, did not enjoy markets free of import competition. More than half the imports in 1820–21 and 1824–25 were manufactures and raw or semifinished materials (table 2.4). Textiles and clothing alone made up about 40 per-

---

[56] In the opinion of Gallatin, Secretary of the Treasury in 1810, American manufacturing's most severe disadvantage was the shortage of capital for the extension of credit and the riding-out of temporary losses, and that "the most efficient, and the most obvious remedy would consist in supplying that capital." North and Thomas (1968), p. 181.

[57] The Waltham interests attempted to have the Massachusetts banking laws altered. Ware (1931), p. 180. Porter and Livesay (1971), p. 71, say that bankers regarded manufacturing as too risky. However, Clark (1929), p. 378, states that "most manufacturers used banking capital in their business," but how much is not indicated.

[58] Clark (1929), I, 94–99. Hazard (1927), p. 36, found no record of shoe exports earlier than 1773.

[59] Ware (1931), p. 91.

TABLE 2.4

*Classification of U.S. Imports, 1821 and 1825* [1]
(PERCENT)

|  | 1821 | | 1825 | |
|---|---|---|---|---|
| Textiles and clothing |  | 36 [2] |  | 44 |
| Cotton | 12 | | 12 | |
| Woolen | 12 | | 13 | |
| Other | 13 | | 19 | |
| Metals and manufactures | | 7 | | 8 |
| Primary iron and steel | 2 | | 2 | |
| Other | 5 | | 6 | |
| Other industrial materials | | 10 | | 13 |
| Comestibles, etc. | | 24 | | 20 |
| Miscellaneous | | 25 | | 15 |
| Bullion, etc. | 13 | | 7 | |
| Other | 10 | | 8 | |

*Source:* Derived from *ASP, Commerce and Navigation,* II, 555–56, and U.S. Special Serial Set 139, House Doc. 148, 10th Cong., 1st Sess., *Report on Commerce and Navigation for 1825,* pp. 116–21.
[1] Years ending September 30, 1821 and 1825.
[2] Subtotals do not add to 36 percent because of rounding.

cent, the major items being woolen and cotton piece goods (8 percent and 7 percent respectively in 1820–21). The main materials imported were rawhides, molasses, indigo, and hemp, along with minor items such as dye woods, burstones, plaster of Paris, bristles and glue, paints and colors, hemp cordage, alum, copperas, coal, gunpowder, and paper and glass products. Pig and bar iron should also be included in this group (about 2 percent of all imports). *Other metals* included tin plates and sheets and a whole range of products (not all separately reported in 1820–21): firearms, wire, nails and hoop iron, and castings (greater detail is provided in the return for 1824–25). Included within *other miscellaneous* were earthenware and glasswares, and minor imports like footwear, cigars, books, and playing cards.

What was the extent of import competition? Unfortunately, it is impossible to estimate the share of imports in the consumption of various commodities. That the manufacturers devoted considerable effort to limiting competition from abroad is some indication that the competition was real. Of course, manufacturers also feared American (including household) competition, maybe more than foreign, but its nature differed.[60] Economic factors affecting one domestic producer (such as a decline in demand) were likely to affect all domestic producers similarly, whereas foreign exporters were influenced as well by events outside the United States. A decline in the British market could lead to a large increase in exports to America; British exports to America were subject to greater fluctuations than British production. Thus it was not so much the level as the variability of import competition that upset business calculations in America,[61] causing what Jefferson called "casual embarrassment" [62] (table 2.2).

Only with substantial guesswork may we cross-classify production and imports, and the following statements should be treated with caution.[63] Products or classes of products with the highest ratios of imports to American production included cotton goods (but not yarn) and woolens, brass manufactures, glass bottles, and refined sugar, followed by bar iron, books, lead manufactures, and some wood products. Relatively free of imports were a range of iron manufactures, ales, cordage, gunpowder, leather manufactures including footwear, marble manufactures, paper, tinware, and window glass.

## Tariffs before 1824

Some of the protective feeling before 1824 arose from experiences in national emergencies. The Revolutionary Army was supplied by public and private industry with boots and clothing, cannon, shot, arms, gunpowder, and wagons. The desire for greater economic self-sufficiency, reinforced by the period of interrupted trade after 1808 and again by the War of 1812, manifested itself in patriotic movements that eschewed foreign goods, in private societies for the promotion of manu-

----

[60] "The limiting force of the expansion of American manufactures during these years, therefore, was to no small degree the resistance offered by household industry to factory production." Clark (1929), p. 252. See also Cole (1936), I, 261.

[61] Clark (1929), p. 254. Against fluctuating import levels, the tariff was not very potent.

[62] Bruchey (1965), p. 120.    [63] Cf. Pitkin (1835), p. 481.

factures, and in local, state, and federal aid to manufacturing.[64] Towns often encouraged the establishment of a grist mill and similar enterprises by land grants and market monopolies. The states, and the colonies before them, had promoted manufacturing by tax exemptions, bounties and premiums, loans, lotteries, exemptions from jury and militia duty, tariffs, and, most importantly, by generous charters and favorable attitudes toward riparian rights. Shipbuilding and shipping were assisted indirectly by laws that required the growing of flax and hemp and by bounties on the production of those fibers and naval stores. Other industries assisted included bricks, cotton textiles, glass, iron, lumber, silk, and stone cutting.[65] The finances of the states did not allow them generosity, however, and apart from the laws of incorporation, state efforts did not have great effect.[66]

Only brief mention will be made of federal policies other than the tariff. Despite differences in social ideals, the first and the fourth Treasury Secretaries, Alexander Hamilton and Albert Gallatin, promoted federal improvements in transport and communications (as did Robert Morris before them as Superintendent of Finance after 1781), thus encouraging westward migration of people and the interregional flow of goods, and building a national market which domestic manufacturers could take advantage of with the help of the tariff.[67]

The dates of tariff acts from 1789 to 1824 can be found in *Public Stat-*

[64] After 1785, societies in Philadelphia, New York, Boston, Baltimore, and Providence promoted manufactures by offering premiums and organizing the sale of articles or by undertaking manufacturing on their own account. Clark (1929), I, 183, 190–91. The popular enthusiasm was tempered by a fear of the detrimental effects that manufacturing could have on moral and physical well-being.

[65] Massachusetts, between 1786 and 1803, prohibited fifty imports while admitting raw material duty-free; imposed a 1 percent levy on foreign hemp and yarn and bounty on domestic; subsidized sailcloth, duck, and twine production; offered manufacturers of glass and hollow-ware bounties and monopolies; encouraged boots and shoes with state stamps of quality; freed from taxation for limited periods some glassworks, cotton mills, brewers, and salt and sugar works. Handlin and Handlin (1947), passim.

[66] Clark (1929), I, 265. Bruchey (1965), p. 133, cites the opinion of Louis Hartz that local aids were more significant than all other.

[67] See Bruchey (1965) for a discussion of early policies for economic development. Bruchey interprets many of the governmental actions as efforts to overcome the shortage of capital available to manufacturing. Balinky (1958) is concerned only with Gallatin's fiscal policy.

*utes at Large,*[68] and of course the tariff acts themselves are in the same source. It proved convenient not to work from the acts themselves, but from listings of the tariffs. For comparison of pre-1824 tariffs with those of 1824, an 1891 list was used,[69] which apparently derived from one of 1872 (which has an interesting tariff history affixed).[70] An 1846 annotated list by Walker was also consulted.[71] Interpretations of some of the valuation provisions can be found in Goss (1897). Selected rates are listed in table 2.5.

One of the reasons for the adoption of the new Constitution was the failure of the Continental Congress to raise sufficient revenue. The first tariff, with its protectionist preamble (that the act was for "the encouragement and protection of manufactures"), passed in 1789 after Madison's proposal for a relatively uniform levy had been rejected in favor of a general 5 percent duty, some specific items for revenue, and some protective duties. There was a continuation of the encouragement previously given by Pennsylvania to its manufacturers of paper, steel, and beer, New York to its brewers, Maryland to its glass makers, and New England to its iron works and distilleries.[72] This Act of July 4, 1789 levied both ad valorem and specific rates.[73] The figure of 7.5 percent was the most common ad valorem duty and applied to blank books and paper, brushes, bullion, goldplated ware and jewelry, cabinetware, canes, clothing, millinery, gloves and mitts, hats, anchors, iron sheet and castings, leather and its manufactures (including saddles), and some pewter and tin manufactures. The rate of 10 percent applied to buckles, chinaware, stoneware and earthenware, glass bottles, gold

[68] Boston: Little and Brown (1845), II, 24.

[69] *Rates of Duties on Imports into the United States from 1789 to 1890, Inclusive, Together with Statistics Relating Thereto,* prepared by the Committee on Finance, United States Senate, Report 2130, to the 51st Congress, 2d Session (Washington, Government Printing Office, February 4, 1891).

[70] *Special Report on the Custom-Tariff Legislation of the United States* (with appendixes) by Edward Young, House Ex. Doc. to the 42d Congress, 2d Session (Washington, Government Printing Office, 1872).

[71] Letter from Secretary Walker to the House, Doc. 25, 29th Congress, 2d Session, December 30, 1846.

[72] Faulkner (1951), p. 159.

[73] The comparisons of duties can conveniently be found in Senate Report 2130 (1891). A discussion of the changes made in 1824 follows. Full details of changes in imposts can be found in Stanwood (1903).

T A B L E  2.5

Selected Tariff Rates, 1789–1824

| | | | | DATES OF THE ACTS | | |
|---|---|---|---|---|---|---|
| NUMBER [1] | NAME | JULY 4, 1789 | MAY 13, 1800 | FEB. 5, 1816 | APR. 27, 1816 | MAY 22, 1824 |
| 1, 16 | Ale, in bottles | Doz. 20¢ | Doz. 20¢ [2] | Doz. 20¢ [2] | Gal. 15¢ | Gal. 15¢ |
| —, 20 | Alum | 5% [2] | 12½% [2] | 30% [2] | Cwt $1.00 | Cwt $2.50 |
| 106, 44 | Axes | 5% [2] | 15% | 35% | 20% | $5% |
| 15, 109 | Brass manufactures | 5% [2] | 15% | 35% | 20% | 25% |
| 24, 140 | Candles, tallow | lb. 2¢ | lb. 2¢ | lb. 4¢ | lb. 3¢ | lb. 5¢ |
| 33, 158 | Carriages and parts | 15% | 20% | 45% | 30% | 30% |
| 59, 221 | Cottons, plain [3] | 5% [2] | 15% | 35% | 25% | 25% |
| 60, 222 | Cotton yarn [3] | 5% [2] | 15% | 35% | 25% | 25% |
| 67, 247 | Earthenware | 10% | 15% | 35% | 20% | 20% |
| 85, 293 | Glass, window < 8 × 10 | 10% | 100 sq.ft. $1.60 | 100 sq.ft. $3.20 | 100 sq.ft. $2.50 | 100 sq.ft. $3.00 |
| 103, 396 | Iron, hammered bar | 7½% | 15% | 35% | Cwt 45¢ | 90¢ |
| 105, 403 | Iron, castings | 7½% | 15% | 35% | Cwt 75¢ | Cwt 112¢ |
| 131, 488 | Iron, nails | lb. 1¢ | lb. 2¢ | lb. 4¢ | lb. 3¢ | lb. 5¢ |
| 116, 447 | Leather manufactures | 7½% | 15% | 35% | 30% | 30% |
| 127, 480 | Molasses | Gal. 2½¢ | Gal. 4¢ | Gal. 10¢ | Gal. 5¢ | Gal. 5¢ |
| 139, 841 | Paper, foolscap | 7½% | 12½% | 30% | 30% | lb. 17¢ |
| 161, 607 | Salt | Bush. 10¢ | Bush. 20¢ | Bush. 20¢ | Bush. 20¢ | Bush. 20¢ |
| 181, 684 | Spirits, grain | Gal. 8¢ | Gal. 29¢ | Gal. 58¢ | Gal. 45¢ | Gal. 45¢ |
| 191, 705 | Sugar, refined | lb. 3¢ | lb. 9¢ | lb. 18¢ | lb. 12¢ | lb. 12¢ |
| 196, 723 | Tea, bohea in U.S. vessels | lb. 6¢ | lb. 14¢ | lb. 28¢ | lb. 12¢ | lb. 12¢ |
| 204, 735 | Tin, unmanufactured | Free | Free | Free | Free | Free |
| 230, 813 | Woolens | 5% [2] | 12½% [2] | 30% [3] | 25% [3] | 30% [3] |

Source: Rates of Duties, U.S. Senate, Report 2130, Washington, Government Printing Office, February 4, 1891.
[1] Item numbers refer to the Comparative Statements in the source, Tables I and II respectively.
[2] Unenumerated.
[3] For minimums imposed in 1816 and 1824, see text.

leaf, gunpowder, and paints. Carriages alone attracted 15 percent. Specific duties were levied on ale and cider, boots and shoes, candles and soap, cheese, coal, cocoa, coffee, cordage and twine, fish, hemp, indigo, iron cables and chains, malt, molasses, salt, spirits and wines, steel, sugar, tea, and manufactured tobacco and snuff. Unenumerated imports paid 5 percent. Ratner has estimated the average duty at 8.5 percent.[74]

The tariff became higher and more extensive over the next twenty years through many amendments and new tariffs in 1790 and 1816. By 1800, 15 percent was the most common ad valorem rate (and the maximum, except for some wines at 40 percent). By 1800, too, the specific list had been doubled in length, with the addition of some more revenue items (cassia, chocolate, cinnamon, cloves, mace, nutmegs, pepper, pimento), some more iron manufactures (anchors, nails and spikes, and sheet iron), and also cotton, currants, plums and raisins, glass, Glauber's salts, glue, gunpowder, lead and its manufactures, lime, ochre and Spanish brown, pewter plate, starch, and tallow. The free list, largely unmanufactured materials, consisted of antimony, brass, brimstone, bristles, clay, copper, cork bark, drugs and dyes, bullion and coin, lapis calamimaris, pewter, plaster of Paris, rags, crude saltpeter, sulfur, tin, wire, wood, wool, "goods for the use of the United States," scientific instruments, and immigrants' effects.[75]

Further extensions and increases were made during the periods 1804 to 1808 and 1812 to 1816, mostly prompted by the needs of the Treasury.[76] It took more than 200 items to describe the tariff on February 5, 1816. By 1804, the usual ad valorem duty was 17.5 percent (up from 7.5 percent or 10 percent in the early tariffs). Specific rates generally had not been raised by a greater proportion than the ad valorem rates; in fact, a number of specific duties had not changed since 1790 (for example, ale and cider in bottles, candles, textile cards, cheese, cotton, fish, lead, malt, pepper, pimento, and soap). Unenumerated imports

[74] Ratner (1972), p. 11. This figure seems a little low.

[75] In 1795, the tariff was levied on the foreign valuation (plus a notional charge for freight); before that year, American valuation was used. Later tariffs were compensated for this reduction in the severity of the rates. Clark (1929), I, 271.

[76] See Stanwood (1903), I, 113, for a detailed argument on this period. He finds a hint of protectionism only in 1804.

now paid 15 percent. All tariffs were doubled during the War of 1812: 30 percent and 35 percent were then the only ad valorem rates, 35 percent being the most common.

The Act of April 27, 1816 represented a substantial increase over previous peacetime rates. The average reduction in the 120-odd specific duties was about one-third, rather than the one-half required to reverse the wartime increases.[77] Ad valorem rates were generally 20 percent [78] or 30 percent,[79] with a few items at 7.5 percent and 15 percent, and textiles at 25 percent.[80] The chief novelty of the new act was the introduction of minimum valuations on cotton manufactures: 25¢ per square yard on cloth; 60¢ and 75¢ per pound on unbleached and bleached yarn respectively. In 1818 there were increases in duties on iron bars, pigs, castings and nails, and on alum, manufactures of copper and glass, Russia sheeting, and some minor products.

*Dallas's categories.* What explanations can be made for the changes in tariffs to 1816? [81] Clearly, fiscal needs of government greatly influenced the general movements in duties and the particular changes in "revenue" items (wines and liquors, tea, spices, sugar, and salt). As for "protective" duties, their relative movements could have reflected comparative advantage but some evidence available from a classification of industries made in 1816 suggests an inversion.

In suggesting a new tariff schedule in 1816, Secretary of the Treasury Dallas, following Hamilton's *Report on Manufactures* (1791), divided American manufactures into three classes according to the firmness of their establishment and their capacity to meet the home

[77] The specific rates on bottles, copper bolts and rods (off the free list), fish, and some sugar increased rather than fell.

[78] At 20 percent were hempen cloth, stockings; types; manufactures of brass, copper, iron, steel, pewter, tin, and lead; cutlery; brass wire; pins and needles; buttons and button molds; buckles, gilt ware; cannon, muskets, and other arms; Prussian blue; chinaware, etc.; other glass manufactures.

[79] The major items at 30 percent were umbrellas and frames; bonnets, caps, hats, millinery; painted floor cloths; salad oils; pickles, capers, etc.; cabinetware, carriages and parts, and wood manufactures; leather and manufactures; paper, etc., and blank books; brushes; canes, sticks, and whips; ready-made clothing.

[80] The rate of 25 percent on cotton textiles was to be reduced to 20 percent after three years, and on woolens to 20 percent after one year. These reductions were not made.

[81] Because the correlation between the rates of 1816 and 1824 is high, the following discussion also applies to 1824.

demand.[82] In the first class, those firmly and permanently established, and which wholly or almost wholly supplied the demand for domestic use and consumption, he put the following:

Cabinetware and all manufactures of wood
Carriages of all descriptions
Cables and cordage
Hats and bonnets
Iron castings, fire and side arms
Window glass
Leather and all its manufactures
Paper and blank books
Printing types

In the second class (what we would be tempted to call "infant industries") he placed:

Cotton and woolen goods of the coarser kind
Metal buttons
Plated ware
Iron manufactures of the larger kind: shovels, spades, axes, nails
Pewter, tin, brass, and copper manufactures
Alum and copperas
Spirits, beer, ale, and porter

In Dallas's third class were those "so slightly cultivated as to leave the demand of the country wholly or almost wholly dependent upon foreign sources":

Cotton manufactures of the finer kind
Manufactures of linen, hemp, and silk
Some woolens: worsted, blankets, carpets
Hosiery and knit and woven gloves
Small hardware and ironmongery
Chinaware, earthenware, and porcelain
Glass other than window glass.

---

[82] *Tariff of Duties on Imports*, by A. J. Dallas, Secretary of the Treasury, February 12, 1816 (Report 470, *ASP, Finance*); all quotations are from pp. 89 and 90.

This classification was used to devise tariff principles. The first class of imports might be prohibited without loss except to revenue. The second class could usefully be aided for a limited period to place them on a stronger footing by duties that "should be such as to enable the manufacturer to meet the importer in the American market upon equal terms of profit and loss." The last class should receive revenue duties. Overall, the policy should be directed at "future safety and independence" to avoid "an increased difficulty of reinstating, upon any emergency, the manufactures which shall be allowed to perish or pass away."

It is interesting to consider Dallas's three classes and their relation to earlier and later import duties. Most of the products still had ad valorem rates at the time Dallas wrote, and apart from carriages, window glass and spirits, products in the first class did not receive higher than average protection before 1816.[83] The new Tariff of 1816 gave most of the industries in the first class the maximum ad valorem rate (30 percent), whereas the second class tended to receive 20 percent (except spirits), and the third class generally no more than 20 percent.[84] The same ranking was preserved by the Act of 1824, with the difference between the first group and the others being, if anything, increased. Industries well established by the end of the War of 1812 were relatively well protected by the 1816 tariff. To the extent that Dallas had correctly judged the ranking of comparative advantages, it would appear that "needs" were not the bases for rates of duty in 1816.[85] To he that hath, it shall be given?

A final explanation (besides revenue and protective "needs") is national defense. The rates of 1816 were designed in part to allow war babies to survive, but it is not clear that newly established industries were more heavily protected than the older industries; rather the contrary, if Dallas's categories are accepted.[86]

[83] This suggests that the firm establishment of the first class was not a consequence of stronger protection before 1816.

[84] The equivalent rates on alum and copperas were considerably higher.

[85] In terms of the protective margin provided to proprietorial surplus by the excess of output tariff over input tariff, there is no pattern of vulnerability among Dallas's categories.

[86] Martial goods were obtained not by tariff protection as much as by direct order by government. In passing, it is worth noting that successive Secretaries had great influence on the early tariff schedules, especially Hamilton in 1792: see Stanwood (1903), I, 101 ff.

## The Tariff of 1824

The Act of 1824 consolidated and raised the rates set in 1816 and 1818. There was an attempt in 1820 to pass a new tariff that failed by one Senate vote; the rates of 1824 were similar to those of the failed bill, but higher than the 1816 rates (see also chapter 3).

To compare the 1824 nominal rates of duty with those of 1816, tariffs quoted in specific terms (a duty per physical quantity or weight) must be reduced to percents or ad valorem equivalents. A set of prices for the period 1821–24 was used to convert specific rates from both acts, so that what are referred to below as the 1816–18 tariff rates are the rates that applied just before the passage of the 1824 tariff, and not those that applied at the time of passage of the earlier acts (see appendix B). The basic price sources were Bezanson, Gray, and Hussey (1937), which gives monthly wholesale prices in Philadelphia for 237 products, far more than Cole (1938); import statistics, *Commerce and Navigation Reports*, which increased considerably in detail in 1824–25; and Congressional reports. In the course of legislative discussions of new tariff bills, the question was raised whether rates were being increased by conversion to specific duties; therefore a number of reports in this period quote the prices of imports, or give ad valorem equivalents of specific duties.[87] Useful for the period before 1824 are reports 470 (1816), 554 (1819), 609 (1821), and 643 (1822) in *American State Papers, Finance*, vol. III. If no price was available for an imported good, then it was assumed that the price of the American product applied.

To compare the Act of 1824 and the Act of 1816 (with its modifications), prices in the period 1821–24 were used. The monthly prices in Bezanson for the years 1821–23 were averaged to even out fluctuations; similarly, the average unit import values for 1821–23 were used

---

[87] There is the difficulty that imports and American products were not identical. If the qualities and therefore prices of an American product and a competing imported product differ, what then is the ad valorem equivalent of a specific tariff? If both prices were available, I assumed that the American product enjoyed a tariff equal to the specific duty as a percentage of the imported price. For example, the tariff in 1824 on bar iron, not rolled, was $18 a ton. Bezanson's price for domestic iron bar is (in December 1823) $89.50 a ton, and for English bar iron $77.50 a ton; I assumed that the American-produced iron price would have been without the tariff equal to: $89.5/[1 + 18/(77.5 - 18)] = 68.7$.

if they provided sufficient detail, otherwise the 1824 values. Whenever possible, price changes were adjusted by deflating with a similar series in Bezanson. For example, a number of prices of spices from *Report 609* were deflated by the ratio of the simple averages of the prices for spices common to that report and Bezanson: chocolate, cloves, cocoa, coffee, nutmeg, pepper, and pimento. Some additional prices were found in the *Digest of Manufactures* (1820), and in the "McLane Report" (1833).[88] It must be noted, however, that in pricing out specific duties my judgment often had to suffice, leaving a fair margin for error.

In appendix A there is a discussion of the "small country assumption," that is, that domestic prices are equal to foreign prices plus the tariff. In comparing the Tariff of 1824 with the previous tariff, this assumption is made, thus ignoring the possibility of redundant tariffs (e.g., on exported goods) and prohibitive tariffs. Consider the wheat tariff of 50¢ a bushel imposed in 1824. One might regard it as redundant, imposed to give the appearance of evenhanded treatment of agriculture and industry. However, its purpose was to protect: there was a border trade in wheat from Upper Canada which competed with wheat from New York; wheat was also exported from the United States. This example, besides indicating the need for caution in interpretation of the ad valorem equivalents of specific duties (because of the geographic variation in United States prices), illustrates the difficulties of deciding whether a duty is redundant. In the explanation of rates of duty in 1824 (chapter 6), tariffs have not always been taken at face value, but they are here when discussing the act as a piece of legislation.

Import prices collapsed after 1816: on a base of 1816 prices = 100, North's index of manufactured and semimanufactured landed import prices takes the value 75 in 1820 and 59 in 1824.[89] To the extent that imports were perfect or almost perfect substitutes for domestic products, a decrease in the landed duty-paid price of imports forced an identical or almost identical reduction in the price of American products, so that an American import-competing industry would have contracted unless its costs had fallen as fast. In fact, the considerable fall in

[88] *Documents Relative to the Manufactures in the United States,* by Louis McLane, Secretary of the Treasury, House Ex. Doc. 308, 22d Congress, 1st Session (Washington: Duff Green, 1833).

[89] North (1966), p. 245.

foreign prices was matched by a similar fall in American prices and costs (not without hardship in the crisis of 1819). It was not merely in goods identical to imports, but a general deflation, albeit relatively more severe in the kinds of products that went to make up manufactures or were consumed by wage earners.[90] Therefore, unless wages fell slower than materials and food prices, the costs of American manufacturers must have fallen at least as fast as import prices.

But American manufactures with specific duties were now protected by higher ad valorem equivalents than in 1816, without any legislative action. If the 1816 equivalent of a specific duty on an import with an average price experience was 25 percent, by 1820 the equivalent would have been 31 percent and by 1824, 35 percent.[91]

Not all the reduction in import prices was due to foreign production costs; ocean freights fell, so that natural protection was eroded. For example, if freight rates fell 40 percent between 1816 and 1824,[92] and if freights respresented 20 percent of the 1816 landed price of an import, then the output of an industry protected by an ad valorem duty would have fallen unless its costs had decreased over 8 percent more than foreign costs of production. However, neglecting this relatively minor effect, and apart from changes in comparative technology, the competitive position of American manufacturers probably had slightly improved on balance.

So far the discussion has been concerned with the comparative costs of American seaboard manufacturers. In a striking image, Daniel Webster made clear the importance of inland freight costs: "Stockholm, therefore, for purposes of the argument may be considered as within fifty miles of Philadelphia." [93] A fall in inland freights increased the

[90] Cole's indexes of Philadelphia wholesale prices of imports and domestic commodities fall almost identically between January 1816 and December 1824. Cole (1938), pp. 146, 148. Note, however, that the prices of American manufactured and semimanufactured exports fell a lot slower than did the prices of materials and foodstuff exports. North (1966), pp. 280, 281, 282. The Warren-Pearson price index had the values from 93, 69, and 54 in 1816, 1820, and 1824. North (1968), p. 970.

[91] $1.25 \times 0.25 = 0.3125;\ 1.41 \times 0.25 \times 0.3525.$ In similar vein, Berglund and Wright (1929), p. 110, find that decreased ore prices raised the ad valorem equivalent of the 75¢ ore duty from 30 percent in 1890 to 50 percent in 1894. See also the speech by Lowndes, *Annals* 16th cong., 1st Sess. (1820), p. 2130.

[92] North's (1966), p. 282, *export* freight index is 1816 = 100, 1820 = 81, and 1824 = 59.

[93] *Annals* 18th Cong., 1st. Sess. (1823–24), p. 2065.

market penetration of imports and manufacturers located at ports with seaboard costs lower than those of establishments inland.[94] It is not at all clear, however, that inland costs of production were always higher, especially for relatively easily transported products made of bulky and low-valued materials: some manufactures of iron and glass, for example.[95] If economies of scale were not very important—as the work of Bateman and Weiss suggests—then there were some inland manufacturers who benefited from falling inland freight.[96]

## The Tariffs of 1816 and 1824 Compared

What were the average rates of duty before and after the Act of 1824, and how uneven? There were 245 items which had ad valorem rates or for which the ad valorem equivalents of specific duties could be calculated. Table 2.6 shows the mean rising from 27.4 percent to 34.5 percent.[97] Surprisingly, the hypothesis that the two means were equal cannot be rejected at the 5 percent level of significance.

The rates on the major revenue items—spirits, sugar, tea, and wines—were much higher than the rates in general (mean 73.4 percent) and were not altered in 1824. Even when the revenue items were excluded, specific rates were higher than ad valorem rates in 1824 (38.2 percent compared with 25.2 percent). The charge that specific rates were used to conceal higher rates of duties is substantiated.[98] Not surprisingly, the dispersion of ad valorem rates was much smaller than the dispersion of specific rates.

[94] An index for internal freight would be difficult to devise. Some indication of the fall in rates is given by Zevin, in Fogel and Engerman (1972), pp. 131–32: dry goods were carried from Philadelphia or Baltimore to Louisville or Cincinnati for 10¢ per pound in 1815–16, and 2.5¢ in 1824.

[95] See Tryon (1917), p. 299.

[96] Bateman and Weiss (1975) report some preliminary work on economies of scale using manuscript samples from the censuses of 1850 and 1860. Only in the South is there any evidence of increasing returns. In face of equal falls in inland and ocean freights, the inland manufacturers would have increased their market shares if their costs exceeded foreign costs of production by less than the tariff, because then the domestic producer would have had more than half the market (in the simple linear case illustrated by figure 4.2) even if foreign freights were zero.

[97] These means include seven unenumerated products (15 percent duty in both years). Generally, such items have been excluded.

[98] See Goss (1897); Stanwood (1903), I, 169.

T A B L E  2.6

*Means and Variances of Nominal Tariff Rates, Before and After the Act of 1824*

| DESCRIPTION | NO. OF ITEMS | 1816 [1] | | 1824 | |
|---|---|---|---|---|---|
| | | MEAN | VARIANCE | MEAN | VARIANCE |
| All duties | 245 | 27.4 | 329.9 | 34.5 | 418.2 |
| Spirits, sugar, teas, wines (SSTW) | 18 | 73.4 | 463.2 | 73.4 | 463.2 |
| Specific in both acts, less SSTW | 71 | 29.9 | 282.3 | 34.7 | 452.2 |
| Ad valorem, both acts | 118 | 21.9 | 54.8 | 25.2 | 68.4 |
| Ad valorem 1816, specific 1824 | 38 | 19.8 | 35.9 | 44.7 | 352.6 |

*Sources:* The text and appendix B.
*Note:* Specific duties were evaluated at 1821–24 prices.
[1] The Tariff Act of 1816 as amended before 1824.

Although the means of the 245 items are not significantly different, the changes made in the act were substantially upward, with very few decreases. The most spectacular changes were in items moved from ad valorem in 1816 to specific in 1824. The mean of these thirty-eight products increased by nearly 25 percentage points (table 2.7), which more than doubled their 1816 rates. The mean change in all rates was a

T A B L E  2.7

*Means and Variances of Changes in Duties, 1824*

| DESCRIPTION | NO. OF ITEMS | MEAN CHANGE | VARIANCE OF CHANGES |
|---|---|---|---|
| All changes | 126 | 13.6 | 180.7 |
| Specific in both acts | 26 | 12.0 | 17.2 |
| Ad valorem, both acts | 62 | 7.4 | 44.2 |
| Ad valorem 1816, specific 1824 | 38 | 24.7 [1] | 331.1 |

*Sources:* The text and appendix B.
*Note:* Specific duties were evaluated at 1821–24 prices.
[1] Table 2.6, bottom line, shows a mean difference of 24.9; the conflict is due to rounding errors.

more modest 13.6 percentage points, but the mean change in ad valorem rates was only 7.4 percentage points. Generally, then, the Act of
1824 increased the rates of protection even though the mean tariffs
were not significantly different in the two acts.

Turning to detail, the main interest centers on the rates of protection
for textiles, iron, glass, and paper. The reduction scheduled for 1819 in
the cotton textile duty from 25 to 20 percent did not take place. The
new tariff raised the minimum valuation (so useful when prices had
fallen after 1816) from 25 to 30¢ for an average protection of over 50
percent. Ready-made clothing retained a 30 percent duty. The minimum valuations and duties set in 1816 on cotton yarns were retained
for a rate of about 70 percent. Raw cotton itself had a duty of 3¢, which
raised the price of imported cotton by 19 percent in 1824. However,
the "protection" of cotton was now no longer significant. The duty on
woolens increased to 30 percent with a promise of 33⅓ percent after
1825, but no minimum was enacted.[99] Carpets now received specific
duties that raised import prices by 30 to 50 percent, although any
benefits to manufacturers were partly offset by an increased levy on
wool of 20 percent in the first instance, rising to 25 percent and then
30 percent in 1825 and 1826; cheap wool (costing less than 10¢ a
pound) remained at 15 percent. Dyes were charged 12.5 percent instead of 7.5 percent, although dye woods still entered free.[100]

Pig iron received 20 percent in 1816, replaced by 50¢ a hundred-
weight (cwt) in 1818 and 1824 (equivalent to about 20 percent). Discrimination in favor of hammered bars had been introduced in 1816
but was progressively reduced until the rates in 1824 were for rolled
bars $1.50 a cwt and for others 90¢ (the former raised import prices
about 57 percent). Most duties within the fine iron classification were
increased from 20 percent to at least 25 percent, firearms receiving 30
percent (except muskets). Of interest to shipbuilders were iron cables
and chains: 20 percent to a specific rate of about 38 percent, with no

[99] In fact there was a kind of reverse minimum whereby cheap woolens paid only 25
percent.
[100] The rates on many "chemicals" were raised: alum (64 percent to 80 percent); refined saltpeter (7.5 percent to 55 percent); Epsom and Glauber's salts (15 percent to over
80 percent); oil of vitriol (15 percent to 71 percent); copperas (94 percent to 188 percent).

drawback.[101] An especially low rate of 12 percent was retained on iron wire for umbrellas.

Glass came in for special attention in 1824, with a much finer classification. Most rates were raised: small window glass from $2.50 per 100 sq. ft. to $3.00; overall, the protection to window glass was about 35 percent. Six separate rates for glass containers (depending on size), averaging about 35 percent, replaced the former single rate. Instead of a single rate for paper of 30 percent, there were eleven specific rates plus one ad valorem of 40 percent. Its raw material, rags, was admitted free.

The duties affecting other sizable industries were as follows. Leather and its manufactures continued to receive 30 percent or so; skins were admitted free. In food and drink, a number of agricultural products such as bacon, beef, and cheese received new specific duties, but only the wheat duties are of interest (26 percent, and wheat flour 122 percent) because they influenced border trade with Canada. Duties on ales and beer were lifted from about 12 percent to 18 percent, still considerably lower than those on wines (50 to 65 percent) and grain spirits (about 100 percent). Rum, made mostly in New England, received about 90 percent, whereas molasses paid 24 percent. Four specific rates protected refined sugar, the most important being more than 100 percent on loaf sugar; raw sugar paid about 50 percent.

Building costs were raised by the imposition of higher duties on nails (up 9 percent from 38 percent), wood screws (up 10 percent to 30 percent) and slate (now 25 percent), as well as hardware and saws (both 25 percent) and window glass.

---

[101] Shipping was also affected by a low (11 percent) rate on sailcloth and the rather higher specific rates (ranging from 50 to 80 percent) on cables and cordage (hemp was unchanged at about 16 percent). Offsetting these disadvantages were the continuing discriminatory duties on products carried in foreign bottoms (an extra 10 percent except that teas had additional specific rates).

# CHAPTER THREE

# Pressure and Congressional Tactics

## PRESSURE AND MEMORIALS

P A S S E D in fairly settled economic conditions, the Tariff Act of 1824 marked a new phase in American tariff history: protection ceased to be in any real sense a national policy but rather became ground for narrow sectional conflicts. Ranged on one side was a tacit alliance between Northern and Southern strict constructionists; on the other, manufacturing interests were supported by Northern and Western agriculture. The period from the end of the War of 1812 to the late 1820s has been called the Era of Good Feelings not for a lack of political strife but for a lack of party, of national coalitions: the logrolling and issue-trading that make possible a party system had not yet taken hold. The Federalists, Madison in particular, had hoped to reduce the ability of any "faction" to become a tyrannical majority by the constitutional separation of powers and, more importantly, by the establishment of a large unit of government covering a diversity of interests.

> Extend the sphere, and you take in a greater variety of parties and interests; you make it less probable that a majority of the whole will have a common motive to invade the rights of other citizens; or if such a common motive exists, it will be more difficult for all who feel it to discover their own strength, and to act in unison with each other.[1]

Unfortunately for political harmony, the major issues of banking, internal improvements, protection of manufacturing, and slavery divided the nation along sectional lines. Great tensions arose, culminating in the case of the tariff in the crisis of the nullification by South Carolina of the 1832 federal tariff law.

The tariff caused great public agitation. In this period, interested

---

[1] *The Federalist*, no. 10, p. 47, quoted in Birch (1971), p. 82.

groups sent petitions (or "memorials") to Congress, addressed to the memorialists' own House or Senate members, asking for modifications of duties. By far the largest proportion of the memorials from 1816 to 1824 were from groups the membership of which did not transcend state lines. The only significant exception was the Philadelphia campaign in favor of widespread protection, which drew some interstate support. Groups of memorialists often formed ad hoc, on town or county lines, although Southern state legislatures or general assemblies were the source of some antiprotectionist petitions; chambers of commerce of the major cities also wrote. The campaign over the tariff was carried to the newspapers, with *Niles' Weekly Register* in the front rank. Apart from such visible signs of pressure, it is assumed that there was other pressure of which we have no convenient historical record. Communications were poor and costly, and in view of the very limited evidence of interstate lobbying, it is reasonable to assert that most interstate and inter-product bargaining took place among the members of Congress, rather than outside Congress. Local pressure groups expected those representing them to press their interests on congressional colleagues and, somewhat inconsistently, to resist the efforts of other local groups.

In some ideal society, representatives would act in the "national interest"; in practice, most would tend to further their own interests unless frequent elections constrained them to act on behalf of their own electors.[2] A consequence of the tension between national and narrow representation was that measures like the tariff had to be defended on grounds of general welfare, or as part of a fairly simple package of policies of benefit to most classes. True, the immediate beneficiaries were the protected industries themselves, but their prosperity was declared essential to national security and progress, and in any case, domestic competition would ensure that monopoly profits did not arise. In 1824 it was a disadvantage for a duty to have been identified in Congress as too local an issue, in that the congressional opponents of tariffs disputed the claims put forward by Henry Clay and others—that further protection was in the national interest—and attempted to op-

[2] Calhoun denied the existence of a "national interest" apart from the vocal interests of powerful groups.

pose each duty on its merits, pointing to the smallness of the numbers who benefited directly. The traditions of the House prevented a vote on the general principles of protection, and items had to be discussed and voted seriatim, unless an opponent had moved to strike the enacting clauses of the bill; none did. There was resistance to protection per se in addition to resistance to particular customs duties.

### Information By Request, 1828

How then were rates of duty to be set? Whatever the principles to be applied, certain information about costs and profits was required. If, for example, revenue was to be assured, there was need for data on comparative costs (and elasticities). Or if duties were to be sufficient for manufacturers to flourish without prohibiting imports, then similar cost data were called for. This issue was pressed by Lowndes of South Carolina in 1820 when high protection was being justified by claims of distress in manufacturing: where were the facts upon which the proposed rates were based? [3]

Reports of committees during 1820–24 refer to information provided, sometimes on request, like woolens cost data from large manufacturers, or ship costs from the Mercantile Society of New York. However, the first Congressional hearing on the tariff of import duties for which there appears to be a record was held early in 1828. There had been much agitation over the tariff in the previous year, and the new Committee on Manufactures had to report on a number of petitions. In addition, the committee wished to make an expeditious inquiry into a few manufacturing interests and, lacking time for collection and presentation to Congress of comprehensive data, decided on the first day of the session to hold hearings to obtain those accurate answers that could only be provided by persons with intimate knowledge of the industries. To that end, the committee was given power to send for persons and papers on December 31, 1827 and decided upon witnesses

---

[3] Lowndes's speech is in the *Annals* 16th Cong., 1st Sess. (1820), p. 2127. The reply was that such data were neither available nor necessary: the tariff sprang from general principles not minute facts. Dorfman (1947), pp. 386–87. The profitable state of Massachusetts cotton factories was pointed at to throw doubt on the kind of despairing pleas found in the *Digest of Manufactures* (1820).

the next day. Hearings began on January 10; the report is dated January 31, 1828.[4]

Twenty-eight persons were interrogated; at least nine were members of Congress; all appear to have had direct interests in one or more products under inquiry; a clear majority were manufacturers. That the range of testimony was narrow is indicated by the comment that the committee examined those subpoenaed together with "all those manufacturers and others, who, up to that time, to the knowledge of the committee, arrived in the city, for the purposes of giving the committee information."[5]

The subjects inquired into and the number of witnesses were: iron (three); steel (three); wool (fifteen); woolens (seventeen); hemp, flax, and sailduck (two); spirits from grain (four); spirits from molasses (five); window glass (two); cotton cloth (eight); paper (two). The changes enacted in 1828 concentrated on these products, many of which had received special attention in past tariffs.[6] The interest in wool and woolens is to be expected from the abortive 1827 Woolens Bill and the Harrisburg convention. Taussig points out that the convention called for increases on cotton manufactures, hemp, flax, iron, and glass, but that these other interests were included as a means of gaining support for aid to the woolen industry.[7]

The three persons appearing on iron were expert witnesses, presenting detailed information about prices and costs. Their requests for additional iron protection were selective and relatively modest. All three spoke briefly on steel, denying much knowledge of the industry; one witness recommended additional steel duties on the general grounds that it accorded with government policy. The evidence on the threat to domestic wool growers from imports was mixed, possibly because all witnesses except one were substantial Eastern manufacturers of woolen goods. Most of those speaking on woolens were happy with additional

[4] *Duties on Imports.* Report 115 to the House, 20th Cong., 1st Sess., by the Committee on Manufactures, January 31, 1828 (166 pp. of collected testimony).

[5] Ibid., p. 3. There is a reference on p. 45 to a deputation of wool growers including one of the witnesses, Aaron Tuffts, who was a woolens manufacturer.

[6] Duties were altered also on annatto, canes, clocks, indigo, mats, bottled salad oil, perfumes, prussiate of potash, scale beams, slate and tiles, precious stones, sugar of lead, and wines.

[7] Taussig (1931), pp. 83 ff. See also Wright (1910).

protection for both wool and woolens. On hemp, flax, and duck, the questions revolved about the suitability of American flax and hemp for manufacturing and whether water rotting of flax rather than dew rotting was necessary.[8] The four witnesses speaking on both spirits from grain and from molasses (one was a retailer) called for higher duties on imported materials, that is, the favoring of grain distillation. All agreed this would benefit farmers. Neither witness on glass argued that higher duties were necessary, at least in their range of products. There was a clear conflict over cottons. A manufacturer of coarse cottons [9] and a seller of yarn [10] thought the present duties satisfactory, but others [11] called for assistance for fine fabrics and prints. The witnesses (one of whom was a manufacturer) agreed that no changes were needed in duties on imported paper.[12] The testimony in general provides a very flimsy basis for the bill reported out of the committee.

## Private Lobbying and Influence

Considering the conflicting nature of public information, it is not surprising to find repeated comments that the tariff rates were set in response to manufacturers' private requests. Since 1789, manufacturers had journeyed to the capital to lobby Congress.[13] Francis C. Lowell is credited with the imposition of the 1816 cottons minimum valuations; Samuel Slater was present in Washington in 1824 to plead his industry's case. Mathew Carey followed his *Addresses* (1819) for the Philadelphia Society for the Promotion of National Industry by secretly fi-

[8] One witness (John Travers of Patterson, N.J.) claimed to be the only man in the country who had spun hemp with machinery. The other witness (James Clark, a Representative from Kentucky) had given up hemp growing in 1823 or 1824.

[9] S. N. Dexter of Delaware, with interests in Oneida Manufacturing Society, Attica Cotton Manufacturing Co., and Whitestown Cotton and Woollen Manufacturing Co.

[10] J. Siddal of Delaware.

[11] Aaron Tuffts of Massachusetts (who had argued against increasing wool duties) and J. Marshall of Hudson, New York (from Manchester, with thirty years experience), in particular.

[12] B. Bakewell cited a report from the paper manufacturer in his city of Pittsburgh, satisfied with the existing duties. He himself was a glass manufacturer and did not ask for higher glass duties.

[13] Herring states that the "old," covert lobbies had been present in the capital, entertaining and bribing, since the first Congress and its debate on the funding of the national debt and assumption of state debts. Herring (1929), pp. 30 ff.

nancing his friend, Condy Raguet, for a week's talk during recess with Baldwin (chairman of the Committee on Manufactures) and others.[14] Most lobbying was ad hoc. The first instance of a group assessing themselves for the expenses of sending an agent to Washington may have been an 1815 Providence cottons committee. Such behavior probably grew common in the next decade, but there was no permanent establishment of lobbies in Washington. Baldwin, speaking as chairman of the Committee on Manufactures in 1820, defended himself against the charge that his was a private committee acting on private petitions, denied having produced "a Pittsburg, a cut-glass bill," claiming more respectable sources, namely, Treasury and earlier committee reports.[15] However, these sources were themselves not unimpeachable. Secretary Dallas had in 1816, it was alleged, recommended a bill identical, apart from iron, to that proposed by Petersburg merchants. The legislation of 1824 was called more "outdoor than indoor": "all sorts of pilgrims had travelled to the room of the Committee of manufactures, from iron masters to the poor manufacturer of whetstones."[16] Cambreleng of New York insisted that the committee had adopted, in every instance, the rates proposed by the manufacturers themselves, especially the fifty or sixty manufacturers who were members of the House.[17] Here, indeed, was the most likely and fruitful entry for pressure. To investigate it is, unfortunately, beyond the scope of this work.[18] We now turn to an important public source of tariff suggestions—memorials.

---

[14] Ware (1931), pp. 56 n5, 71; Stanwood (1903), I, 146; Taussig (1931), p. 35.

[15] "The Committee of Manufactures have not acted, and would not act on the statement, or even the affidavits, of interested persons. . . . I repeat it, that the profits of manufacturers had not been a leading motive, but the public national interest." Baldwin, *Annals*, 16th Cong., 1st Sess. (1820), p. 1943.

[16] J. Hamilton of South Carolina, quoted in Stanwood (1903), I, 237.

[17] *Annals*, 18th Cong., 1st Sess. (1823–24) p. 1578. A similar complaint was made against the Committee on Manufactures in 1820. *Annals*, 16th Cong., 1st Sess. (1820), pp. 1416, 1917, 1143.

[18] John Adams, Jefferson, Monroe, and the then President, Madison (who accepted in person) were elected members of the New York Society for the Promotion of National Industry. Not all these men, of course, were straightforward "friends of protection." Stanwood (1903), I, 161.

## Memorials

The Constitutional right to petition had been well exercised on a range of matters,[19] but the tariff dominated at least until the 1830s. Until 1815, most asked aid for a particular industry;[20] after that year, general agitation started and an organized industrial interest, embracing manufacturers and suppliers of industrial material, began to be felt.[21]

Between 1815 and 1818 four tariff memorials appear in *American State Papers:* two opposing cheap cottons from India; one from 175 New York merchants begging a 10 percent auction duty, prohibition of Indian cottons, and a continuation beyond two years of the present cottons tariff; and a request from Louisiana sugar planters. But there are also committee reports, usually in response to memorials, on woolens, paper hangings, salt, slate, and wines.[22] In 1818, Congress modified iron and other duties, but no memorials were printed. The first session of the 16th Congress (1819–20) narrowly failed to pass a revision that aroused much controversy; about forty memorials were printed, possibly half the total received, and about twice the number printed by the 17th Congress. The 18th Congress was flooded with memorials in unprecedented numbers;[23] table 3.1 presents a partial list.[24] The postwar campaign for protection was launched in Philadelphia and Baltimore, the leading fighters being Mathew Carey and Hezekiah Niles.[25] *Niles'*

[19] For example, the volume of petitions against the embargo and nonintercourse acts.

[20] In 1804, window glass; 1805, hollow ware; 1807, paint, hats (Journeymen Hat Makers of New York), and copperware (Reveres); 1808, twines; 1809, salt, hemp (Kentucky); 1811, hemp, morocco, and iron (New Jersey); 1812, brewers. Stanwood (1903), I, 113 ff.

[21] *Ibid.*, p. 127; Cole (1926), p. 277.

[22] A report to the House dated April 7, 1818 refers to memorials from paper hangings manufacturers of Boston, Rhode Island, Hartford, and several New York towns. The New York Slate Co. memorial is mentioned in *ASP, Finance,* III, 531.

[23] Dorfman does state, however, that in 1803 Congress received an avalanche of memorials. Dorfman (1947), p. 323.

[24] Unfortunately, I was not able to obtain permission in time to examine unprinted House documents, but only those in the Senate archives. *Annals,* 18th Cong., 1st Sess. (1823–24), p. 1481, states that about 100 petitions on protection had been received. There may be duplicate entries in table 3.1.

[25] Before 1817 and his decision to reprint Say's *Catechism,* Mathew Carey was undecided whether he supported free trade. Dorfman (1947), pp. 384–86.

## T A B L E  3.1

### Petitions on the Tariff Presented to the Eighteenth Congress, First Session, 1823–24

| | VOLUME | NUMBER |
|---|---|---|
| PRINTED BY THE SENATE [a] | | |
| S. Slater and others | 238 | 13 |
| Chamber of Commerce, New York City | 239 | 31 |
| Geo. Jones and others | 240 | 48 |
| PRINTED BY THE HOUSE [a] | | |
| Manufacturers of cordage, New York City | 243 | 9 |
| Chamber of Commerce, New York City | 244 | 19 |
| Auctions | | 22 |
| Chamber of Commerce, Philadelphia | | 27 |
| Auctions | | 34 |
| Printing and dyeing | | 35 |
| Manufacturers, etc. of cotton | | 36 |
| New York delegates in favor of manufacturing | | 37 |
| Tariff | | 48 |
| Baltimore auctioneers | 246 | 53 |
| J. Elkins and others | | 63 |
| Citizens of Charleston, S.C. | | 64 |
| Vendors of hardware, New York City | | 65 |
| Albany (woolens) | | 66 |
| Boston merchants | | 67 |
| Chamber of Commerce, New York City | | 68 |
| Merchants of Portland | | 71 |
| Citizens of Richmond | | 74 |
| Citizens of Beaufort | 247 | 81 |
| Merchants of Portsmouth | | 87 |
| Petersburg, Va. (Chamber of Commerce) | | 88 |
| Chamber of Commerce, Philadelphia [1] | | 94 |
| Chamber of Commerce, New Haven | | 96 |
| Citizens of Darien | | 98 |
| Merchants of Baltimore | | 99 |
| Farmers of Pennsylvania [1,2] | | 100 |
| Inhabitants of Darlington | | 101 |
| Boston (tallow) | | 105 |
| New York (tallow) | | 106 |
| Bedford, Mass. (tallow) | | 107 |
| Nantucket (tallow) | | 108 |
| Inhabitants of Fayetteville | | 109 |
| Citizens of Norfolk | | 112 |
| Citizens of Pitman Co., Ga. | | 114 |
| Pennsylvania Soc. Encouragement of Manufactures [1] | | 116 |
| Philadelphia citizens [1,4] | | 123 |
| Inhabitants of St Lukes Co., S.C. | | 124 |

| PRESENTED TO SENATE, NOT PRINTED [b] | |
|---|---|
| Wool growers of Rhode Island | 15 December 1823 |
| J. White (linseed oil) | 23 January 1824 |
| J. Garsed (flax) | 28 January 1824 |
| Umbrella manufacturers of Philadelphia | 2 February 1824 |
| Manufacturers of Baltimore | 2 February 1824 |
| Philadelphia tallow chandlers | 4 February 1824 |
| Senate and House of Pa. | 5 February 1824 |
| Germantown, Pa. (woolens) | 11 February 1824 |
| Legislature of Indiana | 12 February 1824 |
| Charleston, S.C. | 13 February 1824 |
| Savannah,[5] Ga. | |
| Augusta, Ga. | |
| Baldwin Co., Ga. | |
| Burke Co., Ga. | |
| Oglethorpe, Ga. | |
| Sumter, Ga. | |
| Twiggs Co., Ga. | |
| Wilkes Co., Ga. | |
| Farmers of N.Y.[3] | 17 March 1824 |
| E. Littell, Philadelphia (bookseller) | 23 April 1824 |
| Pliny Moore and others (Canada trade) | 28 April 1824 |
| General Assembly of Ohio | |

| | PAGE REFERENCE |
|---|---|
| OTHER PETITIONS [c] | |
| Salem Laboratories, Mass. | 843 |
| Jefferson Co., Ohio (for extra tariff) | 843 |
| Philadelphia inhabitants (iron) | 1083 |
| Friends of National Industry, Ct. (iron especially) | 3124 |
| Merchants of Richmond and Manchester, Va. (cottons) | 3098 |
| Farmers, Van Rensselaer Co., N.Y. (extra duties) | 3132 |
| J. Clarke, Bridgetown, N.J. (iron) | 113 |
| L. Mumford, Cumberland Co., N.J. (iron) | 113 |
| Georgetown, S.C. | 422 |

Sources: [a] Records of publications of the Senate and the House, 13th Cong., 3d Sess. (National Archives no. 13D-B1.)

[b] National Archives files Sen 17A-G2 to 17A-G4 have the originals.

[c] Annals of Congress, 18th Cong., 1st Sess. (Washington, Gales & Seaton, 1854) 41 and 42.

[1] Printed circulars.

[2] Also presented by farmers of N.J.; Pennsylvania was crossed out and New Jersey inserted.

[3] Contains over 1,400 signatures.

[4] At least 30 separate copies, each with many signatures.

[5] These Georgia meetings were held between March 3 and 19, 1824.

*Weekly Register*, which in 1815 devoted a volume to the tariff, was to become the vehicle for the addresses of the Philadelphia Society for the Promotion of National Industry (which had eight members),[26] the American Society for the Encouragement of Domestic Manufactures, and the Friends of National Industry.[27] Delegates from New England, the Middle Atlantic States, and Ohio, with Mathew Carey as secretary,[28] met in New York in 1819 and again in 1820. Their memorial was followed by others from 600 or 700 Maryland "manufacturers," the American Society of New York for the Encouragement of Domestic Manufactures, a similar Pennsylvania society, and the Convention of the Friends of National Industry meeting in Patterson, N.J. These and other large petitions, usually printed up and circulated for signature, were very broad in their requests.[29]

The Senate was swamped with memorials in the first session of the 18th Congress (1823–24). Printed petitions, circulated in Philadelphia, had attracted thousands of signatures. In Baltimore, 1400 manufacturers and mechanics asked for increases in the duties on manufactures of glass, paper, iron, flax, hemp, wool, and silk, besides an extra 10 percent duty on auctions. The Connecticut Friends of National Industry met in Hartford with two delegates from each county. Approval of the new bill was voiced by the General Assembly of Ohio, the Massachusetts Senate and the Indiana legislature. Seventy-odd farmers from New Jersey used a petition printed in and for Pennsylvania to express disinterested support for protection.

This outpouring was not unopposed, with general protests coming from chambers of commerce and Southern legislatures or agricultural societies (especially in Georgia), besides more ad hoc groups like mer-

[26] *Ibid.*, p. 284.

[27] Niles sometimes printed these addresses without comment; e.g., no. 7 from the Philadelphia Society, *Register* of April 17, 1819. For the role of Niles, see Luxon (1947) and Dorfman (1947).

[28] Carey was to complain subsequently that wealthy manufacturers had not reimbursed him for his 2295 pages of memorials and addresses. Stanwood (1903), 248*n*.

[29] Despite its small numbers, the Philadelphia Society had, according to Whitman of Maine "branches in every part of the Union, with which it corresponds, and which it directs and instigates and sets in motion by means of pamphlets and newspaper essays. Its inflammatory and unfounded statements have pervaded every part of the Union. Each member of the present Congress has been favored with enough to make two large volumes." Stanwood (1903), I, 189.

chants in Petersburg, Va. or a convention in Portland. Judged by weight of paper, the supporters won handsomely.

*Pattern of Petitions.* Memorials between 1818 and 1824 fall roughly into three classes, the first being requests, infrequently printed by Congress, from producers or, less commonly, from users of a small range of products. Manufacturers of copper, copperas, cork, footwear, pig iron, silverware, shot, and slate begged the 16th Congress for increased duties, as did some consumers of paper.[30] Boston and Philadelphia merchants urged more favorable treatment of imported molasses and silks, respectively. Memorials in favor of higher textile duties were also presented. Most of the few memorials about specific items submitted to the next Senate (17th Congress) were concerned with hemp manufactures: a dozen or so people each from Bristol, Newport, and Providence argued for drawbacks on cordage exports, whereas forty-three Philadelphia manufacturers of cordage desired a duty at least equal to that on the raw material. The Pennsylvania Society for the Encouragement of American Manufactures claimed that the hemp duty was relatively low at 27 percent equivalent. J. Greene, stating himself to be one of the remaining copperas producers (there had been five), pleaded for more help, as did 122 Philadelphia makers of bridle bits and coach furniture. Requests for lowered duties came from fifteen umbrella makers who protested a prohibitive duty on square iron and from Thomas Jefferson who objected to the duty on learned books. As is shown by table 3.1, less than 15 percent of the eighty-odd memorials were directed at particular imposts: textile manufacture and printing, wool growing, bookbinding, linseed oil; flax weaving, iron, industrial chemicals, and umbrellas (these for increased protection); hardware vending and the Canada trade (reductions); the whale fisheries. Bedford and Nantucket asked for additional duties on tallow and received support from New York but opposition from Boston chandlers.[31]

Most of the petitions mentioned were signed by relatively few indi-

[30] The printers from Baltimore included Hezekiah Niles, and those from Philadelphia, Mathew Carey.

[31] Stanwood's claim that protectionist forces were often defeated in 1824 is borne out by the fact that the 1824 duties were equal to the 1816 rates for umbrellas, iron, tallow, spermaceti oil, molasses, and raw hemp; increases were proposed for most of these products in Baldwin's 1820 bill. Wheat received a duty but no drawback.

viduals from a restricted geographical area, usually a city. This is to be expected, considering the striking spatial and occupational biases in communications: it was easier to raise a petition on a range of products within a city than for a single product in several cities or localities. In reflection of that city's importance in manufacturing and its vulnerability to imports, Philadelphia sent petitions between 1815 and 1824 on bridle bits, candles, cork, hemp, iron and castings, paper, printing, rolled copper, shot, silverware, and umbrellas. In contrast, it is notable that a number of large, widespread industries were not represented at all or barely so: leather and footwear, wood products, iron, hats, grain distilleries, timber, and flour milling.[32] Where petitions seem to have been organized across state lines (and very few were), they were from industries concentrated in a few locations on the eastern seaboards. Otherwise, wider circulation of petitions is found in the second class (petitions on auction and credit) or third (general petitions).

Between cities or towns, information flowed via newspapers, the post and personal travel, all virtually confined to economic elites. In 1820, the annual number of newspaper issues was 5.2 per capita. Postal charges put the mails beyond the occasional use of other than the rich. Travel was slow and costly (the trip from Boston to New York took more than a day in 1820), and was undertaken chiefly by peddlers and migrants.[33] Information flowed more easily within each locality. Among craftsmen, the small area of the cities and the geographical specialization of economic function encouraged close contacts.[34] Pred (1973) has discussed the strong "neighborhood effects" in the adoption of innovations, transmission of economic crises, and the formation of business attitudes, and emphasized "intimate exchanges of information," that is, that "information of local origin was received by individual entrepreneurs primarily from their own peers in various groups" so that most encounters were face-to-face.[35] Inns and coffee houses served as meeting places for the affluent. Chambers of commerce, established in the major cities, were prominent in opposing changes in the "credit" system for collecting duties and in taxes on auctions. Within a city, how-

[32] The only footwear petition came from New York about prunello shoes.

[33] Pred (1973), pp. 21, 179.

[34] *Ibid.*, p. 280, cites examples from New York, Boston, and Norfolk of the 1820s and 1830s.

[35] *Ibid.*, pp. 278, 279.

ever, sharp clashes of economic interest between commerce and manufacturing precluded an early united front. Boston's businessmen
became increasingly outspoken advocates of protection after 1825, but
opinions were divided before then. New York's position also became
more firm after the middle of the decade, except that the tide there
turned against protection. Baltimore had mainly taken the Southern
line in the early 1820s, although generally it was a protectionist city.[36]

Apart from the chambers of commerce and the protectionist societies
already mentioned, few formal pressure organizations existed; certainly
not for particular industries, the reason (apart from the communications
problem) being chiefly the lack of common interest. For example, although the woolen manufacturers of the Boston area met in 1823 to petition Congress, the industry was divided over protection. Some feared
internal competition consequent to increased duties and believed that
their difficulties lay more in the novelty of machinery than in foreign
competition.[37] The chief obstacle to an effective, unified voice was
diversity within an industry. Small firms had needs that differed from
those of large firms; producers in the interior were protected by the
high cost of internal freight but producers near the seacoast were not.[38]

A number of other circumstances may have stirred an industry into
action. In particular, the threat of extinction, or at least of a very
serious decline, galvanized the manufacturers of rum, copperas, tallow,
and cordage. Cottons, bar iron, books and some glass manufactures had
large imports to displace, and in some instances, idle capacity. It is interesting to note that after 1820, the agitation of supporters ceased for a
few years, whereas that of opponents died away more slowly. This was
partly due to improved economic circumstances—the need felt for protection was less pressing [39]—and partly due to discouragement at the
close defeat in 1820.

[36] Dorfman (1947).
[37] Wright (1910), p. 45; Stanwood (1903), I, 229–30. For a discussion of the micro-
economics of protection, see the speech by Tyler, *Annals*, 16th Cong., 1st Sess. (1820), p.
1953. He argued that a lack of profits was a dangerous reason for protection since domestic competition would bid away any increase in profitability in the favored industries, so
that larger and more forceful industries would arise to make further claims.
[38] See chapter 2 and Stanwood (1903), I, 223–34, on the iron industry. The case of the
large cotton producers is well known.
[39] Some petitioning industries were neither greatly threatened nor particularly well
placed to take advantage of extra protection. A proper analysis of the degree of agitation
was not undertaken, but would parallel chapter 6.

*Arguments Used.* The main arguments in the memorials were about the benefits of stimulating manufacturing, the effects on the balance of trade and revenue, and about the equity of the tariff. It was disputed whether manufacturing was in a worse condition than other sectors, [40] and if so, whether that was due to banking policy, unjustified expansion during the war, or extravagant imports and consequent change in tastes. [41] No doubt, the war had prematurely stimulated manufactures, but should protection now be used to nurture "the production of a hot-bed out of season; its curiosity may surprise, but it can never ripen into any degree of usefulness." [42] War is always costly; why exacerbate the cost by further forcing production from its natural (and morally uplifting) channels? [43] In reply, the protectionists claimed that greater self-sufficiency was essential to avoid repetition of the hardships of the last war, and on this they could quote George Washington. Cotton manufacturers in particular decried the great loss of capital that would occur if protection were not increased in 1815. A major dispute surrounded the claim that a steady American demand would avoid agricultural distress due to fluctuations in foreign demand. This did not appeal to Southern cotton exporters who feared the loss of British markets.

The tariff, it was asserted, was unfair; unfair to the poor, [44] to agriculture, shipbuilding, and commerce (especially the coasting and West India trades), and to some manufacturers—particularly those making chocolate, refined sugar, cordage, and rum at Boston. And the benefits were available chiefly to small numbers of proprietors in glass, iron, and textiles, not to workers. [45] These arguments were to be amplified in Congressional debates.

[40] The large profits of the Waltham company were tendered in evidence.

[41] Merchants of Baltimore, "Payment of Duties," *ASP, Finance,* III, 565 (January 5, 1820), p. 450.

[42] Roanoke Agricultural Society, "Remonstrance Against the Tariff," *ASP, Finance,* III, 604.

[43] United Agricultural Societies of Virginia, "Remonstrance," *Annals,* 16th Cong., 1st Sess. (1820), pp. 2323 ff.

[44] Since the present tariff was heavier on the poor, why not raise the protective duties rather than the revenue duties? Such was the question posed in 1824 by some Baltimore memorialists. Both the tariff and excise were, it appears, harsh on the poor, but an "infant industry" tariff especially so, concentrating as it did on the coarse qualities. (Any fall in imports would reduce revenue, it was sometimes suggested, and resort to direct taxes would be needed.)

[45] Merchants of Boston, *ASP, Finance* IV, 467 (1823). It was estimated in 1820 that 100 sugar planters in Lousiana received a "bounty" of $1 million from protection. Philadelphia

## VOTING AND COALITION FORMATION
## IN CONGRESS

The Tariff of 1824 altered about 30 percent of the duties enumerated in the earlier acts, and added about seventy newly enumerated items (most receiving specific duties).[46] The new rates were concentrated in textiles, metals and their manufactures, dyes and drugs, books and paper, glass and some miscellaneous things (ale, coach furniture, candles, cordage, chocolate, marble and slate, and soap); a small number of agricultural duties were added. However, the duties on iron, wool, woolens, hemp and cotton bagging, and distilled spirits received the most attention in the House.

Taussig's interpretation of the passage of the act relies on the theory of sectional interests, that is, that the positions taken by the representatives and senators reflected the economic interests of their constituents: the Tariff of 1824 favored the Middle Atlantic and Western states (or was thought to), and harmed the South, whereas New England's interests were divided. The dynamic elements of Taussig's explanation of the changes in the votes between 1820 and 1824 are, first, the changes in the character of the bills, and second, the changing composition of industrial output in New England, away from mercantile activity toward manufacturing (tables 3.2 and 3.3). On neither of these is there more than a hint of argument or verification; on the latter there is almost a circularity: the vote changed, and therefore the underlying interests must have changed.[47]

Stanwood offers a much simpler explanation. The reapportionment of seats in the House occasioned by the 1820 census meant a large increase in the representation of the "tariff" states of New York, Pennsylvania, Kentucky, Ohio, and Tennessee.[48] However, since the majority in the House in favor of the 1820 bill was larger than that in 1824, Stanwood's reapportionment argument would appear to fail on the face

---

Chamber of Commerce, "Remonstrance," *Annals*, 16th Cong., 1st Sess. (1820), pp. 2424 ff.; and speech by Lowndes of South Carolina, p. 2126.

[46] For details see chapters 2 and 4.

[47] Taussig (1931), p. 72. The sectional interest theory is dealt with in chapters 5 and 6.

[48] Stanwood (1903), I, 198–99, 246. New York and Pennsylvania were prominent in the protectionist movement, according to Foot of Connecticut, because they had suffered greatly in the transition from war to peace. *Annals*, 18th Cong., 1st Sess. (1823–24), p. 2305.

## House Votes on Tariff Bills, 1820 and 1824

| | 1820 | | 1824 | |
|---|---|---|---|---|
| | YEA | NAY | YEA | NAY |
| New England | 18 | 17 | 15 | 23 |
| Maine | — | — | 1 | 6 |
| New Hampshire | — | 5 | 1 | 5 |
| Vermont | 1 | 4 | 5 | — |
| Massachusetts | 10 | 7 | 1 | 11 |
| Connecticut | 5 | 1 | 5 | 1 |
| Rhode Island | 2 | — | 2 | — |
| Middle Atlantic | 58 | 8 | 60 | 15 |
| New York | 26 | — | 26 | 8 |
| New Jersey | 6 | — | 6 | — |
| Pennsylvania | 22 | 1 | 24 | 1 |
| Delaware | 2 | — | 1 | — |
| Maryland | 2 | 7 | 3 | 6 |
| West | 12 | 3 | 29 | — |
| Ohio | 6 | — | 14 | — |
| Indiana | 1 | — | 2 | — |
| Illinois | 1 | — | 1 | — |
| Missouri | — | — | 1 | — |
| Kentucky | 4 | 3 | 11 | — |
| South | 3 | 50 | 3 | 64 |
| Virginia | 1 | 18 | 1 | 21 |
| North Carolina | 1 | 12 | — | 13 |
| South Carolina | 1 | 7 | — | 9 |
| Georgia | — | 6 | — | 7 |
| Alabama | — | — | — | 3 |
| Mississippi | — | 1 | — | 1 |
| Louisiana | — | 1 | — | 3 |
| Tennessee | — | 5 | 2 | 7 |
| Total | 91 | 78 | 107 | 102 |

Sources: The 1820 tabulation was made by applying the *Bio-graphical Directory of the American Congress 1774–1961* (Washington, 1961) to the votes as recorded in the House *Journal* of April 29, 1820. I assumed that the vote by "Reed" was cast by Reid of Georgia and the vote by "Johnson" was by James Johnson of Virginia, who resigned, according to the *Directory* (p. 93, n53) on February 1, 1820, before the tariff vote (April 29, 1820), but presumably continued as Representative. The vacancy was filled by John C. Gray, who took his seat on November 13, 1820. The 1824 tabulation is taken from the 51st Cong., 2d Sess., Senate Report 2130, *Rates on Duties* (Washington, February 4, 1891), p. 118.

TABLE 3.3

## Senate Votes on Tariff Bills, 1820 and 1824

| | 1820 YEA | 1820 NAY | 1824 YEA | 1824 NAY |
|---|---|---|---|---|
| New England | 6 | 4 | 9 | 3 |
| Maine | — | — | 2 | — |
| New Hampshire | 1 | 1 | 1 | 1 |
| Vermont | 1 | 1 | 2 | — |
| Massachusetts | — | 2 | — | 2 |
| Connecticut | 2 | — | 2 | — |
| Rhode Island | 2 | — | 2 | — |
| Middle Atlantic | 8 | 1 | 5 | 4 |
| New York | 2 | — | 1 | 1 |
| New Jersey | 2 | — | 2 | — |
| Pennsylvania | 2 | — | 2 | — |
| Delaware | 2 | — | — | 2 |
| Maryland | — | 1 | — | 1 |
| West | 6 | 2 | 9 | — |
| Ohio | 2 | — | 2 | — |
| Indiana | 1 | 1 | 2 | — |
| Illinois | 1 | 1 | 1 | — |
| Missouri | — | — | 2 | — |
| Kentucky | 2 | — | 2 | — |
| South | 1 | 15 | 2 | 14 |
| Virginia | — | 2 | — | 2 |
| North Carolina | — | 2 | — | 2 |
| South Carolina | — | 2 | — | 2 |
| Georgia | — | 2 | — | 2 |
| Alabama | — | 2 | — | 2 |
| Mississippi | — | 2 | — | 2 |
| Louisiana | — | 2 | — | 2 |
| Tennessee | 1 | 1 | 2 | — |
| Total | 21 | 22 | 25 | 21 |

*Sources:* The votes recorded in the Senate *Journal* of May 4, 1820 and May 13, 1824 were compiled using the *Biographical Directory* (1961).
*Note:* The 1820 vote was to postpone consideration of the bill; I have reversed the record, so that a vote to postpone is recorded in this table as Nay.

of it. Moreover, it must be stressed that although the 1820 bill passed the House, it was defeated in the Senate. In the interim between these dates two states were admitted to the Union, Maine and Missouri. Since both states voted in favor of the 1824 tariff, the additional four votes would have been sufficient, other things being equal, to have converted the earlier defeat into victory.[49] This was not how the vote went. To explain fully the passage of the 1824 Act, one must take into account the possibility that reapportionment allowed the promoters of the 1824 tariff so to restructure it as to win Senate votes, even at the cost of some support in the House of Representatives.

We can regard the bills and tariff motions made in the sessions before the passage of an act as successive steps toward forming a winning coalition;[50] in particular we shall look in some detail at the difference between the 1816 rates, those proposed in 1820, and the ones actually enacted in 1824. First, a whole range of agricultural products were included for the first time in the 1824 bill, for example, bacon, beef, butter, lard, oats, plums, pork, potatoes, wheat, and cheap wool. Most of these articles were of interest to northern and western farmers, although some representatives decried some duties as sham (since the United States exported more than it imported). Southerners similarly ridiculed the increase in the duty on raw cotton. Secondly, Baldwin, manager of the bill, had tried in 1820 to increase import duties on various spices (cloves, nutmeg, mace, etc.), cocoa, chocolate, some tea,

[49] Tables 3.2 and 3.3 show the voting on the two bills in the House and the Senate. Taussig (1931) reports (p. 72n) an 1820 distribution by state so different from Stanwood's (1903), I, pp. 192–93 and mine (which differ slightly) that it must be from a vote on a different motion.

Incidentally, a simplified sectional interest theory of voting has some statistical support. For the states in table 3.2, but excluding Indiana, Illinois, Mississippi, and Louisiana, the fraction of "yea" votes in 1824 ($V$) depended on the per capita value-added in manufacturing ($M$):

$$V = 0.21 + 0.23M$$
$$(1.40)\quad(2.69)$$
$$\bar{R}^2 = 0.25,\quad F(1,\ 18) = 7.26$$

[50] An example of poor coalition formation is afforded by the 1826–27 woolens bill which failed, according to Stanwood, because of the opposition of the "protectionist" Middle Atlantic states to relief for the woolen industry unless the comparatively slight disadvantages which certain of their own local industries suffered under the new tariff were also removed. Stanwood (1903), I, 251.

sugar, and salt; in general, however, the 1824 rates were left at the old levels. All of these products except sugar and salt were noncompeting consumer items, so that Baldwin was clearly attempting to defend his bill against the charge that it sacrificed the revenue to greater protection.[51]

By 1824, revenue was abundant, and some of the bill's supporters (Henry Clay in particular) did not deny that the bill might force the imposition of internal taxes and excises. In the past, revenue had been founded upon imports; in the future, a new system had to be devised in which taxation was divorced from questions of encouragement to manufacturing. This separation was signified by the striking in the 16th Congress of separate committees on ways and means and on manufactures. The manager of the 1824 bill, Tod of Pennsylvania, was willing to go some way toward Clay's position, but generally the supporters denied that the new tariff would greatly harm revenue. However, the bill originated in the Committee on Manufactures, which opened it to the criticism that it ignored revenue.[52]

To turn now to the protective duties, a number of petitioners unsuccessful before 1824 were swept up in the new bill and secured protection for the printing of books, industrial chemicals, corks, flax, hemp and silk manufactures, linseed oil, and slate. (These products had previously enjoyed the 15 percent duty imposed on unenumerated imports.) Many of them had been included in the 1820 bill at similar rates. In addition, requests for increased protection for candles, copperas, cordage, hardware, glass, and shot were acceded to in 1824 (whereas those for prunello shoes and sugar were denied). The rates in the important schedules for textiles, metals and metal manufactures, although increased by the Act of 1824, were generally lower than those proposed four years earlier.[53] The metals schedule was longer and included more specific duties than ever before. (Products barely repre-

[51] Secretary Dallas had proposed greater increases in most of these duties in 1816.

[52] Similarly, the 1820 bill issued from Manufactures rather than Ways and Means. Baldwin, its manager on the floor of the House, regretted having the Secretary of the Treasury pass on the revenue effects of a prohibition of iron and textile imports, but since the other committee was remiss, the bill from Manufactures had to have regard to revenue as well as to protection. Baldwin, *Annals*, 16th Cong., 1st Sess. (1820), pp. 191 ff.

[53] Baldwin had attempted to extend the principle of minimum valuations beyond cotton and wool to other textiles.

sented in memorials or not at all, and for which increased protection
had been proposed in 1820, and which retained their 1816 rates, included boots, cabinetware and other wood products, and leather and
leather products such as saddles.)

What were the sources of the bills and acts? In an arithmetical
sense, the Act of 1816 passed twenty-seven ad valorem rates lower
than those proposed by Treasury Secretary Dallas, and one higher;
twelve lower specific rates and seven higher.[54] Baldwin's bill of 1820
followed Dallas's suggestions only in a few details: books, brushes,
cabinetware, canes, cottons, leather, paper (ad valorem); boots and coffee (specific). In turn, however, his bill was extensively followed by
Tod in 1824: fifty-two of 139 items.[55]

## The Bill in Congress

Meeting as the Committee of the Whole, the House in 1824 began
debate with the item, distilled spirits. The opponents of the increase
argued that the duty would not help agriculture and would harm trade
with the West Indies. In addition, since the bill originated with the
Committee on Manufactures, rather than Ways and Means, it was suggested that revenue would be lost which would be difficult to replace
without recourse to internal taxes. Clay's reply to these arguments,
which he repeated a number of times during the debate on the bill,
was not only to claim that the tariff bill would benefit the country as a
whole, but to point out that if the objections to distilled spirits were
valid, then similar objections must prevail against every other item in
the bill. Time and again he and his supporters attacked the notion that
there is no such thing as the "common good," only the separate inter-

[54] Lower ad valorem: books, brass wire, brass manufactures, brushes, buckles, buttons, cabinetware, canes, cannon, clothing, cutlery, hemp manufactures, iron n.o.p. (not
otherwise provided), Japanned ware, laces, lead n.o.p., leather, muskets, needles, paper,
old pewter, pins, saddles, silk manufactures, steel n.o.p., tin manufactures, types;
higher ad valorem: linen; lower specific: alum, boots, chocolate, coal, cocoa, coffee, copper n.o.p., copperas, iron bar, logwoods, silk shoes (two items); higher specific: wax
candles, spermaceti candles, gunpowder, mahogany, olive oil in casks, brown sugar, lump
sugar.

[55] Thirty-two of 104 specific items and twenty of thirty-five ad valorem items. Tod also
took over one item from Dallas (ale), one from Baldwin's 1822 bill (watches), three from
the 1816 act (duck), and six from Smith's 1822 bill (anvils, butter, flax, indigo, cables,
vinegar).

ests of the individuals who make up the group. Tod, the Chairman of the Committee on Manufactures, also objected to dealing with the bill item by item. For Clay's forces, however, the tactical question was as important as the welfare economics one: supporters of the bill must resist the attempts of its opponents to whittle away at it by arguing that each item benefited one section of the country at the immediate expense of some other section.[56]

There is much to be said for this position. If each representative voted on each item according to whether his constituents' interests were helped or harmed by the item, and with no regard to the import of the whole bill, the bill would most likely have been amended out of existence. It is important to distinguish between the questions of whether a bill *should* have passed (judged by some economic criteria), and whether the bill *would* have passed (that is, commanded a majority). Even if all the separate items in the bill were completely unjustified in terms of welfare economics, it would still have been possible to pass the bill, so long as the majority of the House and the Senate thought that on net it benefited them or their constituents. On the other hand, even if each item were justified on some economic grounds, so long as some states and regions stood to gain while others stood to lose, and so long as each congressman and senator looked only at his local interests, passage would have required a bill that helped at least half of the districts and states. Furthermore, the possibility must be considered that tariffs on some products such as cotton textiles and iron may have been economically justified, but that the tariff bill which was designed, as it were, around these items in order to secure passage, may have been, on balance, economically unjustified.[57]

The supporters of the bill, therefore, wished to have it discussed in

[56] Notice that the question why benefits of the tariff to the nation depended on the passage of the whole bill, and would not be secured, at least partly, by the passage of parts of the bill is not discussed in the article by Edwards (1970). Even the "Keynesian" model that Edwards sees as the basis of some of the protariff statements does not seem to depend on the exact composition of the tariff; it is sufficient if each tariff item itself contributes to aggregate demand.

[57] It is worth noting that an implication of the result of Coase (that any decision rule with transaction cost-free sidepayments will produce only Pareto-efficient results) is that efficient decisions are reduced to purely redistributive decisions: see Buchanan and Tullock (1967), chapter 13.

principle, rather than in detail, so that if the House agreed to the desirability of further protection of manufactures and agriculture, then the Committee of the Whole could hammer out the details.[58] However, the traditions of the House prevented the supporters from moving to strike the enacting clause in order to start a general discussion: when Martindale did this, he was reprimanded, and his motion was defeated quickly and overwhelmingly.[59] The debate thus proceeded, product by product, with the supporters having to treat each item as if its defeat implied the defeat of the whole bill.[60] They argued that, although each item of the bill had an uneven regional impact, the whole bill was designed (or should have been) to equalize these effects.[61] Opponents replied that the bill as a whole was no other than the sum of its parts, and that the latter added up to harm for the South.[62] They added that only by each looking to his local interests could the bill be equalized.[63] In view of this, why not indulge the friends of the bill on an item (wheat) which would do no harm to the South, and was believed to be of essential benefit to other parts of the country? [64]

*Amendments.* In the next stage of the debate, Tod, who had introduced the bill, began to suggest amendments, for example, a reduction of the minimum on woolens. This suggestion, he candidly explained, was made in consequence of an assurance given him by several leading members, now in opposition to the bill, that if this feature were removed they would support the residue.[65] Next, Tod courted Western support by reductions in the rates on scythes, gridirons, and frying pans and an increase on rape seed oil. Furthermore, Tod was willing to make more gradual the increase in the duty on wool in the hope of securing the support of South Carolina, [66] but in so doing angered some firm supporters (especially Martindale of New York).

As a shrewd floor manager, Tod had the task of ensuring that his amendments, designed to capture approval of leading members, did

---

[58] *Annals*, 18th Cong., 1st Sess. (1823–24) p. 1482.     [59] *Ibid.*, pp. 1629 ff.
[60] *Ibid.*, pp. 1484–94, 1495, 1498.     [61] *Ibid.*, p. 1491.     [62] *Ibid.*, pp. 1495–97.
[63] *Ibid.*, p. 1542.
[64] *Ibid.*, p. 1693. This was the kind of argument best directed at the friends of the bill, but was a reply to a staunch opponent, P. P. Barbour.
[65] *Ibid.*, p. 1741.     [66] *Ibid.*, p. 1749.

not in consequence lose him a greater number of votes of early supporters of the bill who were susceptible to the tactics that lost the 1820
bill; it was better to obtain part of the object desired than to form a
perfect bill that failed to pass.[67] Most interesting was his proposal to
reduce the pig iron duty from the recommended $1.12 to 75¢ a hun-
dredweight. This was defeated in the Committee of the Whole; subsequently a reduction to 90¢ proposed by Clark of New York was
agreed to (although the rate was finally left at 50¢ by Senate amendment). The issue revolved around the principle of taxing a raw material, and whether the duty on bar iron would be circumvented by importation of pig. Imports were said to chiefly be Scottish gray iron,
used for small castings and cannon. To tax pig so heavily would force
Massachusetts users to have recourse to pig from New Jersey ore,
four hundred costly miles away. The question of the duty on pig iron
set one manufacturing interest against another.[68]

The bill that passed the House by 107 votes to 102 was heavily
amended in the Senate, and the amendments mostly stuck: the Senate
forced the House to lower the new cottons minimum, to set lower
rates for worsteds, blankets, and cheaper woolen cloth, to moderate
the progression in wood duties, to impose a moderate 30 percent on
cutlery, frying pans, and screws, to liberalize silk drawbacks and silk
duties, to eliminate increases on blank books, cassia, cocoa, copper vessels, flax, prunello shoes, and tallow; also to increase the rates on oats
and pencils. Compromises were reached or the House prevailed on bar
iron (raised to 90¢), hemp, cotton bagging, wheat, and flour. Because
the Senate proceedings were sparsely reported and amendments often
decided without division, i.e., a tally (although votes were often close),
it is difficult to discover the tactics used in winning three extra votes
in New England: Maine (two) and Vermont; four more in the West and
South: Missouri (two), Indiana, and Tennessee; while losing three in
the Middle Atlantic States: Delaware (two) and New Jersey.[69] The "protectionists" lost most of the amendments, including some especially

---

[67] *Ibid.*, p. 1741.

[68] Tod also proposed reductions in rates on printing types, oil cloth, duck, and Prussian
blue, and higher rates on glass, ploughs, currants, and figs.

[69] Apart from these vote switches, Senator J. McLean of Illinois abstained, thereby accounting for the fall in the "free trade" vote between 1820 and 1824.

important ones. There was less faction discipline in the upper house, especially on the protectionist side. Of the twenty-five senators who voted for the bills, ten voted against the majority of their protectionist colleagues in at least one-third of the votes.[70] In particular, the four senators from Maine and Tennessee were in this sense the most inconsistent, one of the former, J. Holmes, voting twice as often with the free traders as with the protectionists.[71]

The danger some friends of the bill tried to forestall was that a few very high duties would condemn the whole bill. Van Buren of New York and Noble of Indiana voiced such a fear.[72] The item in both cases was hemp, on which a revealing series of votes occurred. The Senate first voted 20 to 16 to eliminate the rate of 2¢ a pound; then 6 to 30 against a (slightly higher) duty of $45 a ton; 19 to 27 against $37 a ton; 28 to 19 in favor of $35 a ton. The protectionists modified a high rate for the benefit of the whole bill.[73]

An interpretation of the changes between 1820 and 1824 can be suggested. The customs receipts had picked up by 1824 (Table 2.2), so there was less need for taxes on such foreign items of consumption as spices. These had opened the 1820 bill to charges of taxing the few luxuries of the poor for the benefit of manufacturers.[74] The duties on agricultural products were, in the most part, not protective at all, but a cheap bribe for support.[75] Most interesting were the changes in protective duties. There was both conflict and community of interest among

[70] Other inconsistent protectionists were Benton of Missouri, Knight of Rhode Island, Lowrie of Pennsylvania, Thomas of Illinois and Van Buren of New York.

[71] But siding with protectionists for the important items of silk, worsteds, woolens "minimum," books, hemp, wheat, potatoes, bar iron.

[72] *Annals*, 18th Cong. 1st Sess. (1823–24) pp. 601, 729.

[73] The "protectionists" (those ultimately voting for the bill) voted fifteen against the first amendment, then three, fifteen and twenty-five for the alternative rates.

[74] See, for example, the speech by Tyler against "their rotten manufactories," claiming that the agricultural classes and the poor would suffer from the extortion from their necessities. *Annals*, 16th Cong., 1st Sess. (1820) p. 1958. See also Alexander and Holmes on salt, pp. 2033 and 2086; and Lowndes on sugar, p. 2125.

[75] The wheat duty was, however, requested by farmers suffering Canadian competition. Ironically, the carriage of this wheat was one reason given for building the Erie Canal. An additional factor, discussed later, is that western representatives were impressed by the argument that protection of manufactures would create in the West a "home market."

producers. The obvious conflicts were between producers of intermediate goods and users; supporters of the bill tried to reduce items detrimental to their interest. But beyond that, producers competed for Congressional favors. To put it crudely, the 1820 bill was too sweeping both in rates and breadth.[76] Some large, geographically dispersed industries like leather and woodworking had lower rates offered them in 1824 than in 1820; they were sacrificed to that extent to the remaining industries. The widespread industries had shown (possibly by their relative lack of memorials) that they were not as important to the tariff coalition as was indicated by the number of districts containing them. It was not so much that these industries were absolutely weak politically or weaker than in 1820, but that their interests had been promoted too far in 1820. Similarly, the industries added to the failed, narrow, "woolen" bill of 1827 had not gained political power by 1828: their inclusion was needed for passage just as the partial sacrifice of some industries was needed in 1824. There was opposition in 1824 to protection as a policy, and any duty could be attacked on general principles. The higher the protection, the more severe the attack; the smaller the interest, the more vehement the complaints.[77] All duties had to merit inclusion in the bill by adding more to the spoils for the coalition than they subtracted.[78]

### Wider Bargains: the American System

Thus far the tariff has been discussed in isolation, neglecting the question of expenditure of the revenues collected. Clay's American System was a package of proposals including internal improvements. There may be a good economic rationale for the assertion that the package was more than the sum of its parts, that only the tariff plus improvement of internal communications and transport added up to an economically efficient program of mutually supportive "investments."

[76] McLane of Delaware, although intending to support the 1820 bill, worried that it embraced too much. *Annals*, 16th Cong., 1st Sess. (1820) p. 2094.

[77] For example, Floyd of Virginia asserted that flax was too minor to be worth considering. *Annals*, 18th Cong., 1st Sess. (1823–24) p. 1897.

[78] Riker (1962) discusses political examples of the search for minimum sized coalitions, the point being that the smaller the coalition, the larger the average payoff in some instances.

Clay so claimed. Be that as it may, Taussig for one denied that Western support was justified by a realistic assessment of Western tariff benefits; [79] internal improvements, expected to be of considerable benefit to the West, may have helped swing the balance. [80]

It is worthwhile noting that the discussion of the 1824 tariff bill began on the very day (February 11, 1824) that the House gave its approval to another part of the American System, namely, to a bill that provided for the survey and estimated cost of such roads and canals as the President deemed of national importance, from either a commercial or a military point of view, or necessary for the transportation of the public mail. The managers of the tariff bill were in something of a dilemma when it came to the discussion of the revenue that the new tariff would generate. [81] On the one hand Tod, in replying to arguments that the higher duty on spirits would reduce international trade, stated that the object of the whole bill was to protect home industry by preventing those importations that destroy it. [82] On the other, if insufficient revenue were generated, then the scheme of internal improvements would be jeopardized. [83] In that event, Clay declared himself willing to see an excise tax imposed. [84] This, however, would have made the benefits of the American System contingent on the passage of yet another piece of legislation, one distasteful to some opponents and supporters of the tariff alike. [85]

[79] Taussig (1931), pp. 70, 71.

[80] The assumption used by Pope (1970), p. 17 that tariff revenue was redistributed to the owners of factors of production, does not seem appropriate in a model designed to analyze whether the South was damaged by antebellum tariffs; see also Pope (1971). There is a suggestion in the paper by Passell and Schmundt (1971) that rapid land distribution and high tariffs may have been the combination of policies that best served the manufacturing sector; presumably it was a very poor combination for the South.

[81] The choice between revenue and protection does not arise if the rate is "low," that is, below the revenue-maximizing rate occurring somewhere between zero and prohibitive.

[82] *Annals*, 18th Cong., 1st Sess. (1823–24) pp. 1498–99.

[83] *Ibid.*, p. 1484.    [84] *Ibid.*, p. 1483.

[85] The more complicated the bargain, the more issues embraced, the more costly are the negotiation and sidepayment transactions. Those bargains that are self-financing or self-executing, such as moderate protection and internal improvements, are more suitable for the kind of analysis carried out in chapter 6. There, interest is in the structure of the tariff, and not why a certain bill passed or failed.

## TARIFF ARGUMENTS

Implicit in the attention given, for example, by Stanwood to the debates in Congress, is another explanation of the protectionist victory in 1824, namely, that arguments for protection as a principle caused some congressmen to change their votes, or electors to vote into office men supporting the tariff.[86] It is useful to read the 1820 and 1824 debates together—many of the same arguments were used by the same men. The economic setting of the debate was the prosperity of manufacturers and government suppliers [87] during the War of 1812; peacetime had brought not blessings but distress: vast imports, currency disturbances, and a falling European demand for exports.

The protectionists' basic argument, which related to the structure of employment and to "surplus" population, was well rendered by Silas Wood of New York as follows.[88] There was for each country, depending on population density and the size of towns, a certain fraction of the labor force (about half in the United States) required to produce subsistence—food and drink. A wise government determined the employment of "surplus" population, thereby fixing the political character of the country, whether suspicious, aggressive, or peaceable. China and Egypt, for example, prosecuted vast public works, and Rome, imperial wars; Europe maintained her standing armies,[89] and Britain had taken up manufactures. The more ancient civilizations had not enjoyed the option of foreign trade, for to engage in it would have endangered subsistence by diverting labor from agriculture: a *settled* policy of commerce required a steady excess of production over home demand. Until the late 1810s, some interruptions aside, the United States had employed her labor surplus in the production and carriage of agricul-

[86] Because some of the free-traders' arguments are to be expected of avid readers of Smith, more attention is here given to those of the protectionists.

[87] E.g., Floyd of Virginia and McDuffie of South Carolina. *Annals*, 18th Cong., 1st Sess. (1823–24) pp. 1897, 1677.

[88] Wood, *Ibid.*, pp. 2068–82. See also especially Clay, *Ibid.*, pp. 1966–82 and Clay, *Annals*, 16th Cong., 1st Sess. (1820) pp. 2034–36. Numerous references could be given, even from the Senate: Dickenson of New Jersey, *Annals*, 18th Cong., 1st Sess. (1823–24) p. 695.

[89] Also Clay, *Ibid.*, p. 1971.

tural goods to foreign markets, taking manufactures in return. But this vent for surplus was closed by peace and the determination of Europe henceforth to provide her own subsistence; and the more rapid increase of population in the United States aggravated the problem.[90] It was appropriate, therefore, Wood continued, that legislation direct labor currently idle, and so settle the political character of the nation. Manufacturing industry would temper the passion for military glory with love of property, and bind the Union with mutual ties. Since few nations met their manufacturing needs, foreign sales could be made when prices subsequently fell once American manufacturing, through the skills and experience gained in catering to a secure home market, had overcome the disadvantage of low British wages.[91]

### The Structural Argument

It is necessary to disentangle the two strands of the argument on structure, the one relating to temporary unemployment, the other to more permanent considerations.[92] Taking up the latter, what grounds were used to justify legislative interference even if full employment obtained? The strength and independence of the nation—in short, defense—was a generally accepted argument for assistance to manufacturing, although opponents denied that it could justify these particular bills.[93] Free traders readily acknowledged the need for a secure supply of clothing and arms (obtained by contract as well as tariff), but warned that the front line of defense was the navy and behind it commerce, now under legislative threat. The protectionist position was that com-

---

[90] That more rapid population growth was accompanied by larger surplus was a common theme; e.g. Tod, *Annals*, 18th Cong., 1st Sess. (1823–24), p. 2215. In 1820, P. P. Barbour of Virginia had appealed to Malthus against this proposition. *Annals*, 16th Cong., 1st Sess. (1820) p. 2078.

[91] There are some hints of the "pauper labor" argument for protection in the references to the working conditions of the Russian serfs and the unfortunates in Inverness and Dundee.

[92] For example, Strong of New York, *Annals*, 18th Cong., 1st Sess. (1823–24), p. 2127, "Sir, the question is not so much whether all hands are now employed, as whether they cannot be more profitably employed? . . . But, if we believe the representations made to us . . . there is a want of employment. How, then, can the greatest number of hands be most productively employed?"

[93] E.g., McDuffie of South Carolina, *Ibid.*, p. 1497.

merce would continue under the bill; that the whale fishermen (for whom protection was also sought) could man warships; that commerce itself was a source of international conflict, and, in particular, the cause of the War of 1812; and that security depended not only on the supply of arms but on general self-sufficiency.[94] In this last form, the argument from defense merged with the main question: Would a policy of "let alone" bring about the most desirable pattern of industry and employment?

The answer was no. Commerce, it was claimed, was overblown. It added nothing to the value of items traded; or worse, with the aid of the banks, drained specie from the nation by encouraging an excess of expenditure on foreign goods.[95] Old habits, an unwillingness to await returns from risky investments,[96] and a fluctuating demand exacerbated by British dumping [97] had stunted the natural development of manufacturing. What was needed was a stable American market within which industry would grow and prices fall,[98] bringing prosperity also to suppliers of foodstuffs and materials by extending their home market. A system of internal exchange would displace one of foreign remittance. Besides, commerce had been favored by discriminatory duties on goods carried in foreign ships, by harbor works and lighthouses, and by war fought on behalf of mercantile freedom and seamen's rights. To equalize the benefits of legislative action, a tariff was called for.

[94] E.g., Buchanan of Pennsylvania, Ibid., p. 1710 (on iron).

[95] Martindale of New York, Ibid., p. 1646.

[96] Holcombe of New York, Ibid., p. 2391. Domestic but not great national industries would arise by themselves. McLane, Annals, 16th Cong., 1st Sess. (1820) pp. 2093 ff; "Protection to Manufactures," Annals, 16th Cong., 2d Sess., p. 1586 (reprinted as Report 609, ASP, Finance, III). This is the infant industry idea, popular since Hamilton's report.

[97] The protectionists asserted that British manufacturers had deliberately set out to destroy United States industry after the war. The widely reported Parliamentary speech by Henry Brougham in 1816, suggesting that "it was well worth while to incur a loss upon the first exportation in order by the glut to stifle in the cradle those rising manufactures in the United States which the war had forced into existence contrary to the usual course of things," did nothing to aid the free traders. Quoted in Stanwood (1903), I, 167–68.

[98] The protectionists claimed the tariff would, in the longer run, drive prices down by encouraging domestic competition against foreign sources; internal competition would meanwhile eliminate any monopoly profits: Annals, 18th Cong., 1st Sess. (1823–24), pp. 1476, 1729, 1891, 1897. The price experience of cottons was frequently cited as proof.

## Short-Run Considerations

Clay's position on the "balance of trade theory" is interesting. Although at times he appeared to deny that "commerce regulated itself," he acknowledged that "in the long run" trade would balance, but at the cost of a lengthy period of distress. One reason for protection, then, was to speed up adjustment to the new trading conditions of the 1820s.[99] Many other supporters were simply mercantilists who believed that an excess of exports over imports was desirable, and that foreign intercourse was inferior to a domestic "circle of commerce." They sneered at the advice to buy cheap, claiming that the cheapest source would not buy in return. Others (no doubt drawing on the experience of the immediate postwar period) disliked international commerce for causing an outflow of specie, thereby encouraging, by the use of paper substitutes, debt, bankruptcy, and distress.[100] The West Indies trade in particular was spurned: the islands would take nothing but money in return for their exports.

The telling reply was that, because the United States lacked mines, most of its specie must come from trade, especially multilateral trade involving the West Indies, Europe, China, and Mexico.[101] Opponents generally were confident in their appeals to Smith and Say, but never clearly described the mechanisms whereby a fall in foreign demand would be compensated.[102] The followers of Smith and Say were skeptical about the existence of considerable numbers of persons involuntarily unemployed through want of profitable activities.[103] However, if

---

[99] *Annals*, 16th Cong., 1st Sess. (1820) p. 2045; *Annals*, 18th Cong., 1st Sess. (1823–24) pp. 693, 1712, 1982. Clay went further and proposed that a wise government provide against even distant evils. McDuffie of South Carolina conceded the case for what today is called "structural adjustment assistance," but denied anything could be done in 1824 for the failures of five or six years before. *Ibid.*, pp. 2404–06.

[100] *Ibid.*, pp. 1630, 1639.

[101] *Annals*, 16th Cong., 1st Sess. (1820) p. 2006; *Annals*, 18th Cong., 1st Sess. (1823–24) pp. 1556, 1708, 2016, 2048, 2251.

[102] The closest argument, advanced by Rankin of Mississippi, held that a drying up of foreign credit would terminate an import surplus. *Ibid.*, p. 2019; see also *Annals*, 16th Cong., 1st Sess. (1820) p. 2124; Govan of South Carolina said that Britain's trade surplus was due to her granting extensive credit. *Annals*, 18th Cong., 1st Sess. (1823–24), p. 2124.

[103] *Ibid.*, pp. 2240, 2407.

in 1824 there were still some displaced by the change in the fortunes of agriculture, the correct policy was one of repose; it was undesirable to force labor prematurely into manufacturing.[104] And finally, protection justified by a fall in foreign agricultural demand was paradoxical because the tariff itself would cause a further drop in exports (of this, more later).

This faith did not satisfy supporters of the tariff, who appealed to experience to aid numerous assertions that capital and labor would remain idle for want of markets: war had fostered manufacturing and agriculture through the disruption of foreign trade; the peacetime trade revival had devastated both. It was the duty of a wise and provident government to ensure full employment. How could that be done? The structure of demand had changed, and the interventionists did not believe that market forces would bring about a suitable redistribution of employment without prolonged distress.[105] Clay's disciples refused to concede that labor would merely be re-employed: it was now idle, and should be brought to bear on otherwise useless materials to produce raw inputs for iron, glass, and hemp works.[106]

### Sectional Interests

The outlet for the excess of Western produce over Western consumption was chiefly in the Northern towns and cities. By stimulating manufacturing, the argument ran, protection would increase the demand for industrial raw materials and food, most of which came from the West.[107] Tod, the bill's manager, was explicit: the reason legisla-

[104] *Ibid.*, pp. 1942, 2022, 2298. Roughly, the free-trade position was as follows: If manufacturing was profitable, then government action was unnecessary; if unprofitable, then action was unjustified and unwise.

[105] Mallary of Vermont had grown impatient by 1824 waiting for a natural recovery from the calamity of peace. *Ibid.*, p. 1712.

[106] This theme of Tod's introductory remarks was carried on by many speakers following.

[107] Wright of Ohio said that the object of the high duties on spirits was to give employment. *Ibid.*, p. 1502. However, little could be made of the suggestion that the demand for food would rise. Free traders asserted that the mouths were already being filled, so that any benefit would be entirely through rising prices as labor was diverted into manufacturing; at best, the effects would be local and at the expense of the bulk of agriculture. Floyd of Virginia suggested that all 500,000 manufacturers could be fed from one Western district sixty miles in diameter. *Ibid.*, p. 1897. Garnett of Virginia ridiculed the no-

tion should give one part of the country an advantage over another (the South) lay in the disadvantages of the West.[108] The whole thrust of Clay's strategy was to convince the West that a manufacturing tariff would stimulate Western demand. In 1820 much emphasis was laid on distress in manufacturing; in 1824, a shift occurred to the supposed advantage for Northern and Western agriculture.

What of cotton? Was it possible for the tariff to increase the demand for that staple? The duty on raw cotton was seen largely as a sham, exports far exceeding imports, the latter tending to be of a different quality. The duties on cotton manufactures, especially the minimum on cloth, excluded goods made from foreign cotton and were of minor benefit to planters. However, the South feared that England, exporting cotton goods to many countries, would cease to buy American cotton to the extent that America ceased to buy English manufactures (of which cottons were only a part, albeit a major part). Brazil, Mexico, and India loomed as competitors. McDuffie of South Carolina turned the protectionists' arguments against them: England's policy was to secure foreign markets for manufactures, and she would, accordingly, not follow the principle of "buying cheapest" if her export market in the United States was restricted.

The essential issue, therefore, was the sacrifice of the interests of the South to those of Northern manufacturing and Western agriculture.[109] Virginia and the other Southern states were accused of being "selfish," [110] and Clay went so far as to ask "whether the interests of the greater part should be made to bend to the condition of the servile part of our population? That would, in effect, make us slaves of slaves." [111]

---

tion of "home market" by claiming that local palaces would be as popular with the surrounding farmers as would manufacturing establishments. *Ibid.*, p. 1685. Garnett was explaining the surprising support for the tariff from some agricultural districts.

[108] *Ibid.*, p. 1517. Clay regarded the West as a part of the nation sprung up since Federation, and in need of parental aid. *Ibid.*, p. 1995.

[109] Apart from hemp, Western manufacturing played a minor role in the argument. Nor was household manufacturing frequently alluded to: the tariff was to create great national industries, not household manufacturing.

[110] *Ibid.*, p. 1698.

[111] *Ibid.*, p. 1979; he went on to appeal to the South to "offer, upon the altar of the public good, some sacrifice of her peculiar opinions." Clay also discounted a "conspiracy" against the South. *Ibid.*, pp. 2000, 1690.

Stating repeatedly that the Constitution was no more than a voluntary pact for external relations, Southern speakers denied it could be used to redistribute wealth between classes without courting resistance. The interests of the South had long been neglected on funding, on banking, on taxes, on pensions, on internal improvement.[112] The South must defend its interests, especially slavery (the first step toward the abolition of which was the tariff, according to John Randolph of Virginia).[113] Temporary causes had lasting effects. The accidental stimulation of manufacturing in war had given moral force to the argument, accepted by McDuffie,[114] for some amelioration of the temporary effects of the peace; hence the South had not been uncompromising in 1816. But more protection had been given in 1818, increasing again the size of the manufacturing interest. Now more again was being sought, not to protect infants but to *create* manufactures, and so on until no doubt export bounties would be legislated.[115] A monied manufacturing interest was emerging that had no place in the scheme of the Constitution, which would sway the politics of its workers and ignore the anguished pleas of the minority. The fruits of the bill would be political strife.[116]

[112] *Ibid.*, p. 1686.

[113] *Ibid.*, p. 2253. Randolph recalled Patrick Henry's warning that Congress had the power to liberate the slaves.

[114] *Ibid.*, p. 2404.

[115] This political argument was supported by the remarkably interesting analysis of the effects of the tariff by Tyler in 1820 (*Annals*, 16th Cong., 1st Sess., p. 1953). In 1820, much was made of the low profitability of manufacturing. Tyler argued that protection would drive up profits, but temporarily, as competition would soon equalize profit rates across the various branches of manufacturing. This competition would take the form of bidding for labor against the farmer and merchant in a country where the extensive wilderness already has caused labor to be highly priced. Invited by Congress to invest, the manufacturers would find low profits and an overstocked market, and so have further recourse to tariffs, even to bounties.

[116] These sentiments were echoed by some from the maritime districts: Forrest for the Committee on Agriculture, *Annals*, 16th Cong., 1st Sess. (1820), p. 1653; *Ibid.*, pp. 2002, 2032; *Annals*, 18th Cong., 1st Sess. (1823–24), pp. 648, 1527, 1579, 1684, 2096, 2372; Mercer of Virginia claimed that the tariff on cotton bagging was unconstitutional because it was a tax on exports. *Ibid.*, p. 1558.

As to the monied interest, the opponents wished to have it both ways: that such an interest was behind the bill (e.g., Carter of South Carolina, *Ibid.*, p. 2166 and Taylor of Virginia, pp. 676 ff) but that the Eastern states with most of the manufacturing capital did not want a tariff revision. Foot of Connecticut, *Ibid.*, p. 2305.

### Postscript

Recently Edwards has claimed that the "home market" notion was proto-Keynesian. He suggests that the protectionists saw employment as directly related to the level of production, which in turn was responsive to the level of demand. Demand depended on income, the level of which had been reduced by the cessation of hostilities. The employment problem was not seen as merely structural, but as a question of aggregate demand; of, indeed, a permanent deficiency of demand: "What is important is that in the minds of the tariff advocates there were these essentially Keynesian notions: the level of employment related to aggregate consumption and equilibrium with involuntary unemployment." [117]

This interpretation seems forced. Certainly a speaker of that era might assert that "the want of market . . . effectively limits the exertions of industry" [118] (a notion then commonly applied to particular products); but that does not constitute evidence of a preoccupation with chronic demand deficiency. [119] And of course, the proposal of a Keynesian remedy does not imply a Keynesian insight as to causes. Moreover, Edwards's model, supposed to reflect the essential features of protectionist thought, is itself defective since in it output is exogenous: it needs a mechanism whereby unintended inventory accumulation (due to a deficiency in sales) feeds back into output. Since Edwards makes sales depend ultimately on government and foreign demand, both assumed to be exogenous, a tariff could hardly stimulate sales in his formal model. [120]

Finally, Keynes argued that, barring retaliation, protection could

---

[117] Edwards (1970), pp. 814–18. In supporting his argument with quotations, Edwards makes a number of interpolations which, I believe, distort their meanings. But the differences in our interpretations do not depend on a few isolated sentences.

[118] Wood, *Annals*, 18th Cong., 1st Sess. (1823–24) p. 2073, cited by Edwards (1970), p. 815.

[119] The only quotation Edwards adduces to prove that unemployment was thought of as more than temporary is: "Permanent excess of production over consumption is the only correct criterion by which the necessity of [an international] division of labor is to be determined." But this is from the speech by Wood summarized above, and it is clear that Wood, in the enclosing passage, was concerned with long-run, structural questions.

[120] Edwards gives no detailed documentation of the view that he appears to impute, namely, that output, exports, and government demand were all exogenous.

stimulate employment directly through the multiplier effects of an improved trade balance on aggregate demand, and indirectly through monetary effects. Certainly, monetary benefits were claimed in the 1820s, but (as Edwards points out) of the quantity of specie kind rather than the Keynesian rate of interest sort.[121]

[121] The Keynesian model assumes what the tariff opponents would not concede: a permanent difference between exports and imports (if a permanent direct stimulation to employment was sought). The stimulus of specie inflow does not depend on a permanent improvement in the trade balance, only a temporary one not followed by a temporary change in the opposite direction.

CHAPTER FOUR

# Effects of Tariffs

I T is an argument of this book that the structure of an industry influenced the import protection it received in 1824; yet industrial structure was itself shaped by tariffs. This latter connection is discussed here. The chapter begins, however, with an analysis of how protection altered factor incomes, in particular, quasi-rents.

## TARIFF EFFECTS IN THEORY

The consequences of a change in an isolated import duty can be examined with the aid of a partial equilibrium diagram.[1] The ordinary domestic supply and demand curves in Figure 4.1 are labeled $S$ and $D$; $S_w^*$ is the import supply curve before and $S_w$ after the imposition of a (specific) tariff $t$. As long as imports are not prohibited, the market price rises from $P^*$ TO $P$ by an amount $t$ if $S_w^*$ is horizontal (or more than $t$ if $S_w^*$ slopes upward, so there are two elements in the domestic price effect: the tariff itself plus the change due to foreign supply being less than perfectly elastic). A tariff equal to $O\overline{P} - OP^*$ is exactly prohibitive of imports; any greater is superprohibitive, and will not be taken advantage of fully.[2] As an extreme example, a tariff on iron ore if fully passed on, might cost domestic iron users out of their markets, so that the demand for ore would fall to zero. (The question of derived demand is dealt with more formally in appendix A.)

Figure 4.2 illustrates the spatial effects of import competition and protection on market areas of domestic producers. In the figure it is assumed that customers were spread evenly over a plain bordering the sea. The landed cost of imports at the port was $AB$ and the delivered price is shown by $BC$. Domestic producers at $D$ could have delivered

---

[1] Kindleberger (1968), p. 106.

[2] For the domestic industry, a superprohibitive duty is better than an exactly prohibitive one in that it provides a margin against changes in market conditions.

FIGURE 4.1

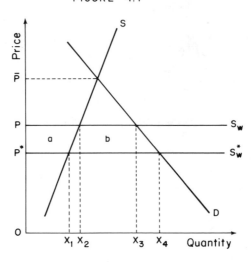

Effects of an Import Duty

at costs including freight indicated by *ED'F* (which, on the assumption of increasing cost, has a steeper slope than would be justified by freight alone). Each production point (and only one is illustrated) had a market area like *HJ* that depended on the tariff and on domestic and foreign costs. By increasing *AB* and raising *BC*, a tariff increased the market area. The typical, small producer in the 1820s had high and rapidly increasing costs, and so the point *D'* was high in relation to *B*, and the angle at *D'* very narrow. As domestic costs fell, and scale economies

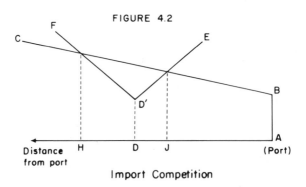

FIGURE 4.2

Import Competition

appeared, the market area *HJ* increased, imports were displaced, and competition with other domestic producers became significant. Until that occurred, these local producers enjoyed some degree of monopoly power.[3] The significance of the spatial effect is that the combination of high internal transport charges and the tariff resulted in less geographical concentration of industry on the seaboard. Because geographical dispersion was to some extent a barrier to obtaining higher import duties (in that it made the forming of efficient lobbies more difficult), previous tariffs helped determine future tariffs through their effects on the structure and location of industry.

Returning to Figure 4.1, the rise in price causes domestic demand to fall from $OX_4$ to $OX_3$ and domestic supply to rise from $OX_1$ to $OX_2$, so cutting imports. Tariff revenue equal to area $b$ is collected. Notice that protection (increases in domestic supply) and extra customs revenue are compatible when the duty is low, but eventually revenue must fall to zero as the duty rises to the prohibitive level.[4] The last effect illustrated is the rise in rent or producer surplus of size $a$, which attracts most attention in what follows.[5] Not only the tariff on the output but also the tariffs on the purchased material inputs may alter the incomes of the factors of production used in the manufacture of an import-competing product, so we need a way to sum up the influence of the whole set of tariffs. A tariff on the importation of a foreign good will generally be welcomed by the domestic import-competing industry, but tariffs on inputs will not. The former tariff protects, the latter does the opposite; what is the net effect?

## The Net Tariff

A fairly obvious answer is the *net tariff*, which can be explained as follows. The tariff on the output in the first instance raises the sale price of the good by the amount of the duty. (We will consider a particular case of tariff redundancy later in which the full tariff will not be used by domestic producers). Assuming for a first approximation that

---

[3] Local monopoly power in 1820 is discussed in the final section of this chapter.

[4] In the linear case illustrated, revenue is at a maximum when imports have fallen to half their free-trade value.

[5] The sum of the small triangles of height $t$ under the demand and supply curves is the deadweight loss.

purchased material input coefficients are constant, the input tariffs reduce the size of the pool available to pay the value-added factors; Corden (1971) calls this pool the *effective price*, but the term *net price* is used here. Writing the (assumed fixed) input coefficients as $a_{ij}$ ($i$ is an input into good $j$), and the (assumed fixed) free-trade landed prices as $P_i^*$ and $P_j^*$, then the *net price of good* j *before the tariffs* is

$$P_j^* - \sum_i a_{ij} P_i^* \tag{4.1}$$

and the *net price after the tariffs* is

$$P_j^*(1+t_j) - \sum_i a_{ij} P_i^*(1+t_i) \tag{4.2}$$

where $t_i$ and $t_j$ are ad valorem rates. Subtracting (4.1) from (4.2) and normalizing by dividing through by $P_j^*$, we have $T_j^*$, the net tariff using observed free-trade coefficients

$$T_j^* = t_j - \sum_i t_i \Theta_{ij}^* \tag{4.3}$$

where $\Theta_{ij}^*$ is the cost-share of input $i$ into $j$, before the tariffs

$$\Theta_{ij}^* \equiv \frac{a_{ij} P_i^*}{P_j^*}$$

A similar formula is implicit in the calculation of the *net protection* of woolens by Taussig.[6]

If the money value of the domestic output of good $j$ before the tariffs is $S_j$ and the quantity sold is $X_j$, then the money value of the change in the pool available in industry $j$ to pay the primary factors is

$$T_j^* S_j = T_j^* P_j^* X_j \tag{4.4}$$

before any other than price adjustments have been made in the economy. $T_j^* S_j$ is the *impact* of the tariffs on the value-added pool in industry $j$. It would seem to be of primary interest in a discussion of the distributional effects of tariffs, despite the restrictive assumptions, but surprisingly it does not seem to have been used in any systematic way in the literature on tariff formation.

If our interest lay in the allocative effects of tariffs, then the net tariff has some serious disadvantages, the chief being that it is the ratio of the change in the net price to the gross price, and as such is hard to

---

[6] Taussig (1931), pp. 75, 194–218.

link to resource allocation. An alternative is the rate of the change in the net price to itself: the effective rate (see appendix A). The simple argument is that the proportional change in the size of the pool of value added determines how much more or less primary factors the industry can afford to hire, assuming that the prices of the primary factors are unchanged. If industry Z has a 10 percent increase in its value-added pool per unit of output, and industry Y a 5 percent increase, then Z can hire 10 percent more primary factors, and Y only 5 percent more. Why should we assume that primary factor prices are invariant? The polar assumption would be that industry Z would be able to pay its primary factors 10 percent more, and hire no more, while Y could raise its pay scales and profits by 5 percent only. What happens will depend on the nature of competition in factor markets. If quantities do change, then clearly there will be general equilibrium effects of the tariffs on factor prices.

If input coefficients are not fixed, then a change in the prices of purchased material inputs would cause a change in the cost-minimizing input mix,[7] and thus in the maximum payment available for the value-added factors. The easier it is to economize on the inputs with a tariff, the less exact will the net tariff be as an estimate of the net price. No attempts were made to allow for input substitution, but some idea of the size of the bias can be gathered. Input coefficients calculated for the *Digest of Manufactures* (1820) are neither free-trade nor equilibrium-protected (1824) coefficients but something in between. They are closer, however, to the latter.[8] Instead of $T_j^*$ we use $\bar{T}_j$:

$$\bar{T}_j = t_j - \sum_i t_i \Theta_{ij} R_{ij} \quad \text{where} \quad R_{ij} = \frac{1+t_j}{1+t_i} \tag{4.5}$$

[7] The much debated question of the choice of techniques, American capital-intensity in manufacturing, and relative factor prices, turns partly on the pattern and height of protection: see David (1975), especially chapter 1 for a summary of the issues. Along these lines, Williamson's (1974) simulation model suggests that the fall in the relative price of capital goods due to Civil War tariffs hastened capital formation and growth.

[8] Formula (4.5) is derived in Pincus (1972), pp. 192–95. The net tariff (4.3) can be refined by using the expression for the rate of change in the material input coefficient ($\sigma$ = substitution elasticity)

$$\hat{a}_{mj} = \sigma(t_j - t_m)$$

Klingaman, Gallaway, and Vedder (1974) estimate cross-sectional production functions for iron using 1820 data, and show that the concept of a value-added production function has doubtful empirical validity.

$R_{ij}$ "deflates" the 1820 cost-share ($\Theta_{ij}$) to provide an estimate of the free-trade cost-share. If the elasticity of substitution is zero, then $T_j^*$ and $\bar{T}_j$ are equal. On the other hand, if the elasticity is equal to unity, the cost-share is a constant because the production function is now Cobb-Douglas, and the difference between the two measures is given in (4.6) for one input $m$:

$$T_j^* - \bar{T}_j = \Theta_{mj} t_m (R_{mj} - 1) \tag{4.6}$$

Thus $\bar{T}_j$ is an overestimate [9] in a Cobb-Douglas model if

$$R_{mj} < 1, \quad \text{that is, if} \quad t_j < t_m$$

*Factor Incomes.* There are two methods—partial and general equilibrium—with which to examine the effects of protection on factor incomes. We will first discuss the latter, beginning with the Stolper-Samuelson theorem which is sufficiently well known not to require a lengthy exposition. It predicts the change in primary factor prices (or, more strictly, factor rentals) from the nominal tariff and data on the production functions (factor intensities). For example, if the labor-capital ratio is higher in the production of the import-competing good than in the exported good, an increase in the domestic price of the imported good will, under certain assumptions, cause an increase in the *real* wage rate, where *real* means the money wage rate deflated by any goods price index. Although the original theorem was proved for a model with primary factors of production only, it has been extended to allow for simple input-output relations. But it is still within the confines of models with small and equal numbers of primary factors and goods. Pope (1971), for example, has a three-sector model of antebellum income distribution; unfortunately, it does not allow him to offer conclusive, quantitative results.[10]

To increase the number of goods substantially within a manageable general equilibrium model requires some "holes" in the matrix of direct primary-factor input coefficients, which indicate that some pri-

---

[9] As an example of the size of the error, assume that the elasticity of substitution ($\sigma$) is unity, $t_j = 0.4$, $t_m = 0.2$, $\Theta_{mj} = 0.8$, then $T_j^* = 0.24$, and $T_j^* - \bar{T}_j = 0.025$.

[10] Baack and Ray (1974) criticize Pope for his indirect approach to Metzler's paradox. A number of other general equilibrium models of the income distribution of the period do not consider the tariff, e.g., Passell and Schmundt (1971) and Passell and Wright (1972).

mary factors of production are specific to some subset of the industries. Although all factor rewards are "rents" in a model with fixed factor endowments, it is reasonable to speak of product-specific factors as earning rents in the usual sense, so that these models with "holes" partly bridge the gap between the typical general equilibrium models (with all factors nonspecific), and the partial equilibrium effective-protection models (all primary factors product specific). For example, Evans (1971) is able to calculate the effects of a tariff schedule using a fixed-coefficients (linear programming) model with one mobile factor, labor,[11] and one factor specific to each industry.

In general equilibrium, the division of the spoils (or how the rent pool made available by tariffs is distributed) depends on the solution of the whole system describing the economy, because competition bids away any differential rent, that is, equalizes factor rentals across industries: for example, according to the Stolper-Samuelson theorem, in the two-good world a tariff on an import which uses relatively much labor would increase wages. Travis (1968) argues without recourse to this theorem that a positive correlation between labor intensity of an industry and its nominal duty is sufficient to establish that the tariff schedule, on balance, protected labor. The argument is not fully persuasive, however. A high duty increases the derived demand for the productive inputs, whereas a low duty does the opposite. Therefore, the aggregate demand for labor is increased if labor-intensive industries receive higher duties only as long as there is not an inverse relationship between labor intensity and the size of an industry: it would do labor little good if all the highly protected industries were both labor-intensive and tiny and the less protected ones were not labor-intensive but huge. (This discussion is continued in appendix A.)

The benefits to labor from a tariff on a particular product would be dispersed throughout the whole economy if labor were perfectly industry nonspecific. For the reasons discussed elsewhere, there would be a small effort (compared to the income increases) by common labor for tariffs which benefit large numbers of people, many of whom might not be employed in the industries obtaining a tariff. The advantages to the workers in the protected industries cannot be fully appropriated by

[11] Because in such a model industries can disappear entirely if relative prices change a little, Evans has to restrain violent output movements in order to achieve realistic results.

them if there is a competitive labor market. What matters, then, is how tariffs affect rents, not value-added.

Rather than follow the general competitive equilibrium route, consider the case of industry-specific factors of production, especially factors in very inelastic supply and essential to production (e.g., marble for burial monuments). These factors are, as it were, the residual legatees of the industry, whose fortunes depend on what happens in the industry in a much more direct sense than for any perfectly nonspecific factor. Specific factors have (need I say it?), a special interest in *their* tariffs.[12] Considering the nature of the 1820s firm, it seems reasonable to identify proprietorial incomes or surpluses with rents, and to regard those who earned the surplus as specific factors of production. Working proprietors, often skilled workers themselves, were very common; besides tools and machinery, establishments frequently owned land, timber, ore and water rights, all relatively immobile between industries.

A sensible question is how the proprietorial surplus would have varied if an industry lost any margin of its output tariff over the extra costs imposed by the input tariffs, or in other words, was exactly compensated for the input duties it had to pay. The consequent fall in the pool of value-added is given in expression (4.5): the fall per unit output is the net tariff. If a reduction in the net tariff to zero leaves wages unaffected, then the proportional fall in surplus is $T_j/\Theta_\pi$ where $T_j$ is the net tariff ($T_j>0$ only being considered) and $\Theta_\pi$ the protected share of surplus in output. (The expression in value-added terms is $T_j/\Theta_v$ in obvious notation. The formula for the effective rate of protection, therefore, answers a relatively straightforward, albeit very partial-equilibrium, question.)

Far more serious for an industry would be to lose its own protective tariff by being put on the free list, and yet still pay input duties. The proportionate fall in value-added would be $t_j/[(1+t_j)\Theta_v]$ and in rents (assuming wages unchanged) $t_j/[(1+t_j)\Theta_\pi]$.[13] For more sweeping

---

[12] Specific factors will not act passively, but attempt to maximize rent or profits by varying output, prices or input mixes, which would make $\overline{T}_j S_j$ tend to underestimate the increase in the rent pool made possible by tariffs.

[13] If wages fell at the same rate as the output price (i.e., at a rate of $1+t_j$), then the proportionate fall in surplus due to the elimination of an output duty would be $t_j(1-\Theta_w)/\Theta_\pi$ where $\Theta_w$ is the wage share before the tariff removal. All these expressions can be put in terms of ratios of changes in rents or values added to their estimated free-trade values.

changes such as the elimination of all protection, these formulae are much less useful.

## TARIFF EFFECTS IN PRACTICE

The literature on the effects of antebellum tariffs is not very full or detailed. Consider revenue. It was claimed in 1824 that further increases in duties would reduce customs receipts; certainly prohibitive duties were not acceptable. Embarrassed by riches, secretaries of the Treasury agreed to cut tariffs; embarrassed by deficits they plumped for increases. The ratio of revenue to imports after 1816 would seem to justify them, for it rose after 1824 and again after 1828, but fell during the Compromise of 1833–42.[14]

As for price, it is extremely difficult to sort out the change due to import duties, for three main reasons. First, the domestic and foreign products may differ in quality (more generally, we do not know cross-elasticities).[15] Secondly, some duties may be prohibitive.[16] (The possibility of a significant number of prohibitive duties in the data is small, not only because of the manner in which price data were collected— mostly from unit import values—but also because the rates of duties were relatively uniform and relatively low considering the comparative disadvantage of the United States: one of the causes of the revival of protective pressures in the period around 1820 was the influx of English goods into the market after the War of 1812.) Thirdly, foreign supply need not be perfectly elastic. For a later period, Fogel and Engerman calculate that reduction in import duties accounted for much of the fall in imported iron prices from 1842 to 1858, and for a 10.8 percent fall in the real price of domestic pig.[17] The *Metzler paradox* (that import duties perversely can reduce the relative domestic price of the import) has been investigated by Baack and Ray (1974), who found no such effect caused by antebellum textile duties.[18]

A question that excited nineteenth-century controversy—Was pro-

---

[14] Dewey (1903), p. 189. No detailed study of the problem has been made.

[15] See Norman (1974). Our study ignores the problem of cross-elasticities.

[16] Travis (1971) calculates maximum prohibitive rates and concludes that many U.S. duties were prohibitive in the 1960s.

[17] Fogel and Engerman (1971), p. 159.

[18] However, their evidence is inconclusive due to simultaneous equation bias.

tection essential to the birth and survival of certain industries?—ceased to be fashionable in a marginalist world. After examining the histories of several leading industries from the vantage of the 1880s, Taussig argued that the early tariffs, although sometimes beneficial, were not crucial.[19] The unexpectedly heavy protection afforded cheap cottons was "a judicious application of the principle of protection to young industries," but probably not essential.[20] Although early protection was vital to stimulate the growth of woolens output, by 1815 the industry was well established.[21] On iron, Taussig concludes that "no connection can be traced between the introduction and early progress of the iron manufacture, and protective legislation."[22] The discrimination against rolled iron did not appear to hasten developments in the United States.[23] However, Fogel and Engerman find that tariff reductions after 1842 caused pig iron output to be 30 percent lower in 1858 than if the 1842 duties had been retained.[24]

## Protection in 1824

All of these conclusions are partial in that they look at an isolated import duty rather than at the effects of the whole tariff schedule. How distortive of the pattern of production and trade had the tariffs become by 1824? Without extensive calculations, no quantitative answer can be given, and unless the duties change in some simple fashion (say proportionately), no definitive qualitative proposition can be asserted.[25] However, we need not be too tentative in concluding that the pattern of in-

[19] Apart from textiles and iron, Taussig (1931) includes glass, earthenware, paper, cotton-bagging, sailcloth, and cordage in his conclusion, p. 6.

[20] Ibid., p. 35. Ware (1931), p. 72, says that no protection was needed for domestic sheeting: the plans to expand Waltham's output were laid before the Tariff of 1816 (notice, however, Lowell himself had pressed for the minimum valuation). See also Clark (1929), I, 308. On the justification of cotton textile protection, see David (1970).

[21] Taussig (1931), p. 45. Cole (1926), p. 149, agrees, but Cole and Williamson (1941), p. 22, seem to dispute this as it relates to carpets.

[22] Taussig (1931), p. 57. Clark (1929), I, 300.

[23] Berglund and Wright (1929), p. 106.        [24] Fogel and Engerman (1971), p. 159.

[25] Johnson (1965) has proposed a separation of the effects of protection into the *production loss* (the reduction in the value of output measured in free-trade prices) and the *consumption loss* (due to preventing consumers from buying at the cheapest source). The production loss could reasonably be calculated in the manner of Evans (1971), for example, using a fixed coefficient model. The consumption loss is more difficult, requiring a knowledge of substitution elasticities: see Fishlow and David (1961) and Bergson (1973).

ternational trade was more distorted than if the early tariffs had still applied in 1824. There are two questions to consider: the height of the duties, and their uniformity. The simple average of the duties undoubtedly rose. Although there are great dangers in using simple tariff averages, and although it would be preferable to have some weighted averages, the direction of movement is clear because most individual items increased. The major exceptions to the rule were some products added to the free list (they would have paid 5 percent in 1789): brimstone, clay, cork, bullion, plaster of Paris, rags, ships' stores, unmanufactured wood, and zinc.[26] This brings us to the second assertion (and here we can speak with certainty only of the ad valorem items): the rates had become less uniform. In the early tariffs 5 percent was charged on unenumerated imports, and 7.5 or 10 percent on the rest except for carriages. By 1824 the free list was more extensive; the unenumerated rate had risen to 15 percent and the most common ad valorem rates were 20 and 30 percent. This is definitely not to say that the protection of all or most of the major American industries increased just because their nominal tariff rates increased (nominal tariff rates or even effective tariff rates do not allow any such easy inferences). On the contrary, those products with rates less than "average" were hampered compared with free trade (where "average" means alteration of the exchange rate necessary to produce the same volume of imports under free trade as occurred under the tariff).[27] In fact, imports of these less favored products might have been larger and production smaller under the tariff than without it—not only *export* industries suffered from a policy of protection.

Tariff escalation was obvious in 1824: repeatedly an input had a lower rate than its output. Therefore, producers' goods tended to receive low rates, and raw materials the lowest—hides, skins and leather, wood, tallow, chemicals and dyes, pig and bar iron, buttons, machinery, and textile combs, for example.[28]

[26] Removed by 1816 from the 1789 free list were unmanufactured cotton, lead, iron and steel wire.

[27] See, for example, Corden (1966).

[28] It is not definite that all these products would have been produced in larger quantities under free trade. On the one hand, they would have benefited from the depreciation in the exchange rate necessary to offset the change in the balance of trade on a reversion to free trade and from the release of productive resources from heavily protected indus-

Within the eighty-two industries with detailed data, those with the most to lose from a reversion to free trade were rum and refined sugar, tarred cordage, millstones, sheet iron, and white cordage made of American hemp. The first two products had negative values-added after tariff deflation [29] because, arithmetically,[30] they had very high output protection (107 percent and 91 percent), lower input tariffs (24 percent and 52 percent), and very high material cost-shares (0.73 and 0.86); economically, assuming the trouble does not lie in postulating fixed coefficients and wage rates, these negative values-added imply that the two industries would certainly have been nonviable under free trade. The other products mentioned had positive free-trade values-added but negative free-trade proprietorial income or surplus (output minus material and wage costs, assuming wage rates unchanged).[31] Under usual price theory assumptions, these industries would also not have survived free trade or a zero net tariff, since they would have been unable to cover costs and show any profit at all, let alone a normal profit. Only if there were a cushion of rents in costs would this conclusion of viability be altered, general equilibrium considerations aside.[32] On the same basis, products with little margin for survival under a zero net tariff were buttons, cotton bagging, cotton wicks, hardware, augers, saws, sickles, sieves and spades, rolled iron, rifles, lead manufactures

---

tries. On the other hand, their derived demand would have fallen when the industries using them as input lost their tariffs. The balance of these effects depends on the elasticity of foreign supply of the inputs: if it were infinite, then a movement to free trade would have stimulated production of these intermediates.

[29] None of the 82 show negative value-added in 1820 prices; note that the relatively few reports of losses were excluded from the calculation of cost-shares.

[30] See equation 4.5.

[31] Estimation of "free trade" surplus requires an assumption about wage rates. Three obvious possibilities are: (1) fixed wages, (2) fixed wage share (which means wages rise and fall with output price via the output tariff), (3) wages varying at the same speed as value-added (that is, according to the usual expression for the effective rate) so that the ratio of surplus to wages is constant. The first assumption is most reasonable when discussing the effect of a reduction to zero of a single nominal or net tariff. The resulting three estimates of the free-trade surplus share are highly correlated.

[32] When "contingent" expenses are included, red lead, glass n.e.s., and white cordage using foreign hemp also have negative proprietorial incomes, on conversion to a free-trade basis. Not too much should be made of this, since contingent expenses were nowhere defined in the *Digest*, and may not be very consistent across products.

and shot, refined saltpeter, and medicines; all had very low positive free-trade proprietorial shares that could easily have been wiped out by small variations in prices and costs.

So far, the likely fates of industries have been investigated on the assumption that an industry lost its input tariffs as well as its output tariff. What would happen, however, if the input tariffs remained and the output tariff were eliminated? The most appropriate measure of the effect of placing a product on the free list is the proportional reduction in surplus (or valued-added) that would ensue, that is, the ratio of the output duty to protected surplus (or value-added). On this criterion, the most heavily subsidized proprietorial incomes were in boots and shoes, bread and crackers, candles and soap, cordage, all cotton goods, iron (augers, nails, sheet, rolled, saws), lead shot, millstones, red lead, refined sugar, rum, and spirits.[33] In all, twenty-nine of the eighty-two products would have been making a negative surplus after the elimination of their protection, even if wages fell at the rate of $(1 + t_j)$.

On the other hand, some industries' surplus did not depend greatly on their output duty: ales, books and printing, drugs, plows, silverware, spirits of turpentine, watches and clocks, sieves, salt, and saltpeter would have lost less than half their surplus if placed on the free list, providing wages had fallen along with the output price.[34]

## THE RATIO OF SURPLUS TO CAPITAL

It is possible to investigate the correlates of the rate of surplus to capital, and it appears that factors other than the tariff were important in 1820. To these we turn, but before doing so, it is useful to recapitulate the main economic events of the decade before 1820. The War of 1812 stimulated the output of a number of industries, and the Tariff Act of 1816 was supposed to nurture these war infants. Immediately on the cessation of hostilities, English suppliers shipped huge quantities of goods to an eager American market that included the West. For a

[33] Value-added would have been most heavily reduced by a loss of protection of boots, candles, cordage, rolled and sheet iron, shot, rum, spirits and sugar.

[34] If wages remained constant, this list would have added to it axes, earthenware, Prussian blue, and tinware.

number of reasons the postwar boom collapsed, causing industrial distress and general price deflation.[35] By 1820 the worst was over and recovery on the way. These circumstances color the data in the *Digest of Manufactures* (1820).

Geographical dispersion of industry meant that some establishments, sheltering to some extent behind high internal freights, had few local competitors. To discover how great this natural protection was requires data on the profitability of establishments by industry and location. Because we have not been able to collect them, we will have to infer the effects from the correlates of the average rate of surplus in each industry.[36]

Geographical competition requires a system for the distribution of products. Domestic and foreign manufactures are not clearly distinguished in the major works on distribution and, as usual, we know most about cotton textiles.[37] The major channels dealt with internationally traded products and, as their volume rose, general wholesale merchants were replaced by specialists, particularly in the export trade. After 1815 imports were frequently sold by auction (especially in New York, where half the receipts in 1818–29 were from European dry goods);[38] jobbers distributed small lots and in the process extended credit to retailers from one end of the Union to the other.[39] American manufacturers sold their standard, good quality products through commission agents and (textile) selling houses; the market was a mass one, not confined to the richer classes [40] and the cities. American cotton textiles in particular and later woolens were the plainer, stronger sort rather than fancy.[41] At the end of the chain were peddlers and general

[35] In anticipation of peace, English merchants established depots at Halifax, Bermuda, and other places. Auctions had been used to sell prizes taken at sea, and proved a convenient method of quick sale of imports after the war (although they aroused strong opposition). See Jones (1937), p. 33.

[36] The surplus is the residual income after wage and material costs. For the data, see chapter 6 and appendix B.

[37] Johnson et al. (1915); Jones (1937); Porter and Livesay (1971) on wholesaling only.

[38] Jones (1937), p. 70. Jones's list of major goods sold in auction included only one American product—olive oil.

[39] Jones (1937), p. 10.      [40] Bruchey (1965), p. 188 ff.

[41] However, Rhode Island's ginghams had difficulty competing with British imports after 1816. Indian cloth had a poor reputation: Ware (1931), p. 71.

stores, the latter acting also as agents for collection of country produce.[42]

A large part of the postwar boom imports was sold to the West: Johnson et al. cite evidence that stores in Pittsburgh, Natchez, and Cincinnati were stuffed with imports around 1816.[43] More than ten years earlier, Almy and Brown had found it difficult but possible to create a Western market for yarn, but for more normal times various opinions about the extent of interregional trade can be found. For example, Pred asserts that inland transport costs virtually prohibited eastern movement of commodities (which implies that sales of manufactures to the West were largely financed by capital movements),[44] but the question is by no means resolved.[45] Notice that the appeal of Clay's American System of internal commerce stimulated by the tariff and tariff-financed internal improvements would be greatly weakened if little trade between the northeast and the West was possible.

The first thing to remark on in table 4.1 is that capital-intensive industries obtained lower surplus per unit of capital in 1820.[46] The decline in markets and prices after the war struck harder the more capitalized industries, where proprietors remained in business as long as possible, awaiting better days: specific capital such as ore and timber lands, riparian rights, forges, and spindles was difficult or slow to shift into the (temporarily) more profitable activities. The following comment on cotton textiles applies with added force to other industries:

> In reviewing the history of the cotton industry, in 1831, Samuel Slater
> said that most manufacturers worked in their factories and that, after

[42] Danhof (1969), p. 9, states that 15 percent of Northern agricultural produce was sold in Northern cities.

[43] Johnson et al. (1915), I, 215. The buying spree resulted from pent-up demand and lower import prices (due to pent-up supply or, it was claimed, dumping), and may have had a lasting effect on farmers' tastes. Clark (1929), I, 276.

[44] Pred (1973), pp. 104 ff. and especially 108–14. Cf. Danhof (1969), p. 9.

[45] See Ware (1931), pp. 48–53, on Almy and Brown; Clark (1929), I, 276, on the effects of the import spree; Tryon (1917), pp. 269, 283, notes that Western textile household manufactures increased after 1818.

[46] Notice that profitability was unrelated to the size of the industry's output, and that a high import duty in 1820 was no assistance to a higher profit rate; although not reported here, the net tariff and the effective rate of protection to surplus had insignificant coefficients when substituted for $X2$.

deducting ordinary interest on their investment and their own wages, their profits would be very small. Manufacturers of this class rarely failed, because their losses fell on all three items—profits, interest, and wages.[47]

Artisans, millowners and, above all, merchants provided capital besides entrepreneurial talent and labor.[48] The handicraft and putting-out system relied on merchant capital and organization. Once established successfully, manufacturers tended to plow profits back into the same business.[49] Around 1820, certainly, profits were elusive, and the *Digest* is replete with complaints of bad times (echoed in the 1830 "McLane" report).[50] Although large cotton factories on the Waltham lines did handsomely at first, subsequently their rate of profit fell.[51] (However, associated concerns in land and water rights continued to do well, as did trading companies.) In 1820, high ratios of surplus to capital were obtained by axes, books, bread and crackers, clothing, combs, gloves and mittens, gold leaf and watches, hardware, lime, seed oils, millinery, Prussian blue, saddles, and saltpeter; there were low ratios in augers, tarred cordage, cotton cloth and yarn, bar and pig iron, lead manufactures, millstones, muskets, red lead, rum, and window glass. Because the numerator of the dependent variable includes the three elements mentioned by Slater, it is as possible that the highly capital-intensive industries had fewer working proprietors per unit of output

[47] Clark (1929), I, 372.

[48] Coleman (1963), p. 83, states that capital for Rhode Island's textile mills did not come from Bristol or Newport. In contrast to early British industrial development, the rural sector was not a significant source of capital for industry; on the contrary, westward migration into the Ohio Valley itself involved considerable capital outlays.

[49] Of course, capital did move beyond manufacturing: Hazard (1921), p. 50, mentions successful shoe and boot manufacturers who subsequently invested in land, lumber, and ships.

[50] The following typical comment about some New Hampshire mills is recorded in the 1820 *Digest:* "The first of the factories was erected in 1806. No dividend has ever been made. The establishment is probably now worth one-third of the original cost. It has been in operation steadily, except from 1815 to 1818. The limited scale on which business has been done, with the continual alterations rendered necessary by the improvement made on machinery, have rendered it a bill of cost."

[51] McGouldrick (1968), pp. 73 ff. Zevin in Fogel and Engerman (1971), p. 144. In 1820, the rate of surplus to capital in the cotton textile industry was about 12 percent, much lower than the average of 80 percent (table B.1).

or value-added, as that the highly capital-intensive industries were less prosperous.[52]

## Local Monopolies?

What we are chiefly looking for is evidence of local monopoly power manifesting itself in profits. Assume that within each region competitive forces acted to squeeze profit rates into approximate equality between industries, but that between regions these forces were weaker. Then we would find,[53] as indeed we do find, a significant relationship between average surplus rates and regional distributions of output: industries with larger fractions of their outputs produced outside the northeast obtained higher surplus rates (variable $X5$ in table 4.1). However, this could have been a passing phenomenon and not merely the result of the natural protection of the West and South. In other words, this result is consistent with but does not prove the claim that *establishments* located in New England and the Middle Atlantic regions suffered more from the crisis of the late 1810s than did their Southern and Western counterparts, or that they lagged behind them in recovery.[54]

[52] High capital-labor ratios: ales, gunpowder, bar iron, lead manufactures and shot, seed oils, red lead, rum, saddles, sugar. Low capital-labor: books, boots, bread, combs, edged tools, hardware, marble works, saddle trees, saltpeter, saws, watches, whips, wicks. The proposition that industries with larger firms (measured by average value-added per establishment) obtained lower surplus per unit of capital (because they had fewer working proprietors per unit of surplus) was not supported.

[53] Unless local monopoly power was taken in higher local wages rather than higher local proprietorial incomes.

[54] This is a difficult proposition to prove or disprove because evidence of the manufacturing revival in different parts of the nation is scarce. Between 1820 and 1823, only 18 cotton mills were erected (and survived to 1832) whereas 19 were put up in 1823 and no less than 15 in each of the next four years. Ware (1831), pp. 37–38. Reported in Niles's *Register*, XVII, p. 117, is that the number of hands employed in Philadelphia manufacturing declined from 9,672 in 1816 to 2,137 in 1819. The table is reproduced in Tyron (1917), p. 282. According to Thorp (1926), the large cotton crop of 1819 found a good price. However, recovery in 1821 was not general, with agriculture still being depressed. Total export and cotton export values continued to fall until 1821 but export volume rose after 1819. North (1966), p. 233. Corn and wheat prices picked up after 1821 and 1820 respectively, but Western land sales did not begin a steady rise until 1828. North (1966), p. 127.

TABLE 4.1

*Regression Results: Rate of Surplus on Capital, 1820*

| INDEPENDENT VARIABLES | VARIABLE NUMBER | EQUATION NUMBERS | | | |
|---|---|---|---|---|---|
| | | 4.1 | 4.2 | 4.3 | 4.4 |
| Constant | | 2.74 (6.86) | 2.45 (6.81) | 2.74 (6.54) | 2.89 (6.54) |
| 1820 Output/$10^5$ | X1 | . . | . . | . . | 0.20 (0.82) |
| 1820 Tariff | X2 | . . | . . | 0.09 (0.13) | . . |
| National industrial concentration | X3 | 0.29 (2.93) | . . | 0.30 (1.37) | 0.38 (2.59) |
| Average state industrial concentration | X4 | . . | 0.45 (2.54) | 0.02 (0.05) | . . |
| Fraction of output in northeast | X5 | −1.44 (3.60) | −1.35 (3.37) | −1.46 (3.50) | −1.53 (3.68) |
| (Capital/Labor) × $10^2$ | X6 | −5.90 (2.53) | −6.16 (2.61) | −5.94 (2.48) | −6.12 (2.61) |
| $\bar{R}^2$ | | .2385 | .2194 | .2186 | .2352 |
| F | | 9.46 | 8.59 | 5.53 | 7.23 |
| (d.f.) | | (3,78) | (3,78) | (5,76) | (4,77) |

*Note:* The *t* statistics appear in parentheses under each estimated coefficient.

A partial test can be made of whether national or local monopoly power was the more significant determinant of average surplus rates. Variable X3 (table 4.1) is an index of national industrial concentration; variable X4 is the average of the indexes of state industrial concentration, each state's index weighted by the state's share in national output of the product. Both variables are of the "entropy" type [55] and have maximum values of zero when the national output was accounted for by

[55] Thiel (1967).

## T A B L E 4.2

### Correlation Matrix, Means and Standard Deviations of Variables, Table 4.1

|  | Y | X1 | X2 | X3 | X4 | X5 | X6 |
|---|---|---|---|---|---|---|---|
| Y |  | −.193 | −.157 | .213 | .190 | −.346 | −.315 |
| X1 |  |  | .322 | −.707 | −.674 | .035 | .111 |
| X2 |  |  |  | −.199 | −.111 | .171 | .193 |
| X3 |  |  |  |  | .887 | .215 | .000 |
| X4 |  |  |  |  |  | .166 | .027 |
| X5 |  |  |  |  |  |  | .179 |
| Mean | .803 | .479 | .280 | −2.047 | −.801 | .692 | 5.785 |
| Standard deviation | 1.250 | .750 | .186 | 1.259 | .699 | .315 | 5.292 |

*Sources:* Appendix B and chapter 6.

## T A B L E 4.3

### Variables: Tables 4.1 and 4.2

DEPENDENT VARIABLE (rate of surplus): value of output less material and wage payments over value of capital installed.

INDEPENDENT VARIABLES

X1    1820 output in hundreds of thousands of dollars.

X2    Rate of import duty, 1820; specific tariffs converted to ad valorem equivalents on prices, 1821–24.

X3    National concentration index equals:

$$-\sum_{i=1}^{N} y_i \ln y_i,$$ where $y_i = Y_i/Y$ is the share of the $i^{\text{th}}$ report in national output, $Y_i$ being the output of a *Digest* report and $Y$ national output; $N$ is the number of reports.

X4    Average state concentration equals:

$$-\sum_{g=1}^{G} y_g \left[ \sum_{i \in S_g} \frac{y_i}{y_g} \ln \frac{y_i/y_g}{1/N_g} \right]$$

where the $N$ reports have been segmented by state $g$ ($g = 1, \ldots, G$), each with a share $y_g$ in national output, accounted for by the $N_g^{\text{th}}$ report.

X5    Share of national output in Maine, New Hampshire, Massachusetts, Rhode Island, Connecticut, Vermont, New York, New Jersey, Pennsylvania, Delaware, Maryland, District of Columbia.

X6    Capital installed/wages paid, 1820.

*Note:* Fuller details of the data can be found in appendix B.

one firm. As can be seen in the tables, the highly collinear variables both have significant coefficients—greater industrial concentration of either type was associated with a higher average rate of surplus on capital. But there are statistical reasons for preferring the national index, $X3$, over the average state index, $X4$, namely, that equation (4.1) has a higher explanatory power ($\bar{R}^2$) and that when both variables are used in equation (4.3), $X3$ is significant near the 10 percent level (one-tailed test) whereas $X4$ is insignificant. Either state boundaries did not delimit market areas, or the particular measure ($X4$) is not appropriate. Until data on profitability by location are collected, a finding that local monopolies were not very profitable can be only tentative.[56]

In summary, manufacturing in 1820 was a small if growing sector of geographically dispersed shops or mills operated by working proprietors and partnerships. The major industries utilized local workers, power, and materials (apart from cotton) to cater to a local demand. Before 1820, manufacturing was alternatively encouraged and rebuffed by external conditions, chiefly European conflicts and the War of 1812. General economic policy was not extremely supportive of manufacturing, and although the tariff moderated the force of foreign competition in more normal times, it proved ineffective against the flood of British goods after 1815. Import competition in the early 1820s was particularly strong in textiles, bar iron, glass bottles, and some wooden products, and in refined sugar and lead manufactures. These last two, together with rum, cordage, rolled and sheet iron, and iron implements, were most vulnerable to changes in duties, prices, and costs.

Early tariffs were low and relatively uniform (although the power of industry pressure was not absent in 1789); rates rose and spread over the first decade, to be doubled during the War of 1812. In the consolidation of 1816 the rates were, if anything, inversely related to comparative disadvantage as the more firmly established were more heavily protected. The rapid collapse of prices after the peace left American industry battered but capable of expansion. The Act of 1824 raised some

---

[56] Bateman and Weiss (1975) rarely find a connection between profit rates in 1860 or 1850 and regional concentration ratios. The suggestion that local monopolies were often undercapitalized establishments barely surviving behind a weak wall of natural protection is made by Green (1975), p. 218. Cf. McDuffie of South Carolina, *Annals*, 18th. Cong., 1st. Sess. (1823–24), p. 2413.

important duties, especially within the finer schedules for glass and iron. Revenue being plentiful, the major sumptuary duties were untouched.

It was argued that the net tariff gives the first approximation to the change in the pool of value-added per unit output and that, due to the prevalence of working proprietors, most of the change fell on proprietors' surpluses. At least some of the industry variation in surplus rates to capital was accounted for by industrial concentration, capital-labor ratios, and concentration in the Northeast, but not by tariff rates.

# CHAPTER FIVE

# Theory of Individual and Group Decisions

## INDIVIDUALS IN GROUPS

T H E first task in developing a positive theory of tariff formation is to examine the responses of interested individuals to the opportunities of influencing tariffs. In order to understand the formation of groups or coalitions, we need to look at things preventing full sidepayments [1] and at asymmetries in transactions costs.

The straightforward way for an economist to analyze economic choice is first, to find out which individuals expected to gain or lose and by how much; secondly (and here the complications arise), to translate the expected gains and losses into efforts by individuals to influence the choice; and finally, to solve for the equilibrium. Armed with knowledge of individual objectives and opportunities, the economist predicts that a line of action will be pursued until, on the margin, the expected benefit of further action just equals the expected cost to the actor. The list of potential actors coincides with the list of the individuals affected and, in its compilation, we must forget the hard-learned distinction between pecuniary externalities and technological externalities. A man's well-being is changed by any change in market prices, and everyone therefore has a motive to intervene in any decision that alters market prices. [2] All persons capable of affecting the decision, be they gainers or

---

[1] A careful reading of Coase's work makes clear that this is the pertinent question to ask. Arrow (1970), pp. 9, 10, dissents from the view that *only* transaction costs prevent the attainment of Pareto-optimality, and gives an example of a game in which the core is empty, at least for single plays.

[2] Pecuniary externalities (or more precisely, exchange externalities) can be avoided only by autarky, that is, individuals or a group of individuals can choose to have no economic contact with others, while having feasible, binding contracts with each other. In contrast, a perfectly competitive market is an institution in which there are no binding contracts; there is instantaneous recontracting and no way to escape exchange externali-

losers, must be considered potential members of the decision group, whether the decision is redistributive or efficient.

The data requirements are large in models of collective choice using distributional information; hence the attractions of using the aggregative Pareto-efficiency approach mentioned in chapter 1 and discussed further in this chapter. Few economic historians are comfortable with all-encompassing groups like the world, or the nation; there are some aggregates intermediate between the individual and the totality which have existence independent of our analytical convenience. Most people belong to numerous groups, collectives or coalitions such as family, work place, union, and political party, and, although they may try to influence group decisions (while leaving intergroup bargaining to others), they continue membership even though the groups do not reflect exactly their individual preferences.

A natural way to define groups, as opposed to mere collections of individuals, is by the community of *direct* interests. An individual is an obvious candidate for inclusion in a group if, without any sidepayments from other group members, he stands to gain along with them from some economic change. (The contrast here is with the universal group that stands to gain *directly or with compensation* by movements toward Pareto-efficiency.) For practical purposes, the requirement that no sidepayments are necessary is too stringent, and it can be relaxed, at the cost of precision, to the requirement that sidepayments be easier within a group than without.

### Sidepayments and Sectional Interests

Consider the sectional interests theory applied by Taussig and others. The interests of, and thus the votes of the representatives of, different regions of the country are identified with the relationship that the major outputs and inputs (including consumption) bear to international as opposed to interregional trade. The South opposed antebellum tariffs because what little it stood to gain from increased trade with the rest of the country would have been far outweighed by its

---

ties. For example, when A switches his purchase from B to C, B suffers but, if the switch is efficient, then the gain to A and C exceeds B's loss. Similarly, most of Davis and North's (1971) examples of improvements in efficiency involve redistribution. See Shubik (1971) for a clear discussion of pecuniary externalities.

losses in the form of increased prices paid for imports and lower prices received for staple exports. New England switched to protectionism in the 1820s—Webster's reversal is the outstanding example—in response to a change in its industrial structure from commerce to manufacturing. Only if the majority of the electors in the area benefits would its representative vote for the legislation, if no sidepayments are possible within the area.

The sectional interests theory tries to say more, however, than that the majority of Southerners were harmed by the tariff. For the theory to be of much interest, we must be able to make some hypothetical compensation test: On balance, did the tariff cost the Southerners more than it benefited them? Or could the gainers in the South have offered the losers enough compensation to win acceptance for the tariff? As long as there is the possibility of sidepayments (with zero transaction costs), then to discover whether the Southern vote against the tariff, or the change in the New England vote, correctly reflected the interests of the individuals in those regions, we may safely add up the gains and losses of the individuals. There is no problem with interpersonal utility comparisons here.

However, once we allow sidepayments, then the tariff would pass or fail according only to whether the tariff was a Good Thing, that is, whether it passed a compensation test for the nation as a whole with no regard for the regional distribution of the gains and losses arising out of the tariff itself. To continue this line of thought, why confine the set of possible bargains to national boundaries? The logical extension of the "efficiency approach," which assumes zero bargaining costs, is that U.S. tariffs should have contributed to the Pareto-efficiency of *world* resources allocation, and would have passed Congress only if they met that condition. *For us to retain the word* sectional, *the transaction costs of making sidepayments within regions must be sufficiently cheap, and between regions sufficiently expensive, for the vote within a region to reflect the failure or success of a compensation test applied to the benefits and burdens arising in that region only.*[3]

---

[3] A full-fledged "efficiency approach" which attempts to predict the set of tariffs from a model that assumes that Congress tried to maximize real national income reverses the procedure of Taussig, who inquired whether at least some of the tariffs passed were justified by their effect on national wealth.

At this level of analysis, then, we can test the sectional interests theory by calculating the net gains or losses to each region, and seeing if the vote on the bill was in accord with these regional calculations. Notice that the tariff is here regarded as standing alone, that is, there are no sidepayments arising out of nontariff issues which could be used to cause a region to vote other than as indicated by the net benefits of the tariff alone.

The task of making the sectional calculations would be formidable and possibly not very rewarding. A simple aggregation of the gains and losses within a region may be a misleading guide to how the region's representatives voted or should have voted. The assumption that sidepayments have zero transaction costs within each region is clearly incorrect, and caution should be exercised in using the results of models with this assumption. In the tradition of the sectional interest theory, Pope has recently reassessed Southern opposition to the manufacturing tariffs with the aid of a general equilibrium, three-sector model. He tends to confirm Metzler's hypothesis about the tariffs—that the elasticity of export demand for cotton was such that the tariff did not damage Southern plantation owners—and concludes that Southern opposition to the tariff was "one of the ironies of antebellum history." [4] If Pope's model had shown that the burden of the tariff on the South was large, would this have explained Southern opposition? The answer is no. A large burden may be necessary, but it is not sufficient. We still need a theory that would tell us how *intense* the effects of the tariffs on individuals in the various regions must be to be reflected in common political action. [5]

In a similar vein, Thomas is concerned with testing the economic interpretation of the American Revolution. [6] As a vital and important first

----

[4] Pope (1971), p. 278. The use of the word "ironies" is very appropriate: Pope's model is complex, and, given the confidence intervals on the parameters, does not yield definite results; it can hardly be used to estimate the *perceived* effects of the tariff. See Baack and Ray (1974) for more direct analysis.

[5] The same comment can be directed at the finding by Passell and Wright (1972) that territorial expansion may have damaged the planter class in the Old South despite the private profitability of slave sales in the new cotton lands.

[6] It should be pointed out that Thomas and Pope were only indirectly interested in the prediction of economic decisions, whereas Davis and North (1971) are explicit in having this as their goal.

step, he estimated the burdens and benefits of membership of the British Empire to the American colonies. Burdens arose from restrictions on trade and shipping; the main benefits were derived from British military and naval protection. The per capita burden in 1770 was estimated to be $1.24; the burden net of benefits was only $0.24 per head. Depending on the estimate of per capita income, one may wish to support the hypothesis that there was not a significant hardship upon the colonies.[7] But these findings, along with similar ones, do not justify a claim that "real economic causes were not very important in stimulating the final break with the Mother Country."[8] The methodology of the "efficiency approach" to politics has crept in unnoticed: Thomas has aggregated the gains and losses of all persons in the colonies. For this he was taken to task by Ransom (1968), who showed that about 90 percent of the burden fell on the Southern colonies.[9] Faced with this fact, Thomas swung to the polar economic theory of political action, Downs's (1957) "passionate minority," and in effect asserted that sidepayments were so costly that we would expect those individuals whose interests were damaged by the British to rebel, and those whose interests benefited to be loyalists.[10] Is there no middle ground between a theory with costless sidepayments and full aggregation, and one with no sidepayments and no aggregation?

Sectional interest theories are really a species of what might be called "Coase-aggregation." In defining sections or groups we implicitly assume for the purposes of a theory of collective action that aggregation is allowable within but not across regions or groups. *The appropriate delineation depends on sidepayments being less frequent and less costly within than between groups.* When there is a common interest (say among proprietors of an industry), the necessity of substantial sidepayments is much less; and when geography, class consciousness, or membership of an association makes for easy communication and agreement within a group, then any necessary sidepayments are less costly. To retain the description "sectional," the number or amount of sidepayments and the cost of making them within a region must be sufficiently

---

[7] Thomas (1965).    [8] Thomas (1968), p. 439.

[9] R. L. Ransom, "The Burden of the Navigation Acts," *Economic History Review*, XXVI, no. 4 (November 1973).

[10] Thomas (1968), p. 440.

small for the actions of the region (or its representatives) to reflect only
the success or failure of a "compensation test" applied to the benefits
and damage *arising in that region.* Taussig used geography as a convenient method of defining or delimiting a group. Not all individuals in a
region or section would benefit directly by a certain tariff but a fair
number would. In addition, any conflicts of interest between individuals within a geographical region would be more easily resolved than
conflicts between individuals in widely separated locations. In an earlier discussion of failures to achieve competitive equilibrium, Arrow
stressed the bias in bargaining costs; [11] what is suggested here is that
biases in bargaining and transaction costs help to *define* groups.

### An Alternative Starting Point: The Distribution of Effects

Rather than assume that sidepayments within regions or industries
or groups have zero transaction costs, let us revert to a more traditional
way of discussing how legislation is formed, by looking at the economic
behavior of those who stand to gain or lose and their incentives for trying to influence the tariff. A change in focus is required, from the pattern of voting on tariff bills to the pattern of tariffs in the bills. The tariff
redistributes economic welfare. It may be justified in some economic
sense, but whether it is or not, only a decision rule requiring unanimity
would ensure that every economic change is "Pareto-approved," that
is, one by virtue of which no one is made worse off. If we regard the
tariff as a redistributive mechanism, then the question arises, Who is
likely to gain and who to lose? It is not sufficient to explain with Taussig that in post–Civil War tariff changes, regard for the producer has
been exclusive unless we can say which producers and when. [12]

The main beneficiaries of protection in the first instance are the
Treasury and the factors of production engaged in import-competition
which enjoy higher factor prices or employment. We would expect the
main pressure for particular duties to come from those receiving direct
benefits. Of course, competition can alter factor prices generally

---

[11] "In real life, monopolizing cartels are possible for a reason not so far introduced into
the analysis: bargaining costs between producers and consumers are high, and those between producers are low—a point made most emphatically by Adam Smith." Arrow
(1970), p. 6.

[12] Taussig (1931), p. 200.

throughout the economy after a tariff change, not just in the protected industries; for example, it can raise the returns to labor at the expense of capital or land. In the empirical analysis of the structure of the 1824 tariff, the general equilibrium repercussions are ignored on the grounds that, especially in the absence of unions, common labor would not be expected to mount a very effective campaign for protection. There is some room, however, for general equilibrium models of income distribution in the theory of tariff formation, and these are touched on in chapter 7,[13] but in this section all that is needed is to postulate that some individuals stand to gain.

## The Voluntary Supply of Public Goods

Economic theory postulates that an individual involved in group decision-making tries to maximize his expected advantage in terms of some economic variables (which I assume are approximated by income), subject to the costs of pursuing his interests. But the public goods nature of a tariff duty prevents the straightforward application of the usual economic theory of individual, maximizing behavior; we have to enquire into the question of voluntary contributions to tariff-influencing efforts. A tariff on a particular import has some of the characteristics of a public good (or evil), in that the benefits are not, in general, fully appropriable by one individual. If the woolen manufacturers secure a duty on their product, they are all affected, irrespective of whether or not each of them expended effort to influence the legislation. Similarly, the duty will harm the users of the protected product, all of whom will suffer, not necessarily identically. (This is to deny, for the sake of convenience, that diminution in price that Clay was often to claim would result from protection.) Apart from this communality, we would expect that each individual would equate at the margin his benefits from protection with his costs of influencing the tariff. But efforts to influence legislation are costly and the benefits are shared, and so we have an example of the problem of cooperative or collective action.

An individual, when attempting to maximize his expected advantage by contributing to the supply of a public good, will *not* equate on the

[13] Chapter 4 discussed in detail the effect of tariffs on factor prices, especially on rents or quasi-rents.

margin the cost of his contribution with his benefit from the good; rather, he will equate the *expected* costs and benefits, that is, will exhibit strategic behavior, an extreme form of which is "free-riding." A free-rider is one who uses a public good but contributes nothing toward its provision. If the good is supplied by voluntary contributions rather than by compulsory levy, then free-riders tempt the law of composition: if everyone rides free, no one rides at all. This is the reason why contributions toward the provision of some public goods are made compulsory, with government supplying the compulsion through taxes. We are interested here, however, in public goods that are voluntarily financed or supplied; ultimately, we shall be concerned with tariff lobbies or pressure groups, and the public good is conceived to be a more favorable tariff rate, that is to say, one which can be enjoyed by all producers of import-competing products whether or not they have helped secure the tariff.

Free-riding is a predictable, if extreme, outcome of individual decisions, and may not be privately irrational. The behavior of an individual who is deciding how much to contribute toward a public good differs from his behavior where a private good is concerned, because of the advantages in not revealing his true valuation. So long as his valuation of an extra unit of a private good exceeds the price of that good, he will demand more of it until equality is achieved, at which point his valuation will be revealed. However, if *his* purchase allows *others* to enjoy the good, and vice versa, he may be tempted to conceal his true valuation. In such circumstances he will not voluntarily pay the supplier until his marginal valuation equals the price of the good. Rather, he will take the risk that others will make sufficient contributions. A strategic element enters, which is absent if goods have no spillover or external effects. The consequence is that the aggregate marginal outlay on a good is not equated with its aggregate marginal cost. The ratio of these aggregates ranges from unity (a private good or a perfectly coherent group), to zero (when everyone attempts to free-ride).[14]

Formally, an individual who maximizes his expected utility will contribute toward a common goal until his marginal contribution produces an increase in his *expected* benefit of an equal amount, where the ex-

[14] Aggregation is here understood in the sense of Samuelson's (1954) discussion of public goods.

pectations are in terms of his subjectively held probability of the achievement of the group goal. Even assuming that *everyone could be made better off* (that the sum of the individual valuations could exceed the total cost), whether the good will be provided at all, let alone in socially optimal quantities, will depend on individual strategic decisions and everyone might decide to contribute less than his "fair share." There is no certainty that a good will be provided by voluntary contributions simply because the sum of its marginal benefits exceeds its marginal cost. In fact, there is no simple relationship between the aggregate benefits and the aggregate outlays or efforts.

What determines where, between zero and unity, the ratio of aggregate marginal outlay to aggregate marginal benefit will fall? That is, how coherent is a group; how closely does its behavior resemble that of an individual faced with the same opportunities? Olson suggested that the significant determinants are the number of individuals, the homogeneity of their interests, and the ease of communications among them, given the public nature of the group's goal. At one extreme groups achieve a joint-maximum like the Samuelsonian optimum. At the other extreme are the free-riders. In between groups differ according to size, homogeneity, and information and transaction costs. When numbers are small (to consider one dimension), the opportunities for profitable concealment of valuation are reduced by the relative ease of mutual surveillance. It seems reasonable to suppose, though it is difficult to prove theoretically, that the outlay-benefit ratio falls as numbers increase, that is, that large groups react less intensely than small groups to identical opportunities. I interpret these ideas of Olson's, therefore, as suggestions about how to form quasi-individuals, or individual-equivalents (analogous to the full-time male-equivalent in labor force studies, in which a group is the equivalent of some fraction of an individual, where the fraction is the marginal ratio between aggregate outlays and aggregate benefits).

The following model shows that it is reasonable to postulate that an individual, seeking selfishly to maximize his advantage, may not contribute at all toward the supply of a public good unless the benefit that he receives exceeds some positive quantity. Further, the contribution he makes will, in general, fall short of the benefits that he would with certainty secure if he were to supply the public good by himself. The effort an individual makes toward gaining a public good is not an accurate indication of the benefits he would receive if that good were to be supplied to him free of cost. It is almost a truism that the interests of consumers are less likely to be catered to by tariffs than the interests of producers, and part of the explanation lies in the public-good nature of the tariff. The cost to each consumer of any particular tariff item is likely to be much smaller than the benefits to the producers (owners of factors of production) of the product. A duty on a product is more likely to be legislated, the more concentrated are the benefits (that is, the fewer who participate) and the more widespread the burdens.

## Formal Models

Consider the analytically simple case of an individual given an opportunity to contribute a positive amount toward a public good that he and others can enjoy. The good is nonexclusive to the group, and there is no crowding in its use. Assume the good to be a goal which requires a minimum expenditure $K$ to be achieved, but that whether or not it is achieved, the contributions are not refunded. For example, the contributions may be time and effort put into lobbying a congressman to vote in a certain way, or to convince a majority of voters to agree to a referendum proposal.

How does the individual decide on the size of his contribution? To keep matters simple, assume that he has to act in ignorance of the *exact* action of other interested individuals, but that he has a fair idea, summed up by a subjective probability density function, $p(x)$ over $x$, of the total contributions of others (figure 5.1). The individual puts a valuation $v$ on his having the good; consider $v$ to be expressed in dollars. Intuitively, he will maximize his expected gains by making a contribution that, on the margin, produces an increase in his *expected* benefits from the good just equal to his marginal contribution. To derive the result, we must first write down the subjective probability of the achievement of the group goal.

Let $c$ (figure 5.2) be the contribution made by the individual, so that the total contribution of all persons is $x + c$. Then the probability that $x + c$ will not fall short of the target $K$ is given by

$$P(x + c \geqslant K) = 1 - \int^{K-c} p(x) \, dx$$

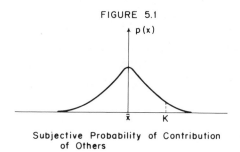

FIGURE 5.1

Subjective Probability of Contribution
of Others

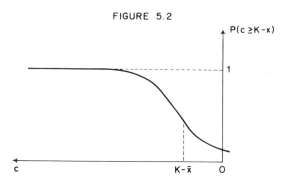

FIGURE 5.2

Probability of Own Contribution Being Sufficient

which is a portion of an ogive. In the case illustrated in figures 5.1 and 5.2, there is an "expected shortfall" when $c = 0$, that is, $K - \bar{x} > 0$, where $\bar{x}$ is the mean. The figures also assume that if the individual contributes nothing, there is still some chance he will enjoy the good; if he contributes an amount $K$, then he is certain to obtain the good. (This last assumption can easily be relaxed to allow for the possibility of negative contributions by others, i.e., opposition.) If this were a private good, then the graph of $P(x + c \geqslant K)$ would coincide with the horizontal axis until $c = K$, and then be a horizontal line from the point with coordinates $(K, 1)$.

Writing $P(x + c \geqslant K)$ as $P(c)$, the problem is to

$$\max_{c} P(c) \cdot v - c$$

The marginal conditions are

$$dP(c) \cdot v - dc \geq 0 \qquad (5.1)$$

$$\frac{d^2P}{dc^2} \cdot v < 0 \qquad (5.2)$$

with equality holding in (5.1) if $c > 0$, as is illustrated in figure 5.3. (The ogive of figure 5.2 is reversed for a more conventional presentation.)

FIGURE 5.3

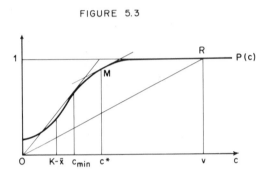

Optimum Individual Contribution

The interpretation of (5.1) is that the increase in the expected gross benefit from the good must just equal the extra contribution. An alternative formulation, $dP(c^*)/dc = 1/v$, is illustrated in figure 5.3: the slope of the ogive at $M$ is equal to the slope of the ray to the point $(v, 1)$.

If the contributions are *refundable*—in the sense that if there is a shortfall so that $x + c < K$, then all is returned, but that any excess $(x + c - K > 0)$ is not returned—then the maximand becomes $P(c) \cdot (v - c)$, and the optimum conditions

$$dP(c) \cdot (v - c) - P(c)dc \geq 0 \qquad (5.3)$$

$$\frac{d^2P(c)}{dc^2} \cdot (v - c) < 0 \qquad (5.4)$$

with equality in (5.3) whenever $c^* > 0$. The first-order condition has a similar interpretation to (5.1): on the margin, the increase in the expected net benefit must just balance the increase in the expected contribution. Alternatively, by rewriting (5.3), the optimum contribution is that which leaves the rate of increase in the probability of success equal to the rate of decrease in the *net* benefit.[15]

Reverting to the *nonrefundable* case, the second-order condition (5.2) implies that the optimum contribution, c*, *can never be less than the amount of the expected shortfall*, that is,[16]

$$c* \geq K - \bar{x} \quad \text{or} \quad c* = 0 \tag{5.5}$$

This has an interesting consequence if $p(x)$ is symmetrical, because the point of inflection at $c = K - \bar{x}$ in figure 5.3 then corresponds with a probability of one-half. That is, for a symmetrical $p(x)$, (5.2) implies that

$$P(c*) \geq .5 \quad \text{or} \quad c* = 0 \tag{5.6}$$

In general, no contribution would be made that is less than the subjective expected shortfall, and unless it left the subjective probability of success no less than that indicated by $P(\bar{x} \geq K)$.

---

[15] In this form the solution is identical with that of Hoffman (1969). The models differ, however, in that Hoffman, and Stigler (1974) confuse the continuous with the discrete case.

If the good is continuous, then the valuation is a function $v = v(x + c)$ and the marginal conditions become:

$$E[v'(x + c)] - dc = 0$$
$$E[v''(x + c)] \quad < 0$$

If instead of maximizing expected utility, the individual maximized the utility of the expected outcome, then the first equation becomes:

$$v'(\bar{x} + c) - dc = 0$$

This can be interpreted: the risk-neutral individual contributes until his last dollar increases by one dollar the utility he would get if others contributed $\bar{x}$. In effect, on the margin he ignores the public-goods character.

No simple scheme for refunding excessive contributions springs to mind; it would be better to investigate some such scheme, because the question arises about what happens to the excess. If it goes to increase the size of public good, then we are in the continuous case.

[16] The second-order condition does not seem to ensure that when c* is positive, $P(c*) \cdot v - c*$ is also positive. This last condition is required whenever $P(0) > 0$ *and* $v > 0$; otherwise, if $P(c*) \cdot v - c* < 0$, then a zero contribution would be preferred. The requirement $P(c*) \cdot v > c*$ is met if the point of tangency $M$ is above the ray $OR$. The model can be applied to many examples of cooperation with "nature."

*Contribution and Valuation.* We can now obtain some standard results. First, free-riding. Rotation of the ray *OR* until it is tangent to $P(c)$ in figure 5.3 gives $c_{min}$, as the smallest contribution that would be made by individuals with the expectations portrayed by $p(x)$, together with the valuation below which no contribution will be made.[17] To use Olson's word, individuals with low valuations "exploit" the more interested individuals. Whether attempts to free-ride succeed, of course, is an open matter. The general relationship between $c$ and $v$ is shown in figure 5.4 (which also illustrates the effects of degrees of certainty).

FIGURE 5.4

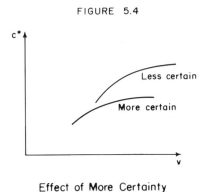

Effect of More Certainty

Free-riding is merely one possible outcome. We can derive the general relationship between the valuations and contributions of individuals with the same expectations by differentiating (5.1) with respect to $v$ at an internal maximum:

$$\frac{dc^*}{dv} = -\ \frac{dP(c)/dc}{d^2P(c)/dc^2} > 0 \tag{5.7}$$

that is, persons with higher valuations contribute more; whether they contribute proportionally more depends, inter alia, on the shape of $p(x)$.[18] On the interim assumption of no interaction between valuations

---

[17] This critical valuation is found by dropping a perpendicular from the point where the tangent ray cuts the line $p(x) = 1$.

[18] If $p(x)$ was normally distributed about $\bar{x}$ with variance $\sigma^2$, then

$$\frac{dc}{dv} \cdot \frac{v}{c} = -\frac{v}{c} \cdot \frac{\sigma}{K - \bar{x} - c} \geqslant 0$$

and expectations, the aggregate contribution should rise with the aggregate valuation.

*Aggregate Contribution, Numbers, and Homogeneity.* Our chief concerns are whether small groups contribute more, under suitable assumptions, than do large groups, and whether diverse groups contribute more or less than groups with homogeneous interests or valuations. We will discuss these questions together, since their answers depend on similar considerations.

First, let the aggregate valuation be constant, but the numbers enjoying the good vary. The extreme case in which there is only one individual with a positive valuation is similar to the case in which there are also some individuals with very small valuations. The one individual with a valuation large in relation to the cost of the good may find it worthwhile to shoulder the entire burden, whereas, if every one of a large number of individuals has the same or similar small valuations (adding up to the same total valuation), all may decide that the project is not worth any effort, and so it fails. There is some presumption, therefore, that concentration of benefits in few hands is associated with larger aggregate contributions.[19]

However, the opposite outcome occurs when, for a given $p(x)$, individual contributions rise less than proportionately with individual valuations. On analogy with the old argument about increasing aggregate demand by a more equal distribution of income, it can be seen that an equal distribution of the total valuation would then produce the largest possible aggregate contribution, as long as all the equals do not attempt to free-ride. Similarly, the more who share in the fixed total benefit, the larger the aggregate contribution as long as none choose to free-ride. Once valuations fall so low that any free-riding occurs, then larger

---

From the interpretation of the second-order condition, and the argument of the second to last footnote, we find that $v/c > 2$, so that for contributions less than $2\sigma$, $(dc/dv) \cdot (v/c)$ is certainly less than unity if there is an expected shortfall (i.e., $K - \bar{x} > 0$).

[19] Olson attempted to show that provision of a public good by voluntary association is more likely if the group is small and the benefits unevenly distributed. Strictly, Olson's argument refers only to the likelihood that one person will be willing to bear the whole burden himself. Olson (1968), p. 24. Stigler (1974) argues that the small numbers case has more relevance than first appears because size distributions of sales or capital (proxies for benefits) are generally highly skewed, so that the few relatively large firms effectively make up a small group. See also Breton (1974), pp. 74 ff.

group sizes or more equal distributions will eventually cause the aggregate contribution to fall. I regard this as the most common outcome.

Thus far $K$, the cost of the public good, has been held constant, and in particular, did not rise with the total benefit. A more realistic assumption when it comes to protectionist lobbies is that, because a larger total benefit causes a larger loss to the users of a protected product, resistance grows with the aggregate benefit enjoyed by the lobby. Take the simple case in which the cost of successful lobbying, the aggregate benefit, and the group numbers vary proportionately (so that the average benefit and average lobbying cost are unchanged).[20] A large lobby is then the sum of smaller lobbies, but the large lobby's effort may not be just the sum of smaller lobbies' efforts. The "pure" effect of group numbers comes into play. Large groups would contribute less in relation to group benefit than smaller groups if, as seems plausible, the effect of increases in the size of the group is to cause expectations to be more uncertain and pessimistic.[21]

*Changing Expectations.* How does an individual's contribution alter when his expectations, summarized in $p(x)$, alter? Consider first a shift in $p(x)$ that leaves its shape unchanged but alters the mean $\bar{x}$, say, raises it. An increase of $\bar{x}$ by $d\bar{x}$ decreases $c^*$ by $d\bar{x}$ (or reduces it to zero). This can be seen in figure 5.2: a rightward shift of $p(x)$ causes a rightward shift of the ogive, so that the point in figure 5.2 corresponding to $M$ in figure 5.3 shifts right by $d\bar{x}$. An individual's voluntary contribution falls pari passu with a rise in $\bar{x}$, but the aggregate contribution remains the same, if his expectations are well founded.

Let us now hold $\bar{x}$ constant and consider two individuals who are identical except in the degree of certainty they have about others' contributions, (i.e., $x$). The upper line in figure 5.4 is the relationship $c^*(v)$ for the less certain individual: he has a higher "threshold" valuation below which no contribution is made, his minimum positive contribution is more than that of the more certain individual, and his contribu-

---

[20] Free-riding is still possible but, in effect, there is crowding: to produce the same average benefit, a larger group requires a larger outlay.

[21] We have so far dealt with three cases. First, the "pure" public goods example: fixed cost, but group benefits rising with group numbers. Second, the case of redistribution of a fixed total benefit (what appears to be the Olson example). Third, the "pure" numbers example, in which the cost of the good rises with the total benefit. The effects of increases in numbers differ among cases.

tion reaches a higher maximum at a larger $v$. Thus, greater certainty leads to higher contribution for any valuation in the high range.[22] An implication is that there will be less dispersion in individual contributions among a group with very certain expectations about the behavior of the group members.[23]

Ideally, we should link the parameters of the group (size, homogeneity, total valuation) with the expectations they hold. For example, if an individual thinks that he is just one of $n$ identical individuals with identical subjective $p(x)$ and $v$, then he can easily carry out the following thought experiment: What happens if $n-1$ others do as I do? He can revise his estimate of $x$; in fact, unless we introduce some stochastic element, he must revise it so that $x = (n-1)c^*$ with probability one. Quickly, we can see that only contributions $c^* = K/n$ or $c^* = 0$ survive such a revision and $n$ identical individuals would all contribute equal amounts or nothing. This special solution to the game-theoretic difficulties of the model is as far as this section goes toward examining the problem of rational expectations.[24]

*Contrasts and Conclusions.* In contrast to the model just developed are Olson's (1968) "by-product" theory of associations and Buchanan and Tullock's (1967) analysis of constitution-making, neither of which is quite suitable for our purposes.[25]

Olson suggests a by-product theory of the existence of voluntary organizations that make both public and private goods available to members. The American Medical Association offers malpractice insurance to

[22] No operational meaning can be put on the words "high valuations," unfortunately.

[23] This could be important if, for example, the reaction of the legislature depended on how "unified" the suppliant industry might be.

[24] The difficulty is that expectations seem to contradict the very behavior they predict. Say a typical group member expects larger groups to contribute less in relationship to the cost of the group goal than smaller groups, in the case in which the group benefits, numbers, and costs rise proportionally. He would then contribute more, according to our analyses of the effects of a shift in the curve $p(x)$. To the extent that he is typical, so would everyone else, thus confounding his expectations. I have benefited particularly from seeing W. A. Brock's notes on game-theoretic models of public goods.

[25] I want to comment briefly on Buchanan's model in *The Demand and Supply of Public Goods* (1968), which concludes that the famous Samuelson (1954) condition for *optimality* in the supply of a public good—that the marginal cost of the good should equal the sum of the individual marginal valuations—is actually the laissez faire *equilibrium* condition! Buchanan proves the case for two individuals by completely ignoring strategic considerations and for no justifiable reason.

members, besides acting as the chief medical pressure group. The theory is a little unsatisfactory, for it fails to explain why individuals should join organizations which supply public goods: an alternative A.M.A. that did not lobby presumably would be able to offer cheaper insurance. A clearer analysis emerges if we concern ourselves with voluntary associations that do no more than provide public goods. One type of such organizations is what Buchanan (1965) has called "clubs." It is useful to distinguish voluntary associations which can exclude non-members from enjoyment of the public goods provided (I hesitate to call these *pure* clubs; perhaps they should be denoted *exclusive* clubs), and those which cannot practice exclusion. By definition, there are no free-riders in an exclusive club, and the individual's decision to join can be analyzed like any other all-or-nothing opportunity.

Buchanan and Tullock (1967) have generalized the notion of the formation of a club in their discussion of the social contract theory of the State. Consider the decision of a person contemplating joining a group—the State—which can impose some costs on him but also can bring benefits. The State will be making a series of decisions under a set of decision rules, and some of those decisions can be expected to hurt, others to help the prospective citizen. A rational, selfish, risk-neutral person would join only if he expected to gain more than he lost. If the constitution of the State protected him from all harmful decisions by adopting a rule of unanimity, there would be very large bargaining costs involved in convincing everyone to agree to each decision under the constitution.[26] Somewhere between a decision rule requiring unanimity and one that allows a single member to bind all others, is the optimal (cost minimizing) rule for any particular kind of decision. The fundamental constitutional agreements are on the set of decision rules: when must there be unanimity, when majority rule, etc. The difficulty is that in general each individual will desire a different set of optimal decision rules to be incorporated in the constitution. Buchanan and Tullock postulate that everyone agrees to the constitution before it is implemented, and so they avoid an infinite regression:

> For individual decision on constitutional questions to be combined, some rules must be laid down, but, if so, who chooses these rules? And so on. We prefer to put this issue aside and to assume, without elabora-

---

[26] The payment of compensatory adjustment assistance to firms and workers harmed by changes in government economic policy tends toward unanimity.

tion, that at this ultimate stage, which we shall call the constitutional, the
rule of unanimity holds (p. 77).

Unanimity would be the optimum rule for a decision if the costs of the
decision-making itself were zero; [27] to *assume* unanimity at the constitutional stage is unsatisfactory. A constitution has some complicated
public-goods characteristics, and its provision by unanimous consent
could be analyzed in that framework.

To summarize, the foregoing model shows there will be a valuation
threshold below which an individual might rationally attempt to free-
ride. Among those who do not free-ride, persons with higher valuations
contribute more, but not necessarily disproportionately more. However, a single individual might reasonably decide to bear the full cost of
a public good, allowing others to "exploit" him, if the good is important
enough for that person. The dispersion in the individual ratios of contributions to valuations decreases with decreasing uncertainty about
the likely contributions of others; in particular, among a group of $n$
identical individuals, contributions will be equal.

As for the aggregate contributions, no firm conclusions were drawn.
Especially, it could not be proved that the ratio of aggregate contribution to aggregate valuation decreased with the size of the group, or
with its homogeneity. [28]

Olson puts forward a common-sense argument, one formally inconsistent with the model above, that with small numbers there is more
opportunity of monitoring to ensure each contributes a fair share.
Clearly, this depends on information costs, and a factor in 1820 as important as numbers was geography: the more geographically dispersed
were the interested individuals, the larger were costs of coordination
and the smaller the opportunities for monitoring others. [29] (The mechanism by which individual contributions are collected and applied to the
provision of the public good or service was not specified in the model.
One such mechanism is the "political entrepreneur," [30] who can be

[27] Buchanan and Tullock (1967), p. 88.
[28] M. McGuire (1974), has shown that the addition of one person to a group (of one)
voluntarily supplying a public good will increase the total outlay.
[29] Olson (1968), pp. 43 ff. Communication costs are discussed in chapter 5.
[30] Frohlich, Oppenheimer, and Young (1974), p. 34, allege the existence of a political
entrepreneur without showing why and to what extent "some donations might be given to
any individual who promised to set up a collection organization and supply the collective
good to the group"; see also their criticism of Olson (1968) on pp. 146–47.

considered either as the agency through which pressure groups sometimes operate, or an individual who actively pursues the job of coordinating the efforts of individuals. A special instance of a political entrepreneur is the elected representative.)

## THEORY OF CONGRESSIONAL COMMITTEES [31]

Leaving aside individuals in Hobbesian isolation and turning to
groups with formal decision rules, consider first simple majority voting
on an isolated issue such as the amount to be spent on a project. It can
be shown that the median committee member determines the outcome
if preferences are single peaked.[32] This model does not seem appropriate for voting on import duties, there being no obvious reason why the
representative of a district specializing in iron, for example, should
prefer a lower to a higher iron duty.[33] More importantly (and we are
still confining our attention to the determination of a single duty), if the
median committee member is to be decisive, it is necessary that intensities of preference not count. Thus a senator with a huge bribe in his
pocket or pressure on his back could not transfer some to others.

If pressures were costlessly transferable, the median would cease to
dominate and what mattered would be total pressure.[34] Consider table
5.1. A prefers outcome 1, B prefers outcome 3, and C prefers outcome
4. Without transfers, outcome 3 would prevail in pairwise voting. But
A would find it profitable to pay C to switch his vote from outcome 3 to
outcome 1, so gaining $9 for himself and C jointly. Since B would be
willing to pay up to $6 to avoid this, A would have to offer C no less

---

[31] I have benefited from discussions with W. A. Brock and S. P. Magee on formal
models of Congress.

[32] See Black (1948). Let $q$ be the continuous variable being voted on and $u(q)$ the utility function of the committee member. Preferences are single peaked when $u(q)$ has an
inverted U-shape. Notice that a rule requiring less than simple majority is "improper,"
that is, two or more mutually exclusive sets of members have decisive voice on the same
issue, so that a decision once reached could be overturned immediately and so on.
Rapoport (1970), p. 212. Also, a committee with a rule requiring more than a simple majority cannot reach *any* decision if preferences are single peaked.

[33] A duty higher than minimum prohibitive gives a margin against changed prices or
costs and is therefore more desirable than a lower duty.

[34] The general proposition that justifies this assertion is analysed in the final section of
this chapter.

TABLE 5.1

*Value of Outcomes*
(DOLLARS)

| PERSONS | OUTCOME | | | |
|---|---|---|---|---|
| | 1 | 2 | 3 | 4 |
| A | 24 | 19 | 11 | 8 |
| B | −6 | −4 | 0 | −1 |
| C | −6 | −4 | −2 | 0 |
| Value to A + B + C (no transfer costs) | 12 | 11 | 9 | 7 |
| Value to A + C (no transfer costs) | 18 | 15 | 9 | 8 |
| Value to A + C (with transfer costs) | 13 | 14 | | |

than $6 (and no more than $13, A's own gain). The result preferred by the median voter (B) does not pass when sidepayments are made cost-lessly but outcome 1, the "socially efficient" result yielding the highest aggregate value, eventuates.

Instead of sidepayments costless to arrange and effectuate, assume that an outlay by either A or B of $9 yields C a net $4 and an outlay of $4 yields $3.[35] The last line of the table indicates that with these transfer costs outcome 2 prevails.

Sidepayment costs occur when C is punished by his supporters for voting for outcomes other than 3. It is one matter if outcome 1 occurs in a congress honestly representing the voters; it is another if votes are clearly being bought. The failure to stop harmful legislation is not punished as harshly as deliberate voting for the same harmful legisla-tion, thereby causing it to pass. Therefore, the figures in the first three rows of table 5.1 are the rewards and punishments for acting on behalf of the voters, not oneself.[36]

Thus, in a congress in which a majority passed a set of duties which

---

[35] To induce C to vote for outcome 2, A would have to lay out at least the $4 that B stands to lose (compared with outcome 3) to yield at least $3.

[36] A member might choose to be recalled or defeated by his electors because he profit-ably ignored their wishes.

maximized the aggregate difference between their rewards and punishments, individual senators and representatives would to some extent
act in the interests of the electors in their district or state. As was
shown in chapter 3, some members strongly opposed to protection
(thereby reflecting the consensus of their electors) were softer when an
industry engaging some of their voters was discussed; others voted in
favor of a duty or bill they expressly did not support personally; agricultural states or districts returned protectionist senators and representatives when convinced by the "home market" argument.[37] None of
these prove the plausible proposition put forward—that a member of
congress would pause to consider the ire of his electors before he voted
directly against their interests—but they are consistent with it. Notice
that the proposition requires that a member cannot costlessly compensate a majority of electors to connive at his voting against their direct
interests.[38]

Reinforcing the tendency for a connection between the votes in
congress and the location of the industry were transaction costs as
usually conceived—it was costly for congressmen and senators to make
bargains, even if the system of geographical representation had no real
meaning in the eyes of the voters. Time and energy had to be spent in
negotiations.

The implication in the table is that the more even the distribution of
pressure on the single issue, the less wastage there was in the course of
transfers of pressure from one member to another. From a given total
of pressure the highest possible duty would have resulted when the
pressure was evenly distributed over the members. The pressure on all
members mattered, not just on a majority or the median: those
members whose district or state desired a low rate of duty suffered
elector disapproval if a high duty were passed without a struggle, and
so all had some incentive to seek to influence the height of the duty.

Of course, bargains were made involving more than one product,

[37] Namely, that protection would stabilize and increase the demand for American
goods and materials.

[38] It is, of course, inconsistent for voters to insist on probity on the part of their own
representatives while still expecting them to attempt to influence the votes of other representatives.

but the discussion of a single duty is still relevant. Congress discussed products one by one, and opposition was aroused by the geographical narrowness of the benefits bestowed by duties. A product lost less pressure during multiproduct bargaining if it were one on which agreement was easy, and therefore the duty obtained depended on more than the total pressure exerted; its distribution also mattered.[39]

With his computer models of committees, Coleman (1973) found that a member of a legislature gains more by concentrating on a small number of issues than by addressing many, which suggests that interests could be overlooked if they never loom large in any electoral district. This implies that in some instances, concentration of pressure could be an advantage by increasing the probability that the pressure in at least one district or state was sufficient to command attention.

In this context, it is often suggested that the wider the electorate, the less chance that "factions" will prevail [40] (to use Madison's term). Therefore, a random distribution of industry would induce more representatives than senators to speak and vote in favor of minor interests.[41] Presidents in the antebellum period, with the widest electorate of all, vetoed bills only on constitutional grounds; that was the limit to Presidential protection of the general interest. The constitutional validity of protective tariffs was not seriously questioned before the late 1820s, and Adams, Monroe, and Jackson were not opposed to protection in these years.[42]

[39] This discussion helps to moderate the force of the criticism by Olson of certain political theories. In *Collective Action*, Olson is highly critical of political scientists in the Bentley tradition (such as D. B. Truman) who extol the virtues of pressure-group politics for a supposed ability to respond to the wishes of majorities. His own theory leads to the opposite conclusion, namely, that large groups are virtually impotent or "latent." Clearly this is going too far. The correct analysis distinguishes two aspects of group size. First, small groups more faithfully reflect the intensity of members' interests. But, secondly, a given amount of pressure from a small pressure group might not be as effective in the legislature as the same pressure from a large group. To distinguish the two effects empirically is a most challenging problem, yet without doing so we cannot make firm generalizations about the characteristics of successful pressure groups.

[40] For example, see Buchanan and Tullock (1967).

[41] However, it is possible that an interest disregarded by every representative would find its champion in the Senate—industry was not random, in other words.

[42] See Stanwood (1903), I. No effort will be made here to discuss formal models of bicameral legislatures.

## DEMOCRACY AND PROTECTIONISM

In their discussion of American commercial policy, Davis and North suggest that the Seventeenth Amendment of 1913 for the direct election of senators made Congress less responsive to protectionist manufacturing lobbies. This, together with the rise of a strong low-tariff lobby, caused a shift away from high protectionism.[43] Yet the fiasco of 1929–30, Hawley-Smoot, has been attributed to the failure of strong executive leadership: direct election of senators was not then sufficient to defeat the efforts of numerous protectionists.[44] The Reciprocal Trade Acts of 1934 and afterward increased Presidential power, and a more selective policy was followed, one that sought export markets at the least cost to American import-competing industries.[45] The success of this policy is indicated by Travis's (1971) finding that most U.S. tariffs in 1962 exceeded their minimum-prohibitive levels by a considerable margin, thereby preventing the exchange of capital-intensive for labor-intensive products. Since 1962, of course, the situation has changed greatly, but up to that date, American import-competing industries were successful in obtaining and keeping protection, despite changes in electoral and trade laws;[46] in fact, they were very successful because a selective tariff, even with lower rates, can give more assistance than that received by the same industries within a very broad tariff.

The literature on European tariffs in the last century places some emphasis on the role of political pressure groups in the determination of tariffs, but there is a distinction between the approach adopted here and that displayed, for example, in work on the German tariffs of 1879 and 1902, or on the repeal of the English Corn Laws in 1846. The distinction revolves around the significance of the type of political system within which tariffs were made. The major theme of most tariff his-

[43] Davis and North (1971), pp. 181–82.

[44] The Hawley-Smoot tariffs attempted the impossible—to protect everyone. The fact that the net gain was zero or negative does not preclude free-riding, for, to change the metaphor a little, each industry had to row hard just to keep up (a little like Alice), but some oarsmen did not put in a full stroke.

[45] See Wilkinson (1960), pp. 113 ff; Mikesell (1952), pp. 66–7. Complaints were made about the early working of GATT that U.S. tariff concessions were being nullified by non-tariff devices. Crawford (1968), pp. 128 ff.

[46] McPherson's (1972) statistical analysis of recent U.S. tariffs is discussed in chapter 6.

tories, European or American, is the triumph of protection over free trade, or vice versa; writers on European tariffs (but not American) have tended to attribute protectionism to a lack of democracy, and free trade to democratic reforms; that is, they have connected the nature of the commercial policies pursued with the degree of representativeness of the political system. Implicit in this argument is the assumption that special favors to particular industrial or agricultural interests are less likely in a fully democratic system. Not surprisingly, this supposed connection between free trade and democracy is mostly absent from the literature on American tariffs, for America was the bastion, the exemplar of democracy; yet the tariff rates of the United States at the end of the last century were in general higher than those of any major European power.[47]

Gerschenkron refers to the speculation of Bastiat (a free trader and democrat) that there was an unfailingly inverse connection between the degree of protectionism in a country and its democratic development (as measured by the width of the franchise).[48] Although Gerschenkron doubts such a simple relationship, the burden of his *Bread and Democracy* is that Bismarck's tariff of 1879 (which brought about the marriage of rye and iron), and Bulow's tariff of 1902 (which remade it) must be explained by reference to the unequal and undemocratic distribution of political power in Germany, by the dominance of the Junkers and the relative weakness of Social Democracy.[49] The German constitution of 1871 created a state that was dominated by Prussia, which in turn was controlled by the large eastern landlords (Junkers). The franchise was very unequal, and the ballot open. Junker political power had been used in the past to obtain economic benefits but not protection from imports. During the 1870s, however, Germany's export surplus of grains vanished; in no year between 1875 and 1900 did rye or wheat exports exceed imports.[50] Hungarian and especially Russian rye competed for the German market. Bismarck formed the "solidarity bloc" of

[47] Little, Scitovsky, and Scott (1970), p. 162.     [48] Gerschenkron (1943), p. 65.

[49] A detailed discussion of German agrarian politics after Bismarck is in Tirrell (1951). Ashley (1920) and Kindleberger (1951) discuss the range of European reactions to the fall in grain prices after 1870; for the Italian tariff politics in this period, see Coppa (1970); for the French, Golob (1944).

[50] Tirrell (1951), p. 20.

industry and agriculture in the 1870s around policies to protect the home market, develop internal transportation facilities, and reform imperial finances without increasing direct taxes. The tariff of 1879, the rates of which were raised in 1885 and 1887, ended free trade in grains, and afforded protection to iron and textiles. After the replacement of Bismarck in 1890, the new chancellor, Caprivi, concluded commercial treaties with Austria and a number of other countries including Russia, Germany's most serious agricultural competitor. These reversals for the agricultural interests were temporary, and in 1902 Bulow had a new tariff passed with higher rates. The solidarity bloc was reconstituted with the agrarians agreeing to the program of naval construction in return for the agricultural tariffs.[51]

It is possible to interpret the repeal of the Corn Laws as an integral part of the dismantling of the vestiges of illiberal economic controls, as part of a movement to substitute individualism for authoritarian regulation, a movement made feasible politically by the reforms of 1832.[52] Kindleberger sees the European shift toward free trade between 1820 and 1875 as part of a general response to the breakdown of the manor and guild system, and suggests that "Europe as a whole was motivated by ideological considerations rather than economic interests." As for Britain, the Reform Bill was not critical, the Manchester School overwhelming those forces it did not convert.[53] A more common view on the Corn Laws does give a role to economic interests. The manufacturers, seeking foreign markets and cheaper wage costs, wanted free trade in grain. The other beneficiaries were the working classes, still relatively weak in political power but always posing the threat of violence. Workers enjoyed the fruits of a competition for popularity between the landowners and the manufacturers, the one group offering them the Factory Acts, the other Corn Law repeal. Both, however, were responding with measures less radical than further electoral reform.[54] It cannot be accepted without argument that ideology, even the ideology of the Manchester School, is interest free.

---

[51] The support of the Catholic party was secured by the promise of the establishment of a widows'-and-orphans' insurance fund. Gerschenkron (1942), p. 62.

[52] Beales (1958), p. 97; Armitage-Smith (1903), p. 24; Fay (1932), p. 100.

[53] Kindleberger (1974), pp. 44–46, 22–25.

[54] Halevy (1961), III, 60 ff, 270 ff; Moore (1966).

This is not the place to sort out the connection between the power of some groups to effect redistribution and the type of political system, but whatever the system, a variety of commercial policies is possible, and in each system the interests and cohesion of various groups cannot be disregarded.[55]

## THE EFFICIENCY APPROACH

Is it necessary to investigate the motives of individuals and the workings of Congress? Is it not possible to call on economic theory for an easier method? One such method is a short cut called "Coase-aggregation" that, by appealing to theorems about Pareto-efficiency, avoids our having to collect information on the distribution of gains and losses and offers instead a simple aggregate criterion. Unfortunately, the efficiency approach is not suitable for most historical problems.

The economics profession has its *pons asinorum:* to prove that individuals, acting to maximize their own utility will, under certain conditions, bring about a Pareto-efficient allocation as an unforeseen consequence of their actions. Once conditions in particular economies are verified, the set of possible allocations can be reduced to the efficient ones. There may be no need to know the distributional detail in order to say something interesting about the outcome. For example, Evans (1971) has a model that predicts how the mixture of outputs would change if a set of tariffs were imposed. He assumes that the economy acts as though it had a single goal, namely, to maximize the value of output. The mechanics of the model, a linear program, need not detain us, for the principle is what matters, namely, that of predicting the allocation of resources by using the theorem that laissez faire is efficient. The collective decision, or strictly, the set of individual decisions, will maximize the aggregate value of production. This simple rule reasserts itself in the Coase model.

Coase's work on social cost points out that the conditions for the theorem on the efficiency of decentralized decision-making are less stringent than many economists had thought. Apparent causes of "mar-

[55] The claim by Davis and North (1971) to have analyzed "arrangemental innovation" is invalid to the extent that they declared exogenous any changes in the political ground rules and in the legal framework of business behavior.

ket failure"—like externalities—may not always prevent the attainment of efficiency. This is because individual profit-seeking can overcome possible inefficiencies introduced, for example, by rules of law that allow some individuals to force others into involuntary allocations; the Coase theorem does require, however, that individuals can escape impositions by arranging sidepayments and buying off those threatening or causing losses, if it is to their mutual advantage. The importance of the Coase theorem for research is that it reinstates the simple aggregative rule—one must search for efficient allocations, those that maximize aggregate income or wealth—and that it allows us to treat a group as though it were an individual faced with the same aggregate opportunities (what we might call "Coase-aggregation" of a group).

To give the kind of example with which Coase illustrated his article, if a dentist and a machine shop occupied adjacent rooms in a poorly sound-proofed building, and the noise of the machine shop disturbed the dentist or his patients, and caused a loss of business, then irrespective of the law of torts, sound-proofing of the walls would occur only if it increased the aggregate incomes of the dentist and the shop by an amount greater than the cost of the insulation. Assume that Mishan's "amenity" laws have been enacted, and that the machine shop is required by law to install sound-proofing if the dentist requests it. If the present value of the increase (consequent to sound-proofing) in the dentist's income stream is $X$, and the cost of silence is $Y$, then the machine shop can pay the dentist any amount $Z$ to accept the noise, where

$$X < Z < Y$$

and both parties will be better off than if the dentist exercised his legal rights. The contract between the dentist and the shop has brought about an efficient solution (more accurately, has prevented an inefficient solution), because the "social" rate of return on the expenditure of $Y$ would have been negative. The same allocation, but a different distribution of income or wealth, would have occurred if the law did not require the shop to install insulation at the insistence of the dentist, since the dentist would not have voluntarily laid out an amount $Y$ in order to increase his income by a smaller amount $X$. By similar arguments, it can be shown that every Pareto-inefficient allocation will be dominated by a Pareto-efficient one.

## Coase's "Theorem"

The essential thing to understand is that the Coase "theorem" is a drawing out of the implication of the definition of a Pareto-efficient resource allocation: if an allocation is not Pareto-efficient, then everyone can be made better off by some reallocation. The maximum amount that losers would be willing to commit to opposition is limited by their losses contingent on the reallocation. Whenever these losses are less than the gains available to others, the gainers have the wherewithal to bribe the losers. A serious threat will induce the gainers to forestall opposition by compensating the losers, justifying the treatment of the group including both gainers and losers as though it were a single individual for decision-making purposes. If the losers were in the (legal) position to decide against the reallocation, an efficient reallocation would still occur, since the gainers could bribe the losers. By similar argument, no inefficient reallocation would occur. In other words, the group of gainers plus losers acts as though it had achieved unanimity. The allocation arrived at is Pareto-efficient, and is independent of which individuals have the legal or formal power to decide on an allocation. All that matters for allocation theory is whether the aggregate gain is positive or negative.[56]

The practical problems with applying the Coase theorem as a research tool are that, if the number of individuals is small then an efficient outcome is at hazard because of bargaining difficulties (the foregoing example involved bilateral monopoly); if, on the other hand, the number is large the individuals might be able profitably to conceal the depth of their interest in the outcome. It was shown earlier that even if everyone in a group could be made better off, it is not certain that all would contribute voluntarily toward securing the public good, let alone in efficient quantity. In addition, conflicts arise when one group attempts to better its economic position at the expense of others.[57]

A theory of voluntary collective action is needed not only for the

[56] Clearly, since the Coase argument disposes of technological externalities, it also removes the danger that reactions to exchange externalities will interfere with the pattern of resource allocation. Incidentally, nonmarket behavior is implicitly ruled out in the Evans model. For example, if the trade union movement used strikes to prevent the reallocation of labor between industries, then Evans's predictions would be in error.

[57] Although there is no substantial game-theoretical difference between the two cases of free-riding and conflict over distribution, the distinction is still useful.

analysis of cooperative decisions, but also because of authoritative or political decisions that result from coalition formation. Consider, for example, a decision which requires majority assent; define the *impact* as the distribution of the gains and losses among individuals before any sidepayments are made. Any policy that does not benefit a majority will not be approved under majority rule unless some sidepayments are made, so that the objective of the managers of a coalition is to modify the impact by sidepayments until at least a majority joins the coalition. In the bargaining that occurs, the revelation problem may arise, because of the efforts by individuals or groups to obtain more favorable distributions. A change that, with or without compensation, could make some better off and none worse off, may still be blocked by individuals holding out for larger shares of the aggregate net gain.

McCloskey, for example, suggests that enclosures were an important source of productivity gain and that a major advantage of the Parliamentary system was the removal of the power each villager had had to veto enclosure under common law, so that "when the benefits exceeded the costs a village was enclosed." Under the Parliamentary system, however, there were still difficulties in obtaining agreement:

> [A] judgment on the equity of enclosure would require no comment in an inquiry into its efficiency were it not that the incentive to enclose could have been affected, at least theoretically, by the distribution as well as the size of the costs and benefits. The method of distributing them may have varied from year to year and from village to village in such a way that an equal social benefit in two villages would produce an enclosure in one and a continuation of the open fields in the other. An explanation of the timing of enclosure is necessary for measuring its impact on efficiency and the timing could have been affected by a mere shift in the incidence of the costs and benefits.[58]

However, no guidance is given about how to predict the timing of the shifts in incidence.

## Davis and North

As a contribution toward the analysis of economic growth, Davis and North in *Institutional Change and American Economic Growth* (1971)

[58] McCloskey (1972), pp. 29–30.

wish to develop, on neoclassical assumptions, a theory of the life cycle of institutions. Their basic approach is indicated by the following: [59]

> An institutional arrangement will be innovated if the expected net gains exceed the expected costs. Only when this condition is met would we expect to find attempts being made to alter the existing structure of institutions and property rights within a society (p. 10).

There are two sources of gain: improved efficiency, and an altered distribution of income and wealth. It is difficult to keep these separate, however.

For example, in the evolution of a national mortgage market in the United States, various profit seekers partly arbitraged regional interest-rate differences. In this context, Davis and North say: "Not everyone would gain [by inter-regional transfers of funds] since firms in surplus savings areas were benefiting from cheap capital. Still, gains were to be realized from arrangemental innovation." [60] The last sentence seems to conclude the matter, but Davis and North later make the following comment:

> In theory, of course, interbank lending could achieve economy-wide mobility at relatively low cost, but throughout most of the late nineteenth and early twentieth centuries, the Comptroller of the Currency frowned on banks in high interest areas soliciting funds from institutions in surplus saving region. [61]

Evidently, the fact that gains were to be made was not enough to ensure arbitrage. Similarly, the rise of chain stores harmed small, local retailers who tried to maintain their economic position through discriminatory taxes. Numerous examples could be adduced from United States economic history of the efforts, sometimes successful, by groups to avoid losses imposed by markets. The point is that such behavior must be easily integrated with the theory, or else the theory begins to give rise to more exceptions than to examples that obey the rules.

At least Davis and North recognize the possible importance of distribution in the two examples just given. But the book is replete with

---

[59] "An institutional arrangement is an arrangement between economic units that govern[s] the ways in which these units cooperate and/or compete." Davis and North (1971), p. 7.
[60] *Ibid.*, p. 108.     [61] *Ibid.*, p. 117.

discussions in which distribution is not given a passing reference. For example, land grant colleges and federally funded research yielded a high *social* rate of return.[62] Does that fact itself explain the extent of the investment, or must one also notice that farmers reaped some of the benefits without shouldering all of the costs?

It is convenient to round off these examples of the treatments that Davis and North give to distributional questions, and consider a long discussion of theirs which, if we carry their logic to its extreme, is irrelevant for the allocation of resources. Their chapter on agriculture discusses, among other things, "land companies which were well placed in government and thus able to persuade public officials to sell or grant them large blocks of land" (p. 89). Davis and North agree with Parker's assessment that the family-sized farm was an efficient production unit in the last century. Why then not argue (and here I recapitulate the argument of the beginning of this section) that, if all the land had been granted to one person, rather than parceled out in small lots, the monopoly landlord would have had an incentive to dispose of land so as to bring about its efficient utilization? Policies of land distribution would have been of distributive consequence only, one presumes.[63]

### Weak Efficiency and A Cyclical Model

Both McCloskey and Davis and North attempt to separate questions of *whether* from *when* a reallocation takes place, and apply what one might call a "weak efficiency approach" that predicts that a change will take place sometime after aggregate benefits first exceed aggregate costs. A difficulty with the weak efficiency approach is that it yields some irrefutable assertions: if some "efficient" reallocation has not occurred, then it is not possible to say whether this is because not enough time has elapsed, or because aggregate benefits in excess of costs are not a sufficient criterion. It would seem better to admit strategic behavior and transaction costs, and attempt to predict from a knowledge of the *distribution* of costs and benefits, not just from the aggregate.

[62] *Ibid.*, p. 103.

[63] Davis and North come close to accepting this conclusion. Notice that too wide a distribution can influence allocation and have a detrimental effect on efficiency: mining and timber companies might have been prevented by small property owners from reaping economies of scale. Bribery and corruption, however, helped smooth the way to a more efficient allocation. *Ibid.*, pp. 91–93.

Strategic behavior and the failure to reach agreement over Pareto-approved changes can partly be explained by the costs of information about the likely actions of others. The weak efficiency approach, an attempt to salvage partially the aggregative approach to collective decision making, is suggested by the argument that the failure to achieve group goals on the first attempt may lead to greater monitoring of efforts, especially of those who stand to gain a lot from the public good, and the bringing of social and moral pressure on them to contribute a fair share, that is, to efforts at reducing transaction and information costs.[64] (We might interpret Olson's by-product theory of large groups along these lines.)

Davis and North try to circumvent these difficulties by defining what they call *primary action groups*, that is, individuals with common direct interests: [65]

> A primary action group is a decision-making unit whose decisions govern the process of arrangemental innovation. This unit may be a single individual or a group of individuals, but it is the action group that recognizes there exists some income—income that their members are not presently receiving—that *they* could accrue, if only they could alter the arrangemental structure. At least one member of any primary action group is an innovating entrepreneur in the Schumpeterian sense, and within the context of this model the group initiates the process of arrangemental innovation.

If we could use Coase-aggregation and the efficiency criterion, then there would be no need for a separate analysis of how conflicts are resolved. An attraction of the efficiency approach is that it provides a single theory to be applied to all changes, redistributive or not. Davis and North say "an institutional arrangement will be innovated if the expected net gains exceed the expected costs": there is no need to ask "gains and costs *to whom?*" Rejecting this, the best we can do is to form quasi-individuals or individual-equivalents, such as Davis and North's primary action group. Then the prospect of conflicts between such groups arises. How are they to be resolved?

[64] In the present discussion, transaction costs, simply conceived, have not been emphasized. Buchanan and Tullock's version of the Coase theorem is that "*any* decision-making rule, with full side payments, will produce only Pareto-optimal situations." Buchanan and Tullock (1967), p. 186. In order then to understand decisions we need to look at things that prevent full sidepayments, as a careful reading of Coase's work makes clear.

[65] Davis and North (1971), p. 8.

For Davis and North, the revelation problem manifests itself not in the coherence of a group and the intensity of its actions (how faithfully the group reflects the aggregate interests of its members), but in the *timing* of its action: if a group can gain from a change, then they predict the change will occur with a lag that depends on the characteristics of the group. Small groups react to opportunities faster than large ones. However, there are two difficulties with the weak efficiency approach. The first, already mentioned, is that, without closer specification, the theory is not testable. The second problem is that it leads to cyclical outcomes.

As it stands, the definition of the primary action group is neutral in the sense that the members could be fighting a rear-guard action in defense of their economic position. The reference to Schumpeterian innovators, however, alerts the reader to what is a strong bias in Davis and North—an almost exclusive concentration on the actions of those who win, and an emphasis on reallocations that are economically efficient, so that groups that oppose efficient reallocations become mere casualties on the inexorable march toward greater efficiency.

Clearly, a group will not act unless its members expect net benefits from action; therefore, the only way to reconcile the weak efficiency approach with the fact that economically inefficient decisions are made is to define the group that makes the decision—the primary action group—to be distinct from the group that suffers the consequences but does not take part in the decision. Without such a distinction, the model of Davis and North is not complete. Yet the distinction is objectionable, because the group that does not make the decision is, in aggregate, suffering from the decision and would gain by its reversal, and therefore, fits perfectly the definition of a primary action group. *An inefficient action creates opportunities for the losers subsequently to reverse the inefficiency.* What emerges is a sequence or cycle of actions and reactions, of decisions being subsequently overturned.[66] Chapter 6 tests on alternative to a cyclical model, one in which both groups act simultaneously but not with equal force or effect.

[66] This important possibility, not seen by Davis and North, is discussed in chapter 7.

# An Empirical Test of a Positive Theory for 1824

B E F O R E putting some of the ideas developed in this book to an empirical test in this chapter,[1] it is necessary to discuss the data gleaned from the *Digest of Manufactures* [2] and to recapitulate the methodology.

## THE DIGEST OF MANUFACTURES

The manufacturing returns from the 1820 census were not made available in the form that Tench Coxe had used in 1813: they were listed by product name, within each county by state.[3] No summary tables were compiled. A most serious difficulty in using the *Digest*, besides problems of coverage and accuracy, is that it does not clearly differentiate among reports on establishments, firms, or even whole counties. In some instances, the comments in the last column record that a number of establishments were aggregated (fourteen tanneries, for example), but where there is no such information,[4] I assumed that there was only one establishment for the purpose of estimating variable Z10 (a measure of geographical dispersion).

A photocopy of the *Digest* was physically rearranged in product order, by county within each state, by the simple method of pasting

---

[1] I am grateful for permission to use in this chapter material published in Pincus (1975), "Pressure Groups and the Pattern of Tariffs," *Journal of Political Economy* 83(4):757–78, copyright © by the University of Chicago.

[2] Price and tariff data are discussed in chapter 4; the details are in appendix B.

[3] Enumeration began in August 1820, and ended by September 1821.

[4] There is a wealth of detail suppressed in the compilation of the *Digest*, for example, price data, number of months worked, information on the original cost of establishments. Copies of some surviving returns for New England are in the Baker Library, Harvard. Most of the returns were sent to the Department of Interior in 1849, and bound into 21 volumes. Wright (1900), p. 76.

each line of the *Digest* in the appropriate place. This method preserved all the detail and avoided transcription errors.[5] Each line was marked with a notation for the name of the county and the state. The returns for Indiana, Illinois, Missouri, Michigan, Arkanasas, and Louisiana were not listed, except for the lead outputs of Missouri and Michigan.

To keep track of products in the computer work, a SIC (Standard Industrial Classification) number was assigned to each product and input in the computer data set. Where the SIC did not provide sufficient detail at four digits, an extra digit was added.

The product list suggested to the census marshals contains about 180 names, but the marshals found these too few. Since many establishments (or firms or counties, whichever was the basis of the report) produced more than one "product," there was a question of how to record the information: whether to attribute it to the chief product or to each product according to some accounting convention. In fact, the report will often list a number of products, such as "bar iron, shovels and spades." With very minor exceptions, all the output reported was attributed *to the product named first,* unless it was desirable to aggregate some products, for example, a number of iron castings; all cotton textiles; all brass manufactures; candles and soap from tallow. Thus, the sales of "bar iron" include some sales of other iron products, just as those products include some bar iron sales. This procedure assumes that the product first mentioned was the major one, and it appeals to the law of large numbers. There are three possible methods of aggregating goods, one each from the tariff acts (taking the product categories of the act), from the tariff listings, or from the *Digest* names. The last was used as much as possible, although, as had already been pointed out, the *Digest* often combines different products in one report or line. The chief difficulties arose in the metals part of the tariff schedule, especially products using bar or pig iron, of which were distinguished the following: guns; rifles; muskets, axes; castings, hollow ware, and stoves; machinery; nails, sheet iron; rolled iron; plow irons; plows; scythes; sieves; saws, augers; spades; sickles; edge tools not otherwise specified. A number of these products had tariffs of 25 or 30 percent, and were distinguished because of the relative homogeneity of the reports in the *Digest,* and because they seemed to have different

[5] Subsequently, some of the data were coded to enable some checking of the arithmetic.

cost-shares. Once the aggregation decisions were made, they were difficult to reverse or alter, because of the nonadditivity of some of the variables used in the regression analysis.

The first processing of the *Digest* estimated output for incompletely reported lines, using the method of means for interpolation and extrapolation. It would have been better to have used regression analysis, but that would have required complete coding of the data. From matched triplets of sales (output), wages paid, and materials cost, the average shares in cost of labor and materials for each product were calculated. (There are some minor exceptions—when too few triplets were available, matched pairs of output/wages and materials costs/output were used.) If the data for output were not reported, they were estimated from the cost of materials, or if that was missing, the wage bill. In some cases a ratio like output/tons of hemp was used, rather than output/expenditure on hemp; or output estimated from the number of workers employed. In a small number of instances it was possible to price out a quantity of output reported. These methods for estimating missing data were carried out at the lowest level of aggregation possible from the *Digest*. In the course of this work, some obvious errors were corrected, but this did not eliminate a difficulty: some reports showed the establishment making a loss in 1820; these reports were eliminated from the matched triplets, and generally the output value recorded was accepted, rather than the cost values.

### Cost-Shares

The most arduous task was to calculate the cost-shares for the individual inputs, an input-output table. In the final data set there are about eighty goods produced in the United States, of which some twenty or so are also inputs of other products, and there are about thirty inputs either not reported in the *Digest* as having been produced in the United States, or for which there were unsatisfactory production data. This is a considerable amount of cross-section work, each product presenting different problems and decisions. Thus not too much is claimed for the detailed figures produced, although the errors should not be too gross.

The *Digest* recorded the quantities of materials used, and their total value. (Some of the losses may have been due to accounting by a cash flow method.) The cost-share for any input $i$ of product $j$, which is written as $\Theta_{ij}$ in the theoretical sections of this book, was then calculated by pricing out the individual inputs. In contrast to the prices used for the conversion of specific to ad valorem tariffs (in which prices for the period 1821–24 were used), for the estimate of cost-shares as of 1820, prices for 1820 were used where possible. Some of these prices could be calculated from the *Digest* itself; some were taken from Bezanson (the prices for December 1819); others from the price sources already mentioned in the discussion of the tariff calculations.

For some products and inputs, the estimation of the input cost-shares was straightforward. If there is only one input mentioned in the *Digest*, all the materials costs were attributed to that input and checked by direct pricing of the average ratio of physical-input to value-of-output. Difficulties arose when more than one input was used. Generally, a small number of inputs were almost universally reported for a product: for example, pig iron used ore and "coal" (that is, charcoal); but there were alternative ways to produce the same output using different inputs, and not just by using the same inputs in different combinations. For example, some establishments produced bar iron from ore, and some from pig iron (possibly purchased from another establishment): the reports were disaggregated into relatively homogeneous groups, one listing ore and the other pig only, in order to estimate cost-shares.

These examples of iron production provide a suitable occasion to comment on the question of redundant tariffs. It was noted in chapter 2, in the discussion of the whole set of 1824 tariffs, that the "small country assumption" was made, namely, that all tariffs were exactly and fully utilized and were neither redundant nor prohibitive. In the work on cost-shares, nonprohibitiveness was adopted, but not nonredundancy. For example, raw cotton had a tariff in 1824 that was assumed redundant. Any input which did not have a tariff, or a redundant tariff, was not priced out to obtain a cost-share—the cost-share for iron ore into pig. Alternative measures of the net tariff or effective protection were calculated, the first of which assigned a 15 percent tariff to nontraded inputs, and the second a zero tariff.[6] The neglect of nontraded input cost-shares greatly simplified the work but detracts from the usefulness of the calculations regarded as an input-output table: it is a *traded* input-output table at best.

[6] The question of nontraded inputs in effective protection calculations is dealt with in Corden (1971).

"Cotton," "cotton wool," and "cotton yarn" were all listed as inputs into cotton cloth, but there seemed no way to distinguish raw cotton from yarn inputs. All the cost of materials was attributed to yarn. A "major" input is one that is almost universally recorded for that product, whereas a "minor" input is one sometimes reported. Two courses were followed on the latter, the first to ignore a minor input if, even it it were used universally in the industry, it would have a very small cost-share; and second, if it appeared that the minor input was used for a variety of the product, the input was treated as major for its own subset of reports. A simple example is tar in cables and cordage: it was assumed that if no tar input is mentioned, that the output was untarred.[7] These two sets were further divided into output from foreign and from American hemp, on the basis of the implicit hemp price difference.[8] As can be seen, the calculation of cost-shares involved a number of detailed and sometimes ad hoc assumptions and decisions, so the results must be treated with caution.[9]

A capital/output ratio was also calculated as the average of the ratios of the "amount of capital invested" to the actual or estimated output. No effort was made to estimate the capital used, that is, to allow for underutilization of capacity. The figure for capital invested is no doubt based on historical values, and includes real and financial capital. No allowance in the input cost-shares was made for the depreciation of the machinery and equipment used, nor does the calculation of the net tariffs or effective protection account for the tariff-induced changes in the cost of capital goods.

## THE THEORY OF TARIFF FORMATION[10]

### Effects

The general argument of this chapter is that tariffs were influenced by pressure from interested persons and groups, acting in hope of

[7] There are two columns with input data in the *Digest*. The first lists the names of the inputs, the second the quantities used, usually repeating the names in the second column, but sometimes omitting the quantity detail, or adding an additional input not mentioned in the "names" column.

[8] American hemp was about half the price of foreign.

[9] A "contingent expenses" cost-share, in the same manner as the capital/output ratio, was calculated but not used for want of guidance on what expenses were included in this cost category; the share was more variable than any other.

[10] This section necessarily involves some repetition of arguments put forward earlier.

some advantage. The important effects of tariffs bore on the incomes of factors of production. The kind of model that should be used to estimate changes in the value-added available to primary factors of production employed in various industries depends on the data available and the problem at hand. A simple, partial equilibrium, fixed coefficients framework seems appropriate to an analysis of expected effects of the 1824 tariffs, where the expectations were those of the historical participants, not those of a modern economist; in this framework, only prices change, not quantities. On the other hand, general equilibrium models might be desirable for the analysis of recent tariffs, or the changing pattern of tariffs over time, rather than the pattern at a particular time.[11] The data available allowed estimation of the impact of duties on value-added in each industry.

The simplest model for estimating the impact of customs duties on value-added is one in which domestic prices change but quantity responses are zero or second-order small. In such a model, the change in value-added depends on the industry's output, tariffs, and input cost-shares. Let $S_j$ be the value of output in free-trade prices, $S_{ji}$ the free-trade value of the $j^{th}$ input used in the $i^{th}$ activity (including the consumption activity), and $t_j$ the ad valorem tariff. Then $t_j$ raises value-added in activity $j$ by an amount $t_j S_j$ and lowers it in activity $i$ by an amount $t_j S_{ji}$. For activity $j$, by changing subscripts on $S_{ji}$ we find the net change in value-added is equal to

$$t_j S_j - \sum_i t_i S_{ij} = S_j (t_j - \sum_i t_i \Theta_{ij}) \tag{6.1}$$

where $\Theta_{ij} = S_{ij}/S_j$ are the cost-shares.[12] The approximation provided by (6.1) is exact if the only effect of the duties was to alter factor and goods prices, and not quantities.[13] Alternatively, the calculation can be

---

[11] Evans's (1971) use of a linear programming model to estimate general equilibrium is discussed in chapter 4. See also chapter 7.

[12] This expression is derived and developed in chapter 4 and appendix A.

[13] The term in parentheses in expression (6.1) is the numerator of simple measures of the effective rate of protection, and what I call here the "net tariff"; Taussig (1931), pp. 75 and 194–218, called it "net protection." To require a set of duties not to lead to an alteration of quantities is inconsistent with profit maximization: if the post-tariff output price is insufficient to cover variable costs, then the profit maximizing output is zero, assuming fixed input coefficients: see the discussion of Z4 and Z5.

said to measure the impact of the tariff before any quantity changes are made.[14]

## Pressure

Various groups organized or formed to put pressure on Congress. How badly or well the groups reflected the interests of members depended on such matters as numbers, homogeneity, and costs of organization. This was because of the "public good" aspect of a duty: the benefits or costs of protection that an individual enjoyed or suffered were not in proportion to the individual efforts made. Pressure was exerted in favor of protection as principle and especially for assistance to particular industries. Most resistance was of a general kind, apart from some memorials against duties on intermediate inputs.

Clearly, a model of collective decisions that is based on the economic theory of rational, selfish, individual behavior, requires, for its empirical application, data on the effects of the decision at the individual level. As a compromise in this chapter, although the pattern of the effects of tariffs was calculated from data averaged across each industry, we may incorporate into the model certain disaggregative characteristics, such as the number of firms, their size distribution, and geographic location, and the division of value-added into wage and proprietorial incomes within the average firm: how closely the behavior of a group resembles that of an individual faced with the same aggregate opportunities depends on these characteristics. At one extreme are groups that have achieved a joint-maximum; at the other, a group all attempting but failing to free-ride. Expressing it slightly differently, we

---

[14] More precise partial equilibrium expressions for the gain to suppliers $G_j$ and the loss to users $L_j$ can be derived using the usual producer and consumer surplus triangles. ($\epsilon_j$ and $\eta_j < 0$ are the elasticities of supply and demand.)

$$G_j = t_j S_j \left(1 + \tfrac{1}{2} t_j \epsilon_j\right)$$

$$L_j = \sum_i t_j S_{ji} \left(1 + \tfrac{1}{2} t_j \eta_j\right) - r_j$$

where $r_j$ is the revenue returned to importers.

Expression (6.1) allows estimation of the benefits of the duties per time period (say, a year). What is required, however, is the discounted value of the stream of expected benefits, which is a function of the rate at which the quasi-rents are bid away by competition. This refinement was not possible. However, the variable Z6 (proprietorial income) and the capital/labor ratio have some bearing on the matter.

can use such variables to calculate (on analogy with "full-time male equivalent" in labor force studies) what fraction, ranging from zero to unity, of an "individual decision-making equivalent" the industry represents. The value unity applies to groups which have completely solved any revelations problems; and zero applies to a group of free-riders.

## Congress

In the representative democracy of the United States, congressmen tended to vote in accordance with the economic interests of their districts and states. This tendency was modified by the advantages to be gained through bargaining. The tariff was made up of a large number of individual items, each fairly narrow in its immediate benefits and broad in its costs (material inputs being exceptions to this rule). In consequence, particular industries would have done best in the formation of a tariff coalition when they were not too narrow.

The pressure group model of tariffs developed here is not meant to preclude the existence of a successful, avowedly antiprotectionist political party. The concern of the empirical part of this chapter is with the variation of duties from the average, not with the height of the average duty. General political circumstances can invalidate the theory proposed here, when, for example, a nation reverts to free trade, or, like the United States after the Compromise Tariff of 1833, to a uniform nominal tariff structure.

## THE THEORY DEVELOPED

To explain the inclusion of explanatory variables in the regression model, and their expected sign, it is necessary to outline in some detail the model of the determination of a single import duty, or more precisely, that component influenced by considerations other than the revenue requests of the Treasury.[15] The model is designed to explain what

[15] The influence of the Treasury and those benefiting from the expenditure financed by duties are both neglected in this chapter. The data required for the former (the Treasury's ideas about elasticities contained, for example, in the Secretary's reports on new duties) are not easily included. Tariff history subsequent to 1824 tends to show that revenue demands led to general movement in duties rather than variation in particular rates (except in the classic revenue items like salt, tea, wines, and spirits): see chapter 7. However, there is one very important consequence of the fact that the tariff was by far the most important source of revenue, namely, that the Treasury was quite opposed to prohibitive duties.

Congress enacted, that is, nominal duties, but the net tariff and the effective rate of protection also appear as dependent variables in a few regressions. The two parts of the model of tariff formation are, first, the determinants of the intensity of pressure group activity, and second, the legislative response to that pressure. Because lobbying pressure was not measurable, or even observable, there are, in the functions estimated, explanatory variables from both parts of the model. This leads to certain problems of interpretation.

In the general form of the estimated relationship, the nominal tariff is written as a function of four classes of variables:

o the *size* of the change in value-added ($Z1$, $Z2$);
o the number of *inputs* and their rates of duty ($Z4$, $Z5$);
o the number of potential *pressure groups* and their distribution ($Z6$–$Z10$);
o *Congressional* variables, representatives and senators ($Z11$).

The theory of tariff formation will now be introduced by a discussion of the first class of variable, industry output size.

### Industry Output Size and Opposition ($Z1$, $Z2$)

Were larger industries likely to have received higher rates of duty? Only to the extent that supporting pressure depended strongly on the size of the gains to be had (which in turn depended on output size), whereas opposition depended not only (relatively weakly) on the size of losses, but also on the height of the tariff duty itself.

In expression (6.1), gains increase with the size of protected output, $S_j$. However, the cost increase $(t_j S_{ji})$ borne by users of an imported good includes the revenue, that is, the gains $(t_j S_j)$ fall short of the losses $(\Sigma_i t_j S_{ji})$. Revenue was not immediately returned to those who paid, so the cost to users exceeded the gain to producers by the amount of duty paid [16] (in fact by more, if we count the deadweight loss of consumer surplus). This excess of loss over gain increases with the height of the duty. Therefore, for a model to be consistent with the passage of any

---

[16] The ratio of imports plus domestic production to production, had it been available, would have been a proxy for the ratio of loss to gain. However, it would also provide an indication of opportunities for displacing imports: an industry with a very low share of imports in total domestic absorption may not seek as high a duty as an industry with a lot of imports to replace (assuming the domestic excess supply elasticities vary less across industries than do the ratios of imports to production).

import duties, either protectionist pressure must be greater per dollar of gain than opposition per dollar of loss in some range of the duty, or protectionist pressure more effective in Congress. We will adopt the first alternative.[17]

Consider the extreme case in which the burden of a particular tariff item does not spur any opposition. There were in fact few memorials against taxes on particular final consumer imports, and for understandable reasons. If there were a large number of duties, and the expected loss from each small, no action might be worthwhile except to support less protectionist candidates or parties in the next election. An individual would not be moved by one item to act on his own behalf unless the advantage hoped for (in this case, avoidance of a loss) exceeded some threshold, assuming there were some fixed costs of action. The threshold would be higher for members of groups that were more numerous, heterogeneous, and dispersed, that is, higher for users (especially of a final product) than for producers.

The threshold argument, relying as it does on there being a very much larger number of users than producers, and on any particular duty being of too small in importance to merit action, is less convincing when the dutiable good is an intermediate input. Input users have the choice, assuming they produce an import-competing good, to lobby for a compensating increase in the duty on the product using the taxed input, as well as to oppose input duties. They will generally do both. Consequently, opposition to duties on inputs cannot be ruled out a priori, and may well exceed support for all but very small duties, thereby giving some explanation of tariff "escalation" (higher duties on final products than on intermediates). See the following discussion of variable $Z4$.

An asymmetry in the response to gains and losses helps explain why import duties are enacted but leaves us with a difficulty, namely, that with no opposition, all duties would be set at prohibitive levels or above. Therefore, what the argument needs is that for some levels of a duty, no or little opposition was stimulated by the widespread losses caused, but that higher levels evoked stronger protests about the burden.

[17] Schattschneider (1935) found that it was more advantageous for users of dutiable inputs to seek compensation than to oppose: free traders did not receive a sympathetic hearing in 1929–30.

We are not yet home. Asymmetry of response is required for a model to produce *any* duties; however, something extra is needed for duties to rise with the size of the industry. This is achieved by adding another restraint to the height of a duty apart from particular opposition, namely, opposition to protection in principle. To the extent that *general* opposition was triggered or stimulated by the *height of a duty*, and not by the *amount of loss*, then a model yielding a nonprohibitive duty is possible, one in which the duties would rise with the size of the gain, that is, with output.[18]

What is the evidence that high duties attracted disproportionate attention.[19] First, some guide to the likelihood of loss of revenue was taken from the level of a tax. Second, sugar began as a revenue item with high rates. Once Louisiana was admitted and the duty became protective also, speakers protested its unusual height. Last, specific duties were used, it appears, to conceal higher rates: the most substantial increases in 1824 were in items switched from ad valorem to specific (see chapter 2).

Formally, let protectionist pressure be $B = B(tS,t)$ and opposition $A = A(tS,t)$, that is, both pressures depended on the size of the gain (made here equal to the size of the loss) and separately on the height of the duty.[20] If the legislature set a duty so that the pressures were equal, then,

$$B(tS,t) - A(tS,t) = 0 \qquad (6.2)$$

---

[18] To illustrate one extreme case, let the unopposed legislative tariff function be

$$t_j = f(B_j); \quad f_1 > 0; \quad f_{11} < 0$$

where $t_j$ is the $j^{th}$ tariff, and $B_j$ the tariff influencing outlay. Assuming a fixed quantity, partial equilibrium model, the duty increases value-added by $t_j S_j$, where $S_j$ is the tariff-deflated value of output. The problem for the protectionists is to maximize $t_j S_j - B_j$ subject to the equation above. The first-order condition is $f_1 = 1/S_j$. Differentiating,

$$\frac{dt_j}{dS_j} = -\frac{(f_j)^2}{f_{11} S_j} > 0$$

that is, larger industries would receive higher tariffs.

[19] For any level of output and imports, the higher the duty, the greater the protests and opposition expected. What is being considered now is whether some high duties attracted more opposition than other lower duties, despite the burdens of the former being greater than the latter. That is, were higher duties opposed per se?

[20] Subscripts are suppressed for convenience. The model would be unchanged if the loss were any constant proportion of the gain.

FIGURE 6.1

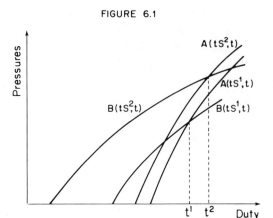

Tariff Formation

Figure 6.1 illustrates the need, given the threshold argument, for the slope of the $B$ curves to be less than that of the $A$ curves; formally, we require the result of the differentiation of (6.2) with respect to $t$ to be negative:

$$S\left(\frac{\partial B}{\partial tS} - \frac{\partial A}{\partial tS}\right) + \left(\frac{\partial B}{\partial t} - \frac{\partial A}{\partial t}\right) < 0 \qquad (6.3)$$

Condition (6.3) is more likely to be met if protectionist pressure depended only on the size of the gain, and not on the height of the duty (that is, if $\partial B/\partial t = 0$). More generally, if $\partial B/\partial tS > \partial A/\partial tS$, then a nontrivial result requires $\partial B/\partial t > \partial A/\partial t$. In other words, antiprotectionist pressure was more responsive to the height of the duty per se than was protectionist pressure.

The condition for the duty to rise with output is found by differentiating (6.2) with respect to $S$:

$$\frac{dt}{dS} = -\frac{t\left(\dfrac{\partial B}{\partial tS} - \dfrac{\partial A}{\partial tS}\right)}{S\left(\dfrac{\partial B}{\partial tS} - \dfrac{\partial A}{\partial tS}\right) + \left(\dfrac{\partial B}{\partial t} - \dfrac{\partial A}{\partial t}\right)} \qquad (6.4)$$

The denominator is expression (6.3) and is negative by construction. Therefore, larger industries would have received higher duties if, for a given duty, antiprotectionist pressure rose slower with the loss than protectionist with the gain, that is, slower with output $S$. Figure 6.1 illustrates this condition that [21]

$$\frac{\partial B}{\partial tS} - \frac{\partial A}{\partial tS} > 0 \tag{6.5}$$

To sum up: it might be possible, by judicious choice of assumptions, to construct a model that yields a clear prediction about the relationship between industry size and the duty. Such a model would seem to have to rely on there being general opposition to higher duties per se, and on opposition engendered by the losses occasioned by particular duties (as long as opposition per dollar of tariff burden for some range of duty was smaller than supporting pressure). To the extent that these kinds of opposition existed, we might expect a positive relationship between industry size and duty, especially if the good is a final output, if we have allowed fully for other influences. The argument is weaker when applied to intermediate goods.

### The Number of Inputs and their Tariffs (Z4, Z5)

We would expect industries with more and higher input duties to receive higher output duties. The demand for inputs is a derived demand, so input suppliers have an interest in the height of the tariff on goods incorporating their products. [22] In addition it might have been easier for industries to obtain protection if they suffered input tariffs: since Congress in 1824 (and here it was not unique) was presented with arguments that protection could benefit all sections of the community, it was open to pleas, supported by input suppliers, to offset the harm caused by input duties. [23] Variable Z5 is the inverse of the number of dutiable inputs, except that Z5 equals zero when there were no dutiable inputs: the support from supplying industries was greatest when

[21] In the figure, $S^2 > S^1$. The vertical distance between the $A$ lines measures $(\partial A/\partial tS)\,dS$ and that between the $B$ lines $(\partial B/\partial tS)\,dS$. Condition (6.5) requires the first distance to be less than the second.

[22] Strictly speaking, an output tariff can raise the price of inputs only if the foreign supply of the input is not perfectly elastic: appendix A develops a derived demand implication.

[23] That Congress was well aware of this problem is shown by the debate on pig iron in 1824 (see chapter 3). In this case, however, the duty on the input (pig) was kept low.

there were a few of them. Variable $Z4$ is the average duty paid on inputs, the weights being the cost-shares.[24]

Tariff historians have attributed part of the strength of the protective movement in the period to war and deflation. The War of 1812 saw the springing up and growth of many industries; the deflation at the end of the decade left the more capital-intensive manufacturers with a greater burden of excess capital, and a greater capacity to expand output cheaply, that is, "investment" in tariff agitation was a relatively more attractive prospect for these industries. (However, since capitalists are included in the category "proprietor," this argument runs somewhat counter to that developed in the next subsection.)

### Pressure Group Variables ($Z6–Z10$)

The *Digest of Manufactures* (1820) provides an imperfect count of the number of establishments in an industry. Some additional information about the severity of problems of communication and coordination of pressure group efforts is offered by the number of counties in which an industry was located. The county was the natural node for pressure group activity, being a geographic, social, and administrative unit. The fewer the number of establishments or counties, and the less widespread geographically, the more intense the pressure.

Enquiring more closely into the motivations of the value-added factors of production, we should notice that owners of *specific* factors benefit more than owners of general factors from a rise in the demand for their products: the relative increases in their factor prices would be greater, and their wealth portfolios, including human wealth, more specialized. And they suffer more from a price fall. Their fortunes are tied to those of the industry; they are the residual legatees. Specific factors might well regard entry into their industry easier than exit, and be concerned about the prospects of large capital losses that would occur if the firm had to shut down. The usual notions about diminishing marginal utility work in this direction: prospects of equal losses and gains do not produce equal agitation.[25] Thus the individuals most con-

---

[24] An alternative explanation of the effects of many and high input tariffs follows.

[25] It is useful to recall from chapter 2 that manufacturing in the 1820s was not dominated as it is today by corporations; on the contrary, "in reviewing the history of the cotton industry, in 1831, Samuel Slater said that most manufacturers worked in their facto-

cerned with the consequences of economic changes are the owners of specific factors. On the other hand, the benefits to labor from a duty on a particular good would tend to be dispersed by competition throughout the whole economy, if labor were perfectly industry-nonspecific. Trade unions might be powerful proponents of protection of labor in general, but workers in any particular industry would not be expected to be very active lobbyists for tariffs on their own outputs, unless labor was relatively immobile in and out of the industry (as is the case today in some important industries).

It is the specific factors of production within the firm which suffer or enjoy variations in rents or quasi-rents, and so we need some theory of the distribution of the change in value-added among the owners of the primary factors of production. The division of the spoils depends on the elasticities of factor supply, and it seems a reasonable generalization that the supply elasticity of proprietorial factors, in or out of an industry, was lower than the elasticity of wage-labor supply. In other words, proprietors were more likely to enjoy rents or quasi-rents of considerable duration than were laborers: the proprietors were better able to appropriate the benefits of the tariffs (or less able to escape the burdens). Proprietorial income is a catch-all category for the residual available to working proprietors (including some skilled workers) and to the owners of factors not currently purchased by the enterprise (such as water rights and some borrowed capital).[26] Proprietorial income in 1820 was a good approximation to rent or quasi-rent.

When an industry is given a new tariff structure that alters quasi-rents, two things may happen. Proprietors already in the industry will change their level of production and purchases in order to maximize their quasi-rents, given the new relative prices. In addition, new proprietors will be attracted to the industries enjoying excess profits at a rate which depends on the importance of barriers to entry and exit, and on the degree of confidence about the level of tariff protection. If

---

ries and that, after deducting ordinary interest on their investment and their own wages, their profits would be very small. Manufacturers of this class rarely failed, because their losses fell on all three items—profits, interest, and wages." Clark (1929), I, 372. Incorporations were more prevalent in cotton textiles than most other industries.

[26] Clark (1929), I, 367–72, discusses working proprietors and the sources of manufacturing capital; see also chapter 2.

new entry is very fast, then there is not much scope for the kind of model of tariff formation being developed here, for we lack evidence on the rate of entry or exit. However, the protectionist principle was still in some doubt in the 1820s, and reversion to a somewhat lower and more uniform rate of duties was a real possibility.

It is expected that industries with low proprietorial income or income share would be more active in seeking protection. The factor reward of a specific factor responds more to variations in the price of output (or other inputs) when the factor's cost-share is small. If $\Theta_\pi$ is the cost-share of the fixed factors before duty, then the proportional variation $\hat{\Pi}$ in fixed factor income is given by $t/\Theta_\pi$; the smaller is $\Theta_\pi$, the larger is $\hat{\Pi}$, given $t$. Larger proportional variations in total income are reflected in larger absolute variations in average income per proprietor, if the average income per proprietor was relatively uniform across industries. Thus $\Theta_\pi$ is a leverage variable.[27]

### Congressman and Senators (Z11)

This subsection discusses whether we can predict confidently that geographically concentrated industries would obtain higher duties. The reader has been forewarned that the interpretation of some variables is difficult because they influenced both the amount of pressure exerted by groups and also how legislators reacted to tariff pressure. The argument has been made that small numbers and geographic concentration should lead to more active pressure groups. We might also expect that pressure to be greater, *ceteris paribus,* the more concentrated the benefits. It was also found that pressure tended to be local, and most memorials did not transcend state lines. Therefore, most interstate and interproduct bargaining took place within Congress.

Thus, there are two relationships to consider. The first is the determination of the amount of pressure arising in a geographical locality, as a function of the size of the local interest (measured by free-trade sales) and the pressure group characteristics (especially the number and diversity of firms). The second relationship is between the local pressures

---

[27] Strictly, for the argument to hold, average income per proprietor, denoted $p$, must be the same in all industries. Let $N$ be the number of proprietors in industry $j$ (subscripts suppressed for convenience), then $p = \Pi/N$ or $N = \Pi/p$, so $\Pi$ is an exact proxy for $N$. Alternatively, the variation in average income is given by $d\Pi/N = tp/\Theta_\pi$. The leverage effect, mentioned by Pigou (1906), is developed in Mussa (1974).

and the resulting rate of duty.[28] Unfortunately, there being no data on the amount of pressure, it is difficult to separate these relationships, and so we have to be content with some amalgam.[29]

---

[28] The use of unrestricted Ordinary Least Squares (OLS) is probably inefficient because of likely restrictions on the coefficients. To keep the example simple, assume that no industry other than $j$ itself makes an effort to influence the $j^{th}$ tariff, and we have

$$t_j = a_0 + a_1 B_{jj},$$

and

$$B_{jj} = b_0 + \sum_k b_k X_{kjj} \qquad k = 1, \ldots, K$$

where $B_{jj}$ is the effort $j$ puts out for tariff $t_j$, and $X_{kjj}$ is the $k^{th}$ determinant of that effort. Substitution yields

$$t_j = [a_0 + a_1 b_0] + a_1 b_2 X_{jj} + \ldots$$

$$= A_0 + A_1 X_{1jj} + A_2 X_{2jj} + \ldots$$

where $A_0 = a_0 + a_1 b_0$, $A_1 = a_1 b_1$, $A_2 = a_1 b_2$, $\ldots$ \hfill (6.6)

There are $K + 1$ equations in (6.6), but $K + 3$ "structural" parameters $a_0, a_1, b_0, b_1, \ldots,$ $b_K$. If some prior or extraneous information made it possible to convert the set (6.6) into linear relationships, with as many equations as unknowns (the $a$'s and $b$'s), then unrestricted OLS regression that does not take into account these relationships among the estimated coefficients will be inefficient. Goldberger (1964), p. 275. I made no attempt to impose restrictions necessary to convert (6.6) into such a linear set of equations.

[29] The model estimated is a more complex linear version of the reduced form of the following system (subscript $j$ suppressed):

$$t = f(L, N) \qquad f_1 > 0, \quad f_2 > 0, \quad f_{12} > 0 \qquad (6.7)$$
$$f_{11} < 0, \quad f_{22} < 0$$

$$L = g(tS, N) \qquad g_1 > 0, \quad g_2 < 0, \quad g_{12} < 0 \qquad (6.8)$$
$$g_{11} < 0, \quad g_{22} > 0$$

Lobbying pressure, $L$, is assumed to depend positively on the benefits to be gained (that is, $tS$) and negatively on the numbers, $N$, in the industry; $N$ is a proxy for a number of variables influencing lobbying strength and Congressional response. In this system, $dt/dS > 0$, but the sign of $dt/dN$ is uncertain:

$$\frac{dt}{dN} = \frac{f_1 g_2 + f_2}{1 - f_1 g_1 S}$$

Stability in the "tariff market" requires $1 - f_1 g_1 S > 0$, as can be seen from the figure, noting that $\partial L / \partial t = g_1 S$ in (6.8). An increase in $N$ lowers (6.8) but may raise or lower (6.7), leaving the sign of $dt/dN$ indeterminate.

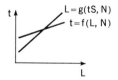

Let us consider the effects of pressure. Electoral districts being mostly smaller than states, it is not likely that the opposing pressure in a district would exceed the pressure in favor. In addition, representatives had fewer calls on their time than senators, so the very existence of a manufactory, even a tiny one, was most likely sufficient to attract the representative's support. It was not possible to make a direct count of those representatives who had an industry in their district; however, a reasonable approximation was made on the assumption that such representatives were in the same proportion to the state's total representatives as were the counties producing the good to the total counties in the state. It is expected that a duty would be higher, the more representatives with electorates containing the industry, because the costs of organizing a majority around a particular duty would have been greater, the fewer the congressmen being pushed by local pressure groups.

In the legislative history of the tariff of 1824, the Senate was particularly important.[30] It is worthwhile exploring the use of data on pressure by state, even though in this instance the data are not available. It is well known that in a committee operating under majority rule, if preferences are single peaked, the median committee member determines the outcome, assuming that members act independently and no bargaining or logrolling takes place.[31] Yet a senator with a huge pressure on his back or bribe in his pocket has an incentive to transfer some of it to the other senators.[32] Consider what happens if only one issue is being decided, or if issues are independent of one another. With pressure costlessly transferable, the median ceases to dominate the outcome, and the total pressure is all that matters.[33] In a system of

[30] It will be recalled that a bill quite similar to that of 1824 was defeated by one Senate vote in 1820 (21 to 20), although it passed the House by 91 to 78. In 1824 the tariff commanded a margin of 107 to 102 in the House, and 25 to 21 in the Senate. It was argued in chapter 3 that the managers of the bill modified it so as to capture Senate votes, even at the expense of votes in the House. Maine and Missouri were admitted between the 1820 and 1824 tariff bill votes; reapportionment after the 1820 census gave more representatives to the "tariff States"—New York, Pennsylvania, Ohio, and Kentucky.

[31] See Black (1948). This discussion draws on chapters 3 and 5.

[32] W. A. Brock and S. P. Magee are working on formal models of Congressional behavior; I benefited from their comments. Some senators or congressmen may have been influenced by the considerable tariff debates of the period: see Edwards (1970) for an interesting analysis, and Stanwood (1903).

[33] Tullock (1959) argues that logrolling (or vote-trading) leads to an "overinvestment" in activities decided by majority vote.

geographical representation, however, transfer costs arise, firstly, from the simple costs of bargaining, and second, from voter disapproval of neglecting local interests wholly or partly. The rewards offered to individual senators and representatives by industrial pressure groups were not costlessly transformed by the recipients into rewards offered to other senators and representatives to alter their votes (away from the pattern based solely on geographical representation).

The more even the distribution of pressure, the less wastage there was in the course of transfers of pressure, one senator to another.[34] From a given total of pressure the highest possible duty would have resulted when the pressure was evenly distributed over the senators. The pressure on all senators mattered, not just on a majority of senators: those senators whose states desired a low rate of duty suffered elector disapproval if a high duty were passed without a struggle, and so all sought to influence the height of the duty.

### REGRESSION RESULTS FOR 1824

Reversing the procedure, typical in industrial economics, of explaining the characteristics of an industry such as profitability or size by variables such as concentration ratios and tariff rates, this chapter instead postulates a causal chain running from structural characteristics to rates of duty, using data from 1820 to predict the Tariff of 1824.[35] To the extent that the 1820 data may have been shaped by a relatively unchanging tariff structure, there is danger of spurious or biased results, a question referred to below.

The Tariff Act of 1824, the first general revision since the postwar Act of 1816 (itself passed with nationalistic enthusiasm), raised somewhat the rates of duty to levels similar to those in the narrowly defeated 1820 bill. In describing the Tariff of 1824 as the first seriously protective measure, Taussig and Stanwood were referring not so much to the level of the duties as to the intensity and nature of the Congressional debate, especially the Southern opposition. Free trade had

[34] Was it on balance an advantage for an industry to have been located in the larger states? Each senator had but one vote, but those from larger states would have had more with which to swing the votes of other senators, if we think of pressure in a transferable form like a bribe. On the other hand, the larger the state the more numerous and diverse the calls on the senator's time.

[35] Stigler (1970) uses a similar approach.

T A B L E  6.1

*Regression Results: Nominal Duties on Manufactures, 1824*

| INDEPENDENT VARIABLES | | R1 | R2 | R3 |
|---|---|---|---|---|
| | Constant | .329 | .345 | .276 |
| | | (8.31) | (9.20) | (7.75) |
| Z1 | Output | .394 | .481 | |
| | | (3.28) | (4.14) | |
| Z2 | (Output)² | −.074 | −.082 | |
| | | (1.98) | (2.22) | |
| Z3 | Pressure | | | 2.136 |
| | | | | (4.09) |
| Z4 | Input duties | 1.340 | 1.203 | 1.318 |
| | | (5.04) | (4.54) | (5.15) |
| Z5 | (Input number)⁻¹ | −.128 | −.122 | −.119 |
| | | (3.28) | (3.14) | (3.19) |
| Z6 | Proprietorial income share | −.958 | −1.024 | −.815 |
| | | (5.17) | (5.64) | (5.50) |
| Z7 | Establishments | .335 | .369 | .599 |
| | | (3.00) | (3.24) | (5.81) |
| Z8 | Industrial concentration | .026 | .077 | .013 |
| | | (1.11) | (2.80) | (0.56) |
| Z9 | Sales dispersion | . | .102 | |
| | | | (2.03) | |
| Z10 | County dispersion | −.258 | | −.270 |
| | | (1.93) | | (2.10) |
| Z11 | Senate | .011 | −.005 | .012 |
| | | (1.42) | (0.61) | (1.67) |
| $\bar{R}^2$ | | .6325 | .6345 | .6492 |
| F | | 16.49 | 16.72 | 19.73 |
| (d.f.) | | (9,72) | (9,72) | (8,73) |

*Note:* The *t* statistics are in parentheses under each estimated coefficient.

never been the policy of the United States, but the rates of 1824 were more obviously products of economic interests than general principles.

Tables 6.1 and 6.2 report OLS estimation of linear relationships.[36] The results were generally satisfactory. It appears that the most intense pressure came from industries with lower proprietorial incomes and presumably fewer proprietors; with higher industrial concentration of output and therefore concentrated tariff benefits; and with fewer prob-

[36] The original results were obtained with the assistance of A. Kum, using the Massager program supplied by the Bank of Canada, and put up by C. Macurdy. The program originated with M. C. McCraken at Southern Methodist University. Subsequent results were obtained with the help of W. C. Naughton and M. J. Pokorny.

Table 6.1 Notes

| VARIABLE | DEFINITION |
|---|---|
| $Y1$ | Nominal ad valorem or equivalent duties on 82 manufactures. |
| $Z1$ | Tariff-deflated 1820 output, scaled $10^{-6}$. |
| $Z2$ | $(Z1)^2$ |
| $Z3$ | Pressure. Equals $Z1/(Z7 \cdot 10^3)^{1/2}$ |
| $Z4$ | Cost-share weighted sum of input duties, 1820 rates. |
| $Z5$ | Inverse of the number of costed inputs, except $Z5$ equals zero if the number is zero. |
| $Z6$ | Proprietorial income share in output, deflated to a zero tariff, assuming money wage payments unchanged. |
| $Z7$ | Recorded number of establishments (see text and appendix), scaled $10^{-3}$. |
| $Z8$ | Industrial concentration: |

$$-\sum_k y_{ik} \ln y_{ik}; \quad y_{ik} = Y_{ik}/Y_i$$

where $Y_{ik}$ is the output of the $k^{th}$ establishment (report) of product $i$, and $Y_i$ the total output; note the negative sign.

| | |
|---|---|
| $Z9$ | Sales dispersion: |

$$\sum_j y_{ij} \ln y_{ij}; \quad y_{ij} = Y_{ij}/Y_i$$

where $Y_{ij}$ is the output of the $j^{th}$ state, and $Y_i$ the total output.

| | |
|---|---|
| $Z10$ | County dispersion: |

$$\sum_j p_{ij} \ln p_{ij}; \quad p_{ij} = P_{ij}/P_i$$

where $P_{ij}$ is number of counties in state $j$ producing good $i$ and $P_i$ the total.

| | |
|---|---|
| $Z11$ | Senators. Equals the number of states producing the product. |

## T A B L E 6.2

Correlation Matrix, Means and Standard Deviations for Variables, Regressions R1 to R3, Table 6.1

| | Y1 | Z1 | Z2 | Z3 | Z4 | Z5 | Z6 | Z7 | Z8 | Z9 | Z10 | Z11 |
|---|---|---|---|---|---|---|---|---|---|---|---|---|
| | | | | | | CORRELATION MATRIX | | | | | | |
| Y1 | | .190 | .116 | .246 | .531 | -.068 | -.184 | .293 | -.130 | .007 | .194 | .180 |
| Z1 | | | .932 | .824 | .018 | .072 | .836 | .638 | -.706 | .468 | .586 | .751 |
| Z2 | | | | .667 | -.046 | .113 | .745 | .588 | -.552 | .326 | .414 | .583 |
| Z3 | | | | | .196 | .111 | .690 | .248 | -.520 | .327 | .516 | .608 |
| Z4 | | | | | | .392 | -.222 | -.112 | .003 | .021 | .053 | .000 |
| Z5 | | | | | | | .000 | -.122 | .084 | -.055 | -.098 | -.059 |
| Z6 | | | | | | | | .473 | -.614 | .455 | .513 | .654 |
| Z7 | | | | | | | | | -.617 | .459 | .466 | .598 |
| Z8 | | | | | | | | | | .775 | .893 | .877 |
| Z9 | | | | | | | | | | | .697 | .774 |
| Z10 | | | | | | | | | | | | .883 |
| | | | | | | | | | | | | |
| Mean [1] | .339 | .358 | .427 | .044 | .057 | .646 | .092 | 64.0 | -2.04 | .172 | 1.25 | 6.34 |
| Standard deviation | .188 | .550 | 1.18 | .042 | .063 | .372 | .154 | .151 | 1.26 | .171 | .716 | 4.27 |

Source: Appendix B.
[1] Z7 is here not scaled down by $10^3$.

lems of communication due to geographical dispersion. Pressure was more effective if it was evenly spread across a larger number of states and supported by the presence of large numbers of establishments and thus electors. In an alternative formulation (Z3), the quantity of pressure is represented directly in an effort to investigate the combined effects of size of output and number of establishments.

### Size of Industry Output (Z1, Z2)

Because the increase in value-added allowed by a duty is, on first approximation, in proportion to the free-trade value of output, it was predicted that any association between output and duty would be positive.[37] Generally speaking, however, larger "free-trade" output meant lower duties except in the low ranges of output and proprietorial share, $\Theta_\pi$; or there was no connection at all: if proprietorial share, $\Theta_\pi$, was substituted for proprietorial income, Z6, then the coefficients of Z1 and its squared term Z2 were both insignificant.[38] Free-trade value of output was estimated by "deflating" the observed 1820 value by unity plus the ad valorem rate of duty, assuming supplies were perfectly elastic abroad and perfectly inelastic at home. If higher rates of duty elicited larger production, there is a danger of statistical illusion, lessened

---

[37] The difference between the results for final and intermediate products did not prove important.

[38] Regression R2 becomes, on substitution of $\Theta_\pi$ for Z6,

$$Y1 = .431 + .012Z1 - .005Z2 + 1.368Z4 - .128Z5$$
$$\phantom{Y1 =}(7.88)\quad(0.11)\quad(0.13)\quad(4.22)\quad(2.91)$$

$$- .295\Theta_\pi + .465Z7 + .067Z8 + .089Z9 + .0002Z11$$
$$\phantom{-.2}(3.04)\quad(3.68)\quad(2.14)\quad(1.56)\quad(0.02)$$

$$\bar{R}^2 = .5331, \quad F(9.72) = 11.28$$

If $\Theta_\pi$ is added to regression R2, it has an insignificant coefficient. In the regressions reported in the table, noting that $Z6 = \Theta_\pi \times Z1$ but ignoring the low ($r = -.20$) covariation of $\Theta_\pi$ and Z1, the turning points are approximately where output equals $10^6 \times (3.0 - 6.3\Theta_\pi)$. The relationship was positive only in the lower range of output and for low $\Theta_\pi$. The means of $\Theta_\pi$ and Z1 were .32 and .36, and their standard deviations .20 and .55 respectively.

If the elasticity of supply is $\epsilon$, then the "true" of free-trade output would be $Z1(1+t)^{-\epsilon}$; the assumption made is that $\epsilon$ equals zero. Even if the value of $\epsilon$ were known (and not zero), there would still be a simultaneous equation bias because a positive error in the duty set in 1816 and 1818 (and hence most likely in 1824) would have caused a higher value of output in 1820.

somewhat but not eliminated by the severe price deflation of the late
1810s. Such a spurious positive correlation between output and duty
was not in evidence.

### Input Numbers and their Duties (Z4, Z5)

Industries suffering in 1820 from larger average input tariffs obtained
higher duties in 1824. It is possible that, just as in 1929–30,[39]
Congress had a working rule to compensate industries harmed by input
duties; the coefficients of Z4 are not different from unity, that is, exact
compensation.[40] In addition, the more numerous were the dutiable inputs, the higher the output duty, but the effect was less than proportional. These results are consistent with the hypothesis that input suppliers influenced output duties, but there are other possible
explanations.[41]

### Pressure Groups, Numbers and Politics

In 1824 the structure of the tariff was influenced by the willingness
of proprietors to bring pressure and by the responsiveness of congressmen. Both presure group activity and political bargaining were involved. Higher duties went to industries with low proprietorial income

[39] See Schattschneider (1935) for a discussion of the principles implicit in the Smoot-
Hawley revision. Ideally, simultaneous equation methods are called for, but because the
endogenous variables (the other tariffs) enter the equations as weighted sums, OLS was
used. The term $\Sigma_i t_i \Theta_{ij}$, the coefficient of which is reported here, was calculated using the
pre-1824 duties. The results do not alter appreciably if the duties in the 1824 act are
used. Nor is there much change if 15 percent, the duty on unenumerated imports, is
charged to all material inputs for which no separate cost-shares were calculated. (Some
importable inputs were uncosted because of data difficulties; most of the uncosted inputs
were nontraded goods.)

[40] N. R. Norman has suggested to me an explanation of tariff escalation, namely, that
domestically produced goods are not always perfect substitutes for imports, particularly
the more highly finished manufactures. Higher nominal tariffs are needed to give highly
finished manufactures the same proportional price rises as are obtained with lower rates
of duty by cruder products.

[41] For proprietors in 1824, prospects of equal gains and losses would not have produced equal agitation, and so firms vulnerable to damage from input tariffs would have
tried harder to influence the duties that affected them, including their own output tariffs.
Schattschneider (1935) found that the legislature in 1929–30 was more responsive to
requests for compensatory duties than for reductions of harmful ones. The results in Z4
are compatible with this explanation, but Z5 is inappropriately defined; if the actual
number of inputs is used instead of Z5, it has no significance.

(a proxy for the number of proprietors) or low income share (high leverage), with firms more concentrated geographically, and with higher degrees of industrial concentration, which are all consistent with the model of pressure group behavior. The strong pressure groups had fewer proprietors, in relatively easy distances for communication, and were able to capture for themselves most of the quasi-rents from the tariffs. However, pressure was brought to bear within a political system of geographical representation. Evidently, although pressure came mainly from the relatively few, larger establishments,[42] the mere existence of numbers of smaller, dispersed firms helped lend weight in Congress, so industries with many establishments and with sales spread more evenly across states or with establishments in many states obtained higher duties. Now the details.

Industries with low proprietorial incomes or income shares obtained higher tariffs in 1824. There are a number of ways of estimating what proprietorial income shares would have been without tariffs, depending on what is assumed about money wages, but the results did not depend on the method chosen: when the regression was run using actual 1820 proprietorial income rather than $Z6$, the sign was still negative and significant.[43] However, whether income, $Z6$, or share, $\Theta_\pi$, was used did affect the significance of the squared output variable, $Z2$.

Two "entropy" measures of geographical dispersion were calculated, the dispersion of output by state, $Z9$, to be considered below, and of producing counties by state, $Z10$. The latter appears to be a substitute for the index, $Z8$, of industrial concentration: industrially concentrated industries or those in geographically concentrated counties obtained

---

[42] See Stigler (1974).

[43] Denoting actual 1820 profits as $Z6'$, the regression $R2$ becomes

$$Y1 = .339 + .365Z1 - .049Z2 + 1.748Z4 - .136Z5$$
$$\quad\;\; (7.73) \quad (2.22) \quad\;\; (1.14) \quad\;\; (6.18) \quad\;\; (3.01)$$

$$- .625Z6' + .960Z7 + .104Z8 + .130Z9 - .005Z11$$
$$\quad\;\; (2.20) \quad\;\; (4.10) \quad\;\; (3.12) \quad\;\; (2.18) \quad\;\; (0.50)$$

$$\bar{R}^2 = .5062, \quad F(7,92) = 10.23$$

If tariff lobbying were financed out of existing proprietorial incomes, we would expect to find a *positive* coefficient on $Z6'$. The evidence is weak that capital-intensive industries obtained higher duties. Travis (1968) found a positive correlation between labor input coefficients and contemporary duties.

higher tariffs. The free-rider problems of pressure groups were smaller when geographical location reduced costs of communication, and when the benefits of action were not diffused.

Although the direct measures of political importance of industries— the number of senators, $Z11$, and representatives [44] with the industry in their electorates—did not always have significance, there was ample additional evidence that politics did matter. First, in those regressions in which $Z11$ had low signifiance, higher duties went to industries with more even distributions of output (and therefore tariff benefits and pressures) across states, $Z9$. This confirmed the notion that too local an interest raised the number and size of sidepayments needed in Congress.[45] Secondly, in general, industries with more establishments and hence more electors obtained higher rates of duty.[46]

### An Alternative Formulation ($Z3$)

Because some factors could have influenced both the strength of lobbying and the effectiveness of pressure in Congress, no firm theoretical predictions could be made about their signs. The number of establishments, $Z7$, is one of these. According to pressure group theory, its sign should have been negative, but it was in fact positive, which has been interpreted as indicating that political considerations outweighed pressure group ones—it was important to have had a large number of electors in your industry. Another result that was surprising (although less so) was the lack of a positive relationship between output and the tariffs. An alternative formulation was tried that made "pressure," $Z3$,

[44] The approximation for the number of representatives did not have significance when substituted for $Z11$. In earlier versions of this chapter, before a count of the number of establishments was available, representatives did have a significant, positive coefficient.

[45] The coefficient of the sales dispersion term, $Z9$, was less than that of county dispersion in absolute value, so that the advantages from an even spread of output were less than the disadvantages of geographical dispersion of producing counties. Notice that infant industries had the desirable pressure group characteristics but the undesirable political characteristics of smallness and localness.

[46] The *Digest* did not report separately every establishment, but often used aggregations, noting, in many instances, the number of firms included. Where firms were small, aggregation to the county level was more common; where large—textiles in New England—individual firms were reported more often.

depend positively on output and negatively on number of establish-ments:

$$(\text{pressure}=Z3) = (Z1=\text{output})/(Z7 \times 10^3 = \text{establishment})^{\frac{1}{2}}$$

A doubling of both output and establishments was assumed to have increased pressure by less than double. The results are reported in regression R3. Industries exerting more "pressure" obtained higher du-ties; more "pressure" was generated by more output but fewer es-tablishments, although Z7 itself still had a positive coefficient.[47] (If Z1 is added to this regression it has an insignificant coefficient without changing the significance of any other; Z3 squared has no significance either.)

## Net Tariffs and Effective Rates

Although Congress set nominal tariffs, what import-competing indus-tries sought was protection, and that was not determined solely by out-put tariffs. The net tariff $(t_j - \Sigma_i t_i \Theta_{ij})$ and the effective rate are superior measures of the benefits obtained by industries. A simple transfer of variable Z4 $(\Sigma_i t_i \Theta_{ij})$ from the list of explanatory variables to the left-hand side of the equation leaves the qualitative results virtually unchanged.[48] However, a similar modification does not work well in explaining statistically the pattern of effective rates.

It is pointed out in appendix A that there may be many sets of nominal tariffs all yielding the same pattern of effective rates of protec-tion: if the Congress desired to set effective rates, then we would not

---

[47] Ignoring the rather high positive correlation between Z1 and Z7 $(r = .61)$, the partial derivative of Y1 with respect to the number of establishments is negative everywhere ex-cept very low in the range of numbers of establishments. The assumption justifying $\Theta_\pi$ as a leverage variable was such as to make Z6 a good proxy for the number of proprietors; a referee of the article mentioned in the first footnote of this chapter pointed out that Z7 might be a better proxy. The use of Z3 almost eliminates the contrast between the effects of more $\Pi$ and of more establishments.

[48] The modification of R3 is:

$$Y1 - Z4 = .194 + 3.780Z3 - .111Z5 - .679Z6$$
$$(4.31) \quad (3.36) \quad (2.95) \quad (5.50)$$

$$+ .558Z7 + .013Z8 - .341Z10 + .020Z11$$
$$(4.63) \quad (0.53) \quad (2.47) \quad (2.62)$$

$$\bar{R}^2 = .4553, \quad F(7,74) = 10.67$$

expect to be very successful in explaining nominal rates, and vice versa. Whatever the reason, most of the variables used in chapter 6 have no power to explain effective rates. The most respectable regression result is

$$\overline{EP} = .302 + 22.836Z3 + 1.086Z12$$
$$\phantom{\overline{EP} = .30} (1.46) \quad\; (2.81) \qquad (2.41)$$

$$\overline{R}^2 = .1199, \quad F(2,79) = 6.52$$

where $\overline{EP}$ is the effective rate to 1820 proprietorial income (explained in appendix A) and $Z12$ is the fraction of output of the industry accounted for by New England.[49] This is the only instance in which a variable from the strict "sectional interest" theory had significance, and in view of the poor power of the equation, no great emphasis should be placed on it.

## CONCLUDING REMARKS

The results reported here are considerably more encouraging than those of McPherson (1972), who applied a "political exchange" model to 1954 and 1963 U.S. manufacturing tariffs. The two studies differ more in their economic and political context than in the models used. In 1824, the United States was embarking on a long transformation from commerce and agriculture to manufacturing. It is not possible to characterize the comparative advantage of the United States in the 1950s and 1960s in simple terms of process (manufacturing or non-manufacturing) nor factor-intensity (skill-, labor-, capital-, or resource-intensity). Some manufacturing industries have no need for protection, but, on the contrary, advocate freer trade, and so the results here are to be compared only with McPherson's on import-competing industries. For 1954 he found that higher duties were obtained by industries with fewer, geographically concentrated firms offering more employment, but that the concentration ratio (percentage of total shipments

---

[49] $Z12$ did not have significance in regression for nominal or net tariffs. In an earlier version, a more successful looking result was reported, but the form was not well justified and could suffer from some spurious correlation. Pincus (1972), pp. 178–79. Hawke (1975), p. 96, says that the 1883 Tariff Act involved a "setting of nominal tariffs in such a way that they were more influential in ranking industries in the order of the effective protection which they were accorded."

accounted for by the eight largest shippers) had a totally unexpected negative coefficient, causing him to place little reliance on the other co-efficients. A similar concentration measure (for the five largest output reports) did not have significance in 1824, although the "entropy" measure, Z8, did in some regressions, tending to be displaced, however, by the meaure, Z10, of county dispersion: location seemed more important than market shares.[50]

The Tariff Act of 1824 more faithfully reflected pressure group successes than do modern tariffs because firms today seek, besides tariffs and quotas, various subsidies, tax credits, military procurements, freeways, some of which might be more easily secured or more attractive than protection, even for import-competing industries. In other words, McPherson's dependent variable—nominal tariff rates—is only part of what his independent variables explain.

Possibly the most significant change in the process of tariff formation since 1820 has been that no longer is a new structure of rates arrived at by, as it were, a *tâtonnement* among senators and representatives. Since the 1929–30 revision, and especially since the Reciprocal Trade Acts, the tariff structure has been revised by the president in bits and pieces, and so a cross-sectional approach is less appropriate—as is, for that matter, a cross-time comparison (which McPherson also attempts) that assumes that observed values are "equilibrium" values.[51]

---

[50] The only possible but not very plausible explanation of the perverse sign on Mc-Pherson's concentration variable, apart from specification error, must be that it was a serious political disadvantage for an industry to be dominated by a few firms. McPherson (pp. 19, 20) was aware of the difficulties in predicting the signs of the coefficients of variables like Z7 (number of establishments) and Z9 and Z10 (geographical dispersion). His equation for the import competing products in 1954 was

$$y = 12.42 - 4.63N - 16.43K + 2.38E + 20.04GC + 1.94LI + 12.12D$$
$$(0.40) \quad (2.69) \quad (3.33) \quad (1.67) \quad (3.07) \quad (0.47) \quad (3.84)$$
$$\bar{R}^2 = .54, \quad n = 48$$

The independent variables, except the consumer industry dummy $D$, were in logs and were the number of firms, concentration, employment, geographical concentration, and the employment/value-added ratio.

[51] The main changes in the process of tariff formation were the Seventeenth Amendment of 1913 for direct election of senators, and the Reciprocal Trade Acts of 1934 which put tariff-making in the hands of the president, and gave a voice to foreign producers.

A final comment on the results. Beginning with Taussig, economic historians of the antebellum tariffs have had as a chief concern the theory of sectional interest: that the Congressional voting on the tariff bills in 1820 and 1824 reflected the economic interests of the various regions of the United States. Since the United States at the time was a net importer of manufactured goods, manufacturing industries were the only ones that stood to gain directly from the tariff. Some benefits might flow to the suppliers of inputs into manufacturing, but these could scarcely be the driving force behind protection. Manufacturing industries were not spread evenly throughout the nation, the South being especially deficient; that pattern had traditionally been part of the explanation of Southern hostility to the tariffs. In general, concentration of an industry in New England or the North (measured by the fraction of all counties reporting the industry) did not prove a significant explanator. However, the results throw light on a necessary condition for the theory of sectional interests, namely, that Congressional bargains were costly in a system of geographical representation.

CHAPTER SEVEN

# *Toward a Positive Theory of Tariff Change*

A N examination of the pattern of protection at a single time takes us only part way toward a theory of tariff policy. In the last century, tariffs were altered frequently in response to economic and political forces; chapter 1 presents a sketch of this.[1] This final chapter outlines a theory of tariff change for the nineteenth century that builds partly on ideas presented earlier.

Let us first recapitulate the explanation of the "static" or cross-sectional pattern of protection. The underlying comparative advantage, the accidental boost during the War of 1812, the disruptive postwar import boom, crisis, and deflation, other tariffs—all these helped fashion a certain industrial structure in the early 1820s in terms of what was produced, where, how, in what amount, and how profitably. This industrial structure in turn fashioned the pattern of tariff pressure by influencing the intensity with which expected benefits were reflected as pressure. Congressional response to pressure was conditioned by belief in the efficacy of protection and its proper place in the development and defense of the nation. The effectiveness of a particular industry's claim depended systematically on the tension, exacerbated by sectional interests, between alleged national benefits and obvious "local" advantages to specific individuals, establishments, or districts.

This cross-section model is the starting point for dynamic and historical analyses: if in time each industry went through the same stages, then the cross-section would be a good guide to the time series. The first step, therefore, is to generate a cross-section of industry structure

---

[1] What remained constant, however, was the use of import duties as almost the sole instrument of protection policy (drawbacks—duty remissions—were important to a few industries such as rum distilling in New England; only later were quotas, subsidies, and tax concessions used extensively). Also, despite the advent of tariff commissions, protection was decided by Congress; after 1934, the chief executive was given the power.

by postulating a stylized industry life-cycle—birth, maturity, decline—through shifts in comparative advantage. This "product cycle" [2] is accompanied by changes in ability and desire to obtain protection.

An adequate dynamic theory has to go further. Each product could not pass through exactly the same stages if only because the granting of protection to some early industries altered the growth and tariff of industries appearing later. The second step in the analysis, clearly, is to consider how one year's tariff influenced, through economic processes, the duties passed subsequently.

The third and last stage in the discussion is to convert a dynamic theory into a historical one by consideration of the effects on the pattern and height of protection of exogeneous shocks, especially wars, fiscal crises, and political upheavals. [3]

## GENERATING A CROSS-SECTION: INFANT INDUSTRIES

Consider a new product or process to be developed in country A (called the "advanced" country). In the early stages of the product cycle, scale of output is small, the highly skill-intensive techniques poorly explored, acceptance by consumers slow, and price high. Through improvements of the learning-by-doing type, the price falls and sales increase. In the meantime, technology has moved on and the product becomes suitable for standard, even unskilled production. The industry is relatively comfortable and achieves further scale economies through exports (after time $t_1$ in figure 7.1). Eventually, however, other products arise to draw skilled labor and capital from the now mature industry. Factor endowments at home and abroad also change, pushing the industry into a declining phase, and imports become possible. [4]

After some time, import replacement starts in the "follower" country B (figure 7.2), possibly with the aid of protection (needed because B is relatively short of the skills required, despite the simplification of pro-

[2] The term is from Vernon (1966).

[3] The "product cycle" depends on smooth, mostly exogeneous changes rather than shocks. Standard tariff histories tend to emphasize the influence of shocks on the general level of protection. Notions about endogenous forces, although present in Taussig (1931) and Stanwood (1903), are not systematically developed.

[4] We are here abstracting from protection. Note also that a phase, of zero trade around time $t_2$ is possible but is omitted for simplicity.

FIGURE 7.1

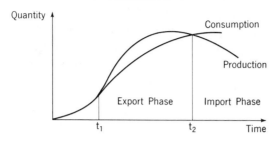

FIGURE 7.2

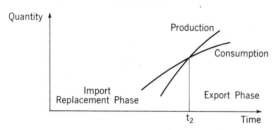

duction). With the aid of learning-by-doing, and internal and external economics of scale, the follower country may eventually become an exporter to advanced or to third countries.

A cross-section of industries, therefore, will capture different products at different stages. To give focus to the discussion and to tie in with the literature, we will concentrate on infant industries.

### Infants in the Antebellum

Infant industries exercised tariff power through cohesive groups seeking considerable and longlasting benefits. Saliency of protection was high for infants with low supply elasticities, low value-added or proprietorial income shares, and large imports to displace. Cohesiveness was high for those with geographically and industrially concentrated establishments. But some of these same characteristics increased legislative resistance to narrow interests.[5] In contrast, well-established industries (in this cross-sectional analysis) had less cohesive pressure

[5] Resistance was moderated to the extent that the electorate desired the creation of external economies.

groups but commanded more Congressional support due to their size and spread. Declining industries, those facing extinction without aid, are in a special category, because their interest in protection may well be the most intense, and their case the most appealing, even if wrong: defend us against inroads made by cheap labor, and from dumping.

It was not possible in chapter 6 to make simple arguments relating the value of output or the number of establishment to the size of duty obtained; the empirical results were complex also.[6] However, higher duties were obtained by industrially concentrated industries (a characteristic not exclusive to infants), whereas wide geographical dispersion, indicative of maturity, was associated with lower duties.[7]

There is some other evidence for the early period. Echoing Hamilton's *Report on Manufactures* (1791), Taussig concluded that

> the primary object of the protective legislation of the earlier period had been attained in 1842. The movement was, after all, only an effort, half conscious in its aim, to make more easy the transition from the state of simple agriculture and commerce which prevailed before the war of 1812, to the more diversified conditions which the operation of economic forces was reasonably certain to bring about after 1815.[8]

This is an "infant sector" not an "infant industry" argument, since for none of the industries he examined in detail (cottons, woolens, iron) did Taussig conclude that protection was essential to their successful establishment. Note that this is not exactly the question posed here, which is rather: Did infants receive special attention? A tentative answer, no, was put forward in chapter 2 in the discussion of early tariffs and Dallas's 1816 categories of industries.

Take the example, made familiar by Taussig, of the early U.S. cotton textile industry. The "first best" policy would have been to subsidize production, maybe of a pilot plant.[9] However, a textile duty may still

[6] Except when the alternative variable, Z3, a composite of output and establishments, was used. See chapter 6.

[7] Low proportional shares meant higher rates. It is not obvious how to link such low shares with the degree of infancy because they compound working proprietors' wages, returns to capital, and pure profit. The argument could be made that technologically new industries would be high in capital intensity (raising the share) but low in proprietor intensity (lowering it). In a well-established competitive industry, the last component, pure profit, would be zero. Probably the biggest influences on the proprietorial share were *temporary*, that is, business conditions in 1820.

[8] Taussig (1935), p. 106. See also Schumpeter (1951).     [9] David (1970).

have been better than nothing at all, so let us assume that was the case. It is probable that a policy of free trade which exempted textiles would not have commanded a majority in Congress, and that many inefficient tariffs (or other types of logrolling) were the price of passage.[10] That such a special trade policy obviously benefited greatly the small group of owners of textile factors of production would have contributed to the rejection of a fairly efficient outcome, that of duties on textiles alone. Effective opposition would have come less from the consumers of textiles (having to pay temporarily higher prices) than from producers in other industries.[11] Infants, therefore, had more chance of achieving protection (apart from accidents like war) through a general tariff revision. A source of infant industry tariff power—that the infant could have afforded to repay the losers, not now but in the future—was not decisive.

The fate of the 1827 woolens bill is a case in point. Conflicts between the users of fine and course wools were submerged in a strong drive for additional protection. Nevertheless, the bill was defeated by representatives of other import-competing industries, especially in the Middle Atlantic states, who were unwilling to adopt a disinterested stance. (The Tariff of 1828 should have been the vehicle for the aid sought in 1827, but its erratic design, a result of political machinations, reduced its usefulness.)

### Infants in the Postbellum

As the century progressed, the import-competitiveness of manufacturing changed, as did the industrial structure. Much more important than the effects of protection (to be discussed later) were the consequences of mineral discoveries, changes in export demand, accumulation and international flows of capital and labor, and not least, technological changes in transport, industry, and agriculture.

In the early part of the century, manufacturing was scattered, small scale, and suffering severe comparative disadvantages (which must have been worsened by the rapid growth of American exports, espe-

---

[10] Cottons did receive some special treatment, but the great protective effect of the minimum valuations was not to be forseen in 1816, depending as it did on the subsequent deflation.

[11] The argument is made in a variation on the theme of "localism." See Hartz (1948) and Scheiber (1969).

cially cotton and grains). Growth was of an extensive kind, with new establishments following the westward spread of population. What large-scale firms existed tended to locate near the eastern seaboard and were vertically integrated, producing, as did the large cotton manufacturers, their own capital, machinery, materials, and final product, and marketing their own output. After the Civil War, the northeast central states began to develop as a major urban manufacturing region. The various scattered markets became a national market with the fall in transport costs. Together with changes in technology and improvements in the capital market, the growth of domestic demand resulted in increases in specialization and scale.[12] The United States began to challenge Europe in world markets for consumers' and producers' goods.

A priori, it is difficult to predict whether the dispersion of rates of duty could have been expected to increase over the century as a result merely of changes in industrial structure (taken as exogenous).[13] Therefore, attention will be confined to the effects on the success of infants, and here the most significant change was that new industries in the later decades were less likely to be severely comparatively disadvantaged. Consequently, new industries in the postbellum period would have had less incentive to seek protection than their antebellum counterparts.

### What Facts Do We Have?

After the Civil War, the protective umbrella was extended beyond coarse cottons, woolens, hemp and bagging, iron, glass, paper, and leathergoods to some new industries: copper, nickel, steel, rails, rubber products, tinplate, and fine fabrics. The attention given by some writers to relatively few but important industries may prevent us from noticing that the list of industries in the tariff was becoming longer and longer. So widespread had the tariff become that Taussig stated that "the protective system has gradually been brought to include almost every article, whatever its character, whose production in the country

---

[12] Toward the end of the century, however, a number of industries were remarkable for vertical and horizontal integration.

[13] Greater dispersion of rates would have occurred (assuming unchanged the form of the tariff function estimated for 1824) if there had been greater dispersions across industries of output, industrial concentration, geographical concentration, tariff leverage, and ratios of imports/domestic absorption (a variable that could not be measured in 1824).

is possible." [14] In the proliferation, were infants nurtured? For the last decades of the century, Hawke (1975) did not find that higher effective protection was given to industries that subsequently grew exceptionally. Not only did early infants fail to mature sufficiently to be placed on the free list but some (like the iron industry) received additional protection long after their firm establishment in the country.[15] Latecomers, therefore, found difficulty securing particularly high rates. We now turn to the complications introduced by endogenous tariffs.

## ENDOGENOUS TARIFFS

### Contemporaneous Interaction

At a given time, the duty obtained by one industry is influenced by the duties in other industries. A final producer suffers taxes placed on intermediate inputs; it was argued in the preceding chapter that one would expect higher duties to be awarded to products with larger cost increases from this source, and indeed, such was the cause in 1824. The explanations are that such industries were more agitated over protection [16] and that Congress favored low rates on intermediates: we have direct evidence of the latter in the Congressional debates. Protection was of consumer industries in the antebellum period; after the Civil War, capital goods and other producers' goods were important.[17]

### Effects over Time

Ideally, learning-by-doing (possibly aided by a more general availability of skilled workers) should eventually have rendered protection

[14] Taussig (1935), p. 236. See also *ibid.*, pp. 174–75, on how "preposterous" errors became the "foundations of the policy of a great people."

[15] Baack and Ray (1973).

[16] Greater agitation would result from the fear of losses due to unexpectedly high input duties.

[17] The kind of external economies being sought were more apparent in the prewar consumer-goods industries: dew-rotting of flax was not as worthy of aid as attempts to weave it by power. It is worth noting that the early New England textile firms were vertically integrated, producing their own finance, water power, machinery, yarn and cloth, and acting as their own selling agents. To the extent that producers of intermediate goods enjoy increased derived demand from the protection of final products, they would add their pressure to that of the final producers themselves. There is another interaction between duties at a point in time. Just as attempts to pass a narrow tariff were fruitless (in 1827), so were attempts to pass too wide or high a tariff (in 1820). This has been fully discussed in chapter 4.

otiose. This happy result was not universal, largely because of the consequences of protection itself: once an industry received an import duty for whatever reason, its ability to secure future duties was enhanced.

*A Single Duty.* Consider the effect of protection limited to one product (or a rise in one duty only). By increasing the demand for American substitutes, an import duty resulted in some combination of higher prices and increased output, depending on the nature of domestic competition and cost conditions. Higher prices and profits increased the ability of an industry to finance a lobby but opened it to attack as a "monopoly." [18] The greatest enhancement of an expanding industry's political pull came when output grew through new locations being brought into production, rather than merely through proliferation of firms. [19] These developments were, however, complicated by questions of access to materials. Iron ore was given a relatively modest 10 percent duty in 1861, raised to 20 percent in 1870. The specific rate of 75¢ was equivalent to about 35 percent when introduced in 1883, 30 percent in 1890, and 50 percent in 1894. [20] (Later in that year the rate became 40¢.) The Lake Superior ores that fed the great steel industry of the center could not compete at the coast with Cuban ores. The protection of ore, therefore, divided the interests of coastal and interior producers. This kind of conflict was not uncommon. [21]

In understanding the cumulative effect of a duty, it is worth recalling that there is no such thing as marginal protection of a competitive in-

[18] Note the ups and downs of the Sugar Trust.

[19] Proliferation of firms is a common consequence of protection, especially of infant industries, with inevitable difficulties for a substantial proportion of the entrants. Each hopeful entrepreneur expects to solve the production difficulties fastest and to capture buyer loyalty. The Australian Tariff Board (now the Industries Assistance Commission) has recently decided that market forces under protection are too slow in weeding out the sick firms, and that a burst of import competition is needed to speed up rationalization. Tariff Board (1973).

[20] A fall in price explains the variation between 1890 and 1894. A specific duty can result in pressure for new duties if it causes the importation of more expensive substitutes: prior to the initial duty, consumers or users were unwilling to pay the price for the higher quality import; after the duty, they switch expenditure to the good that is made *relatively* cheaper.

[21] On conflicts among Northern businessmen during Reconstruction, see Coben (1959) and Sharkey (1967).

dustry: if price exceeds costs (including "normal" profit), then output expands until equality is achieved.[22] Therefore, a once-and-for-all settlement of the question of protection in the last century was unlikely. Duties were passed which temporarily boosted profits in some industries, and competition then caused a reversion to lower, "normal" levels. A subsequent decline in profitability (for whatever reason) would then have left those industries in need of further aid, and possibly with an enhanced ability to get it. Once granted, a duty may be hard to remove. These kinds of considerations disturbed Tyler and others in the 1820s, that the tariff would give rise to a more powerful tariff lobby and so on.[23]

*Many duties.* Protection was not often given in isolation, and increases in merely one or a few items were quite rare. We have argued that infant industry protection was more likely within a general tariff, but we should also note how tariffs begat tariffs.

In the first place, by reducing imports, protection was a partial substitute for exchange depreciation. Some industries that would not have suffered import competition without the tariff, did suffer it, and may have ended up with protection.[24] Secondly, there are general equilibrium repercussions to consider. A broad change in the tariff may disappoint some of the protected industries through factor price changes. Unless there are effects (which we will ignore) on supplies of primary factors of production, tariff-induced expansion of some industries must be at the expense of contraction in others, contraction that will not be confined to export industries or to industries with zero import duties. An industry will find its protection illusory if cost increases it suffers

[22] This argument makes nonsense of claims for a "scientific" or "competitive" tariff, that is, one that sets foreign and domestic producers on par. No matter how large or small, as long as the domestic industry continues to exist in the face of imports, it receives a price equal to the delivered, duty-paid price of foreign substitutes. Ex post, a duty is always "justified" by competitive cost comparisons.

[23] Were protection and other federal policies—land, banking, internal improvements—powerful in changing sectional economic interests and political power? See Passell and Schmundt (1971), Passell and Wright (1972).

[24] An exchange appreciation (or effective appreciation) has a uniform propositional effect on values-added as long as specific tariffs are fixed in terms of foreign exchange, not domestic currency (neglecting changes in input coefficients). As the exchange rate appreciates, we enlarge the set of import-competing activities by moving down the list of industries ranked by comparative advantage, rather than by re-ordering the list.

from tariff-caused factor price variations exceed the enhancement in price it enjoys from its own import duty. Therefore, an industry that is quite satisfied immediately after a new tariff act could find itself without lasting benefit. [25]

To conclude, infants may have been helped, but not especially. As they grew, they tended to retain their tariff levels (so that subsequent infants could only be assisted by obtaining higher than average duties). Further, the transition from protected import competition to exporting was impeded both by protection in export markets and by the spread of protectionism at home. The United States was more a technological follower before than after the Civil War, when it became an economy rich in capital and skill. Industries losing comparative advantage for reasons both internal and external to the United States were often able to shore themselves up with protection directed not so much against foreigners as against domestic industries successfully attracting productive factors away from the mature industries.

## FISCAL FLUCTUATIONS

Tariff agitation varied with the Treasury surplus or deficit. Customs receipts, the major revenue source, were unstable before the 1880s in consequence both of tariffs and of movements in the quantity (and to a lesser extent, price) of imports. The most striking causes of fluctuations in imports were embargoes and wars; during the latter, duties were increased substantially in an effort, more successful in the Civil War than in the War of 1812, to increase revenues. Extraordinary expendi-

---

[25] Taussig was often indignant, even surprised, when an industry that he singled out in an earlier edition of his book as having been well catered for in previous acts, begged once more for help. We may speculate whether unforeseen general equilibrium repercussions are part of the explanation. The deterioration of profitability of an industry, say industry A, as a result of duties on other products not inputs of A, depends on the disparity between the rates of duty on A and on the others, as well as on how close substitutes they are in production and consumption. Clearly, A benefits from high rates of duty on close substitutes in consumption. (It is a common characteristic of tariff schedules that substitutes in use receive similar rates of duty; this causes importers to attempt to have foreign goods reclassified, for example, by minimal embroidery on linen to distinguish it from plain linen). However, A suffers if products with similar input coefficients receive protection. (Technically, the production possibilities frontier would then be almost flat and small differences in relative output prices would lead to larger changes in the output mix.)

tures called for extraordinary revenues. Once the emergency was over, however, and Treasury surpluses appeared, tariffs were harder to reduce than they had been to raise: war rates became the norm.[26]

Imports and revenue responded to economic conditions, which in turn were attributed to protection.[27] The long slump after 1837 was blamed on the Compromise, and similar conclusions were arrived at from the near-coincidence of crises in 1857 and 1872 with tariff reductions; on the other hand, prosperity under the low Walker tariff was credited to that act. No satisfactory statistical connection has been established, however, between tariff changes and subsequent economic conditions.

Generally, it does not seem that duties, at least before the Civil War, were appreciably above their revenue-maximizing levels. When more revenue was required, rates were raised rather than lowered. Protectionist strategy was to eliminate "revenue" duties first, followed by raw material taxes if need be, and to spend or distribute any threatened excess receipts.[28] In periods of surplus, proposals for reduction

[26] Of course, the withdrawal of the South from the Union altered the composition of Congress. Some reasons for the "ratchet" effect are given above, but it should be remarked here that, as with the international balance of payments, a surplus is more readily tolerated than a deficit. Also, see Taussig (1935), pp. 192–93.

[27] No analysis of the effects of changing attitudes toward protection will be attempted. For a discussion of Congressional debates in 1824 and 1894, see Edwards (1970).

[28] Were protectionists reluctant to agree to deficit financing in wars?

During the period 1862–69 the leading spokesmen for protection—Henry C. Carey, Thaddeus Stevens, William D. Kelley, Peter Cooper—were also supporters of soft money: see Sharkey (1967), especially chapter IV. Sharkey argues that, because the rise in the greenback prices of gold (foreign exchange) was greater than the rise in domestic prices to 1864, there was an improvement in American manufacturers' competitive positions; in the deflation, the gold price fell faster than any other price, harming import-competitive industries. Therefore a number of protectionists opposed McCulloch's contraction (although New England manufacturers were not so keen on higher tariffs and soft money).

The advantages for import-competing industries of having the gold price at 200 for seven years (as Carey desired in 1865) flow from the avoidance of problems in the *transition* to a lower exchange rate and price level, not from the high price of gold itself. In the movement from a lower to a higher gold price, brought about by expansion of the domestic money supply, manufacturers could benefit if their costs rose slower than their prices, and if they were, on balance, debtors. But before seven years were up, exchange rate, price and cost relationships would have been restored, and the advantages of soft money evaporated. (Of course, domestic inflation under fixed exchange rates would have been a different matter, and detrimental to the same manufacturing interests.)

abounded when opponents attempted to remove the revenue-raising burden from manufactured imports, but they were not always successful.

## POLITICS

To explore fully the relationship between the economics and the politics of protection is beyond this book. However, we can note some of the chief reasons for increases and declines in the strength of the protectionist element in nineteenth-century politics: changes in attitudes, in political alignments, and attention.[29]

Protectionists benefited until the 1830s from being members of a successful coalition of interests, a coalition that had sectional lines— Northeastern manufacturers and Westerners whose voices were strengthened by westward movements of population. This coalition weakened for a number of reasons, not the least being that the South made it clear that the spoils would be hard won, and that the West became less convinced of the benefits of the American System.

The removal of Southern representatives and senators upon secession and war silenced passionate opponents. This great political upheaval had lasting effects on protection, for reasons outlined earlier. Protection had a double justification in the Civil War, as revenue, and as compensation for internal taxes. The restoration of the Democrats to power did not lead to significant revisions, chiefly owing to the distraction of silver. The antiprotectionists could not capture attention.

Finally, we must consider the effects of tariffs or tariff politics. Embedded in the explanation of the structure of 1824 are elements of an endogenous, cyclical kind already alluded to at the end of chapter 5. Recall that an asymmetry in responses to tariff gains and losses seems necessary for a theory to predict any import duties at all: roughly, that beneficiaries were more alert to the hope of gain than loser to the prospect of equal loss. Now, from the point of view of the model in chapter 6 it was not necessary for losers to be totally inert. On the contrary, some reaction to substantial losses was essential if all tariffs were not to be prohibitive, *and could have taken the form of future support of less*

---

[29] The following two paragraphs need to be read in conjunction with the last section of chapter 1.

*protectionist candidates and parties.* That is, response to tariffs was partly a delayed counterattack (possibly an attack on the policy of protection itself, rather than being solely directed at the particular tariff item or tariff bill). Therefore, losses imposed by a tariff act may have sparked forces that subsequently destroyed or modified the act. The protectionists, however, were relatively easily mobilized for another onslaught. And so on.

The increasing number of industries pressing for protection could, theoretically, have had an effect on the method of granting it. In his well-known review of the work of Bauer, Pool, and Dexter, Lowi classified the "traditional" tariff as "distributive," that is to say, favors were dispensed

> unit by small unit, each unit more or less in isolation from other units and from any general rule. . . . [Distributive policies are those] in which the indulged and the deprived, the loser and the recipient, need never come into direct confrontation. . . . They are policies that are virtually not policies at all but are highly individualized decisions that only by accumulation can be called a policy.[30]

Contrasting with distributive policies are "regulation" and "redistribution," both of which involve conflict between the indulged and the deprived—in regulation, between basic industrial sectors; in redistribution, between social classes.

Tariffs from 1789 to 1842 do not fit Lowi's distributive category. Detailed decisions were made, but not piecemeal, not in isolation and "without regard to limited resources." Southern planters and Northern merchants were active in opposition. There was a limit to the duties passed, therefore, because individual decisions were seen to add up to a policy, a policy of protection that supported other decisions inimical to the planters' economic and social interests.

The conflict that blew up in 1832 was resolved temporarily by the Compromise, whereby duties were progressively lowered until 1842. A new, higher tariff passed in 1842 was soon replaced by the Walker rates which were, in effect, a broad set of regulations. This sequence gives some support to the suggestion by Salisbury and Heinz (1970), following Lowi, of a tendency for a fragmented decisional system (such

[30] Lowi (1964), p. 690.

as characterized tariff-making before 1833 or 1846) to give way to an integrated or regulatory one as the number of minute decisions increases. The support is meager, however, because in 1861 the system reverted to its old style, to remain essentially unchanged, despite Tariff Commissions, until the Reciprocal Trade Amendment of 1934.[31] The feedback from decisions to the decision mechanism was weak and slow.

[31] Reciprocity provisions in the McKinley Tariff were removed in 1894. No serious use was made of the flexibility provisions of the Fordney-McCumber Act of 1922. Ratner (1972), pp. 38, 49. The tariff does not fit the full sequence proposed by Salisbury and Heinz (1970) as easily as does, for example, the Ohio canal policy: Scheiber (1968). The sequence goes something like this. A policy is initiated that is (possibly) justified on grounds of economic efficiency but that has very uneven distributional effects. In the early stages, it is used temperately, but as pressure builds up for its extension, criteria are relaxed. More and more groups successfully lobby for inclusion, until the legislature finds itself unable to give any great consideration to individual cases, and develops short-hand methods of decision, delegates authority, or becomes a passive partner through general legislation. Eventually, a revulsion may occur, and the policy be abandoned.

# The Redistributive Effects of Tariffs

THERE are five sections to this appendix. The first discusses the partial equilibrium concept of the net tariff (the numerator of the effective rate of protection), the separate bits of which were used in chapters 4 and 6. The second introduces derived demand. The Stolper-Samuelson theorem and Travis's (1968) method, alternatives to the use of net tariffs, are discussed in the third and fourth sections, the former being found insufficiently rich in information and the latter being confined to qualitative statements only. The final section discusses the relationship between nominal and effective tariffs. The objective of the appendix is to explain the use of partial equilibrium international trade theory and to investigate alternatives. Readers familiar with trade theory will find this appendix easy going; the third section should not be skipped by the general reader.

## SYMBOLS USED IN APPENDIX A

$\hat{} =$ the proportionate rate of change of the variable over which it appears

$* =$ a value under free trade, excepting $T^*$

$a_{ij} =$ input coefficients of factor $i$ (any factor), $v$ (value-added), and $m$ (the intermediate factor) in the unit output of $j$

$\delta_i =$ proportionate increase in $P_i$ which reduces to zero the rent in industries having $i$ as input

$\delta_i$ max $=$ maximum nonredundant tariff at stage $i$, assuming the tariff on the final stage is fully utilized

$EP'_j =$ proportionate rate of change of unit value-added using free trade input coefficients and goods prices, and the assumption that $\sigma_j = 0$

$\widetilde{EP}_j =$ proportionate rate of change of unit value-added allowing for input substitution

$EP_j =$ proportionate rate of change in unit value-added, using tariff-deflated protected input coefficients

$\overline{EP}_j = EP_j$, except protected net price is used as dominator

$\Theta_{hj} =$ cost-shares of factor $h$ per unit output of $j$; $h = i, m, v$ as above;
$\qquad$ $h = \pi$ for profit or rent share

$g_{kj} = k^{\text{th}}$ direct-plus-indirect coefficient for industry $j$

$P_h =$ price of products $h = j, i, m$

$p_j =$ Travis's notation for the price of $j$

$R_{ij} =$ cost-share tariff-deflated, equals $(1+t_j)/(1+t_i)$

$S_j =$ market value of domestic output of good $j$, before the tariffs

$S'_j =$ market value of output $j$ net of intermediate usage of $j$

$S_{ji} =$ intermediate usage of $j$

$\sigma_j =$ elasticity of substitution between inputs $m$ and $v$

$T^* =$ net tariff calculation using free-trade input coefficients

$\overline{T}_j =$ net tariff using tariff-deflated protected coefficients

$t_h =$ ad valorem tariff on goods $h = j, i, m$

$\tau_{hk} =$ partial effective rate of a tariff $t_h$ on industry $k$

$V_h =$ money value-added in $h$

$w_k = k^{\text{th}}$ primary factor price

$X_j =$ physical quantity corresponding to $S_j$

## NET TARIFFS AND EFFECTIVE PROTECTION

Protection has at least two meanings: the change in the output mix, and the change in factor incomes that result from tariffs; we are interested here in the former only insofar as it throws light on factor prices and employment. Not only the tariff on the output, but also the tariffs on the purchased material inputs may alter the incomes of the factors of production used in the manufacture of an import-competing product, so we need a way to sum up the influence of the whole set of tariffs. A tariff on the importation of a foreign good will generally be welcomed by the domestic import-competing industry, but tariffs on inputs will not. The former tariff protects, the latter does the opposite; what is the net effect?

This question has been dealt with in chapter 4, where the concept "net tariff" was derived. To recapitulate, the "net price" of good $j$ before import duties is (assuming the landed prices $P_j^*$ and $P_i^*$ are fixed)

$$P_j^* - \sum_i P_i^* a_{ij} \qquad\qquad (A.1)$$

and the net price after the tariff is

$$P_j^*(1+t_j) - \sum_i a_{ij} P_i^* (1+t_i) \tag{A.2}$$

where the $t$'s are the ad valorem rates of duty. Subtracting and normalizing by $P_j^*$, we have $T_j^*$, the net tariff using observed free-trade coefficients:

$$T_j^* = t_j - \sum_i t_i \Theta_{ij}^* \tag{A.3}$$

where $\Theta_{ij}^* \equiv a_{ij} P_i^*/P_j^*$ and are the cost-shares before the tariff.[1]

Let the physical quantity of domestic output be $X_j$ and its value prior to protection be $S_j$, then the change in the money value of the pool available to pay primary inputs is

$$T_j^* S_j = T_j^* P_j^* X_j \tag{A.4}$$

before any other than price adjustments have been made. In chapter 4, this was called the *impact* of the tariffs on values-added.

An important variation on the net tariff is the effective rate. Corden (1971) defines the effective rate of protection as the proportional change in the *net price* (what he calls the "effective price"), not in the *unit value-added*, on the grounds that a change in the latter compounds what it is desirable to keep separate: a change in the prices of value-added factors and a change in their input coefficients. In a partial equilibrium framework, Grubel and Lloyd (1971) derive the formula for the rate of change of the price of the single, specific, primary factor of each industry, assumed available in imperfectly elastic supply (p. 96). There are some difficulties with their model.[2] If we are content with knowing the change in unit value-added, then the result is

$$t_j + (1-\sigma_j) \cdot \frac{\Theta_{mj}^*}{1-\Theta_{mj}^*} \cdot (t_j - t_m) \tag{A.5}$$

where $\sigma_j$ is the elasticity of substitution between the single, specific, primary factor and the single intermediate good, $m$, and $\Theta_{mj}^*$ is the cost

---

[1] See Taussig (1931), pp. 75 and 194–218, for the application of a similar calculation to woolens.

[2] Because their formula (10), p. 97, does not involve the elasticity of supply of the primary factor, implicitly the elasticity is zero. Otherwise their attempt to capture only the change in price of the primary factor must be invalid, since it neglects supply. But if the primary factor is in perfectly inelastic supply, then why worry about the distinction between changes in unit value-added and changes in the price of value-added?

share of $m$ in free trade. A similar expression can be derived using protected values.[3] Effective protection was designed to enable inferences to be made about free-trade values and quantities from a knowledge of protected values and quantities, or vice versa. It is not as much a partial equilibrium concept as a method of partial information: the Corden concept requires complete knowledge of the production or cost functions, and is thus of less practical interest than a mismatched measure combining, say, equilibrium protected input coefficients with free-trade goods prices and tariffs. The justification of such mismatches is the assumption of fixed coefficients; alternatively, the rationale is that they measure the impact of a change in tariffs in the short run (all primary factors fixed in their present occupations).

No attempts were made to allow for input substitution, but some idea of the size of the bias can be gathered. Because the input coefficients from the *Digest of Manufactures* (1820) are used in chapters 4 and 6, we have neither free-trade nor equilibrium protected input coefficients in the work on the tariff of 1824, but something in between, which is closer, however, to the latter. Instead of $T_j^*$ we use $\bar{T}_j$:

$$\bar{T}_j = t_j - \sum_i t_i \Theta_{ij} R_{ij} \tag{A.6}$$

where

$$R_{ij} = \frac{1+t_j}{1+t_i}$$

$R_{ij}$ "deflates" the 1820 cost-share, $\Theta_{ij}$, to provide an estimate of the free-trade cost-share. If the elasticity of substitution is zero, then $T_j^*$ and $\bar{T}_j$ are equal. On the other hand, if the elasticity is equal to unity, the cost-share is a constant because the production function is now Cobb-Douglas, and the difference between the two measures is given in (A.7):

$$T_j^* - \bar{T}_j = \Theta_{mj} t_m (R_{ij} - 1) \tag{A.7}$$

---

[3] Formula (A. 5) is derived in Pincus (1972), pp. 192–95. The net tariff (A. 3) can be modified to include $\sigma_j$ by using the expression for the rate of change in the material input coefficient:

$$\hat{a}_{mj} = \sigma_j(t_j - t_m)$$

Thus $\overline{T}_j$ is an overestimate [4] in a Cobb-Douglas model if

$$R_{ij} < 1$$

that is,

$$t_j < t_m$$

It is fortunate if the researcher has observations on input coefficients under both free trade and the tariffs. If the latter only are available, it seems advisable to avoid a protective rate formula, $\widetilde{EP}$, which "deflates" the observed protected coefficients:

$$EP_j = \frac{t_j - t_m \Theta_{mj} R_{mj}}{1 - \Theta_{mj} R_{mj}} \tag{A.8}$$

$\widetilde{EP}$ explodes when

$$\frac{1 + t_j}{1 + t_m} \equiv R_{mj} \rightarrow \frac{1}{\Theta_{mj}}$$

($\Theta_{mj}$ is the observed cost-share after the tariffs). An alternative, used in chapter 6, which was proposed by Soligo and Stern (1965) to avoid some complications of negative rates, but which does not explode, is $\overline{EP}$:

$$\overline{EP}_j = \frac{t_j - t_m \Theta_{mj} R_{mj}}{1 - \Theta_{mj}} \tag{A.9}$$

## THE SMALL COUNTRY ASSUMPTION AND DERIVED DEMAND

We are interested in the total variation in value-added in the industry, so we have to multiply the per unit variation by the number of units of output. $\overline{T}_j S_j$ is the change in the money value of value-added in industry $j$, $S_j$ being the sales or output value before the tariff. If the number of units produced changes, then this may be a biased estimate: industries with high net tariffs might be expected to have large output increases, industries with small net tariffs might suffer output de-

---

[4] As an example of the size of the error, assume that $\sigma_j = 1$, $t_j = .4$, $t_m = .2$, $\Theta_{mj} = .8$; then $T_j^* = .24$, and $T_j^* - \overline{T}_j = .025$.

creases.[5] Considerable literature has been published recently which examines whether the *EP* is a reliable predictor of output changes, or resource reallocation; rather than reviewing it, let us investigate some more elementary problems with *EP* and the net tariff, which have to do with the partial equilibrium interpretation and involve output changes.

Anderson (1970) has shown that even if the world were characterized by the assumption of fixed input coefficients, the usual formula for *EP* could not accurately predict resource reallocation, because the "small country" assumption on prices is inconsistent with general equilibrium: when there are $r$ primary factors of production, and $n$ goods $(n > r)$, in general equilibrium we can expect no more than $r$ goods in a small country to be produced at prices (= costs) equal to the parametric world price $P_j^*$ times unity plus the ad valorem tariff. The model has even more serious problems than those spelled out by Anderson. Attempting to interpret *EP* as the change in rent as a proportion of free-trade value-added, Anderson identifies the short run as the period within which one factor of production (capital) cannot be augmented. With fixed coefficients, and all factors fully utilized initially, this assumption ensures that output cannot increase; however, outputs can decrease. There are still variable costs in this model, unless there exist contracts which prohibit the short-run downward variation in the supply or purchase of factors: the supply schedules of factors would have to be vertical. Otherwise, whenever the net price falls so low that the gross price does not cover variable costs, profit-maximizing behavior in the short run would reduce output to zero. Putting it another way, output would fall to zero if the fall in the net price were greater than the pre-tariff profit or rent.

The discussion so far has accepted the small country assumption: the domestic price of any imported good is equal to the parametric foreign price $P^*$ times unity plus the tariff:[6]

$$P_j = P_j^* \ (1 + t_j).$$

---

[5] In standard trade theory, output is cost of supply determined; demand is neglected except in models with nontraded goods.

[6] For a trenchant criticism of the use of this assumption, see Norman (1974). Norman, in effect, wishes to assert as a more reasonable assumption that domestic output is, strictly, nontraded, but less than perfectly substitutable for imports.

Is this a reasonable assumption, within a short-run partial equilibrium model? I wish to investigate some circumstances under which the domestic manufacturers of import-competing products will not raise their prices to the full extent of the tariff, and the tariff becomes wholly or partly redundant. The focus of the analysis is on the concept of derived demand.

Intermediate factors of production face derived demand, and their ability to take advantage of a tariff on competing imports depends on the elasticity of that derived demand. If the output of the industries using the intermediate falls to zero, then the output of the intermediate must also fall to zero, and the tariff is of no benefit to the producers of the intermediate output.[7] The output of an industry will fall to zero if the fall in the net price is greater than the pre-tariff rent. But the net price can fall only if the output tariff falls and/or input prices rise. Confining ourselves to the partial equilibrium, fixed coefficients model, and disregarding the possibility of decreases in tariffs, it is obvious that the domestic producers of inputs would not take full advantage of their own tariffs if to do so forced their own customers out of production.

It is worthwhile to explore the derived demand argument in a more rigorous framework. Assume that the matrix of the fixed input coefficients is triangular. Let industry $j$ use input $i$ and, for simplicity, assume that no tariffs other than $t_j$ and $t_i$ exist. The variation in unit value-added in $j$ is

$$dP_j - a_{ij}dP_i$$

or in proportional terms,

$$\hat{P}_j - \Theta_{ij}\hat{P}_i \tag{A.10}$$

If there were no tariff on good $j$, and foreign supply were perfectly elastic, then any increase in the price $P_i$ would make domestic producers of good $j$ uncompetitive with imports, unless the increase in $P_i$ were absorbed by the rents in $j$. The producers of $j$, with no tariff on their output, cannot pass on any of the cost increase occasioned by the increase in $P_i$. The best that the input producers can do is to reduce the rents in $j$ to zero, which occurs when the proportionate increase in $P_i$ is $\delta_i$

---

[7] It is assumed the intermediate product is import-competing.

$$\delta_i = \frac{\Theta_{\pi j}}{\Theta_{ij}} \tag{A.11}$$

where $\Theta_{\pi j}$ is the pre-tariff rents share in industry $j$. $\delta_i$ is found by reducing the rent in $j$ to zero, that is, setting the rent share before the tariff equal to the proportional variation in rents given by (A.10). More generally, if the proportional variation in $P_j$ is $\delta_j$, we have

$$\delta_i = \min\left(t_i, \frac{\delta_j + \Theta_{\pi j}}{\Theta_{ij}}\right) \tag{A.12}$$

The extent to which an industry can raise its price above that of foreign supplies is determined not only by its own tariff, but also by the tariffs and rents in all subsequent stages in the production process.

Iteration of (A.11) using (A.12) yields the *maximum nonredundant tariff* at any stage $j$ as

$$\delta_j \max = t_n \left[ \prod_{k=j}^{n-1} \Theta_{k\,k+1} \right]^{-1} + \sum_{i=j+1}^{n} \Theta_{\pi i} \left[ \prod_{k=j}^{i-1} \Theta_{k\,k+1} \right]^{-1} \tag{A.13}$$

assuming that the tariff on the final good, $t_n$, is totally utilized. This formula requires that all

$$\delta_k \max = t_k, \quad k = j, \ldots, n$$

Such a set of tariffs would enable the $j^{\text{th}}$ stage to capture all the benefit of the tariff on the final stage, plus all the rents in any industry using $j$, directly or indirectly, as an input. Since all cost-shares are less than unity, $\delta_j$ max can be quite large in comparison with $t_m$.

To illustrate the use of the ideas just outlined, take the case where the stage $j$ is a nontraded input, and all tariffs on it would be redundant (say, iron ore). What interest have the owners of iron ore deposits in the tariffs on pig iron, bar iron, or axes? Tariffs on these direct or indirect users of ore allow increases in the pool of value-added that the ore producers might be in the position to appropriate. This possibility is overlooked in the usual *EP* literature, because it confines its attention to the economic relations between one stage and the next, ignoring the derived demand for outputs using inputs with a tariff.[8]

Formula (A.13) has the ore owners appropriating not only the increase in rents occasioned by the tariffs, but also the rents that existed

---

[8] Corden (1971) does make some comments along this line. See also Ray (1974).

before the tariff. If they are able to do the latter, then the tariff was not necessary to reduce all other stages to zero rents—the ore owners clearly had monopsony power. (They do not have to fear imports of ore, by assumption.) A more interesting case might be one where the ore owners wish to achieve a proportional increase in their own price, $\hat{P}_i$, consistent with leaving rents in all other stages unchanged. This is achieved when the net tariffs on all stages above ore are zero. Solving yields a *"harmonious set" of nonredundant nominal tariffs* with respect to $\hat{P}_i$:

$$t_j = \hat{P}_i \prod_{k=i}^{j-1} \Theta_{k\,k+1} \qquad j > i \qquad\qquad (A.14)$$

assuming that all goods for $j > i$ are import-competing.

Formula (A.13) assumes that the elasticity of demand for the final output is zero, and that the final tariff is fully utilized. Redundancy or partial redundancy of the tariff on the final good modifies the analysis, as does consideration of less restrictive supply assumptions. These points are not further pursued.

## DIVISION OF THE SPOILS: STOLPER-SAMUELSON

The central question for the theory of tariff formation is how the rent pool made available by tariffs is divided up. In general competitive equilibrium, the answer depends on the solution of the whole system describing the economy, because competition bids away any differential rent, that is, equalizes factor rentals across industries: for example, by the Stolper-Samuelson theorem (discussed next paragraph), in a two-good world, a tariff on an import that uses relatively much labor would increase wages. The benefits to labor from a tariff on a particular product would be dispersed throughout the whole economy if labor were perfectly industry nonspecific. For the reasons discussed in chapter 3, there would be a small effort (in proportion to the benefits) by common labor for tariffs which benefit large numbers of people, many of whom might not be employed in the industries obtaining a tariff. The benefits to the workers in the protected industries cannot be fully appropriated by them if there is a competitive labor market. What matters then is how tariffs affect rents, not value-added.

The Stolper-Samuelson theorem is sufficiently well known not to require a lengthy exposition. It predicts the change in primary factor prices (or, more strictly, factor rentals) from the nominal tariff and data on the production functions (factor intensities). For example, if the labor-capital ratio is higher in the production of the import-competing good than in the exported good, an increase in the domestic price of the imported good will, under certain assumptions, cause an increase in the "real" wage rate, where real means the money wage rate deflated by any goods price index. Although the original theorem was proved for a model with primary factors of production only, it has been extended to allow for simple input-output relations, but is still within the confines of models with small and equal numbers of primary factors and goods; to increase the numbers of goods and factors to three, Philip (1969) had to assume some "holes" in the matrix of direct primary factor input coefficients, which indicate that some primary factors of production are specific to some subset of the industries. Although all factor rewards are "rents" in a model with fixed factor endowments, it is reasonable to speak of product-specific factors as earning rents in the usual sense, so that these models with holes partly bridge the gap between the typical general equilibrium models (with all factors nonspecific), and the partial equilibrium, effective protection models (all primary factors product-specific).

The general equilibrium models, even with holes in the matrix of input coefficients, do not provide sufficient detail for prediction of the effects of a large number of tariffs. Rather than follow the general competitive equilibrium route, consider what happens when there are industry-specific factors of production, especially factors in very inelastic supply and essential to production (e.g., marble for burial monuments). These factors are, as it were, the residual legatees of the industry, whose fortunes depend on what happens in the industry in a much more direct sense than for any perfectly nonspecific factor.[9] Specific factors have, naturally, a special interest in *their* tariffs. Specific factors will not act passively but will attempt to maximize rent or profits by varying output, prices, or input mixes, which would make $\bar{T}_j S_j$ tend to underestimate the increase in the rent pool made possible by tariffs.

In the regressions of chapter 6, since I am concerned ultimately with

[9] Evans's (1971) model, a linear program, is of this character, but allows some primary factor prices to be endogenous.

the explanation of the Act of 1824, the dependent variable is usually the set of nominal tariffs, not net tariffs or effective rates. The other elements of the effective rate formula—the cost of input tariffs and the value-added shares—do enter, as explanatory variables, however. One thing should be noted in view of the discussion in chapter 5 about the importance of specific factors. It is usual to regard the effective rate as protection to value-added. If there are specific factors, then it seems more appropriate to consider effective protection to rents or profits. Not only is it in accord with price theory to worry about profits or rents, but also it fits better with my own interest in the causes rather than the effects of tariffs. The effective protection concept emphasizes that a certain net tariff means a small proportionate boost to value-added in an industry which already has a large value-added share, and a large boost in an industry with a small value-added share. Going further, we can say that a given effective rate (to value-added) means a larger proportionate boost to rent, the smaller is the initial rent share, assuming that the specific factors appropriate the benefits of the tariffs. It is assumed in chapter 6 that all the benefits of tariffs are appropriated by the residual income claimant called "the proprietor."

## TRAVIS

Travis (1968) rejects effective protection for a number of reasons, and claims to test whether a tariff structure protects a general factor (i.e., not product-specific to any proper subset of industries), say labor, by correlating the direct-plus-indirect labor input coefficients with the nominal tariff rates. A high positive correlation is taken to indicate that the tariff structure protects labor, that is, raises the wage rate above its free-trade level (pp. 453–61). The argument is in two parts: the first is to show a causal link between product prices and primary factor prices; the second is to derive the appropriate test. I will treat them in that order.

Let $r$ be the number of primary factors, regarding any intermediate factor not produced at home as a primary factor (p. 454). Let $n > r$ be the number of goods, both final and intermediate, produced at home. Then the cost functions of the economy can be written as

$$\mathbf{p} = H\mathbf{w} \tag{A.15}$$

where **p** is the vector of goods prices (equal costs), **w** is the vector of primary factor prices, and $H$ is the $n \times r$ matrix of direct-plus-indirect primary-factor input coefficients, the elements $g_{kj}$ of which depend only on the relative factor prices $\mathbf{w}_k$. Since $H$ is not invertible, the factor prices, **w**, cannot be solved from the product prices but, as Travis argues,

> Any $r$ commodity prices and the corresponding $r \times r$ submatrix of $H(\mathbf{w})$ can be picked out to obtain a potentially invertible system which will give all $r$ factor wages a function of the chosen prices. . . . The determinant of the chosen submatrix of $H(\mathbf{w})$ . . . may conceivably disappear for some particular set of $\mathbf{w}_k$'s so that it is possible that a given vector of $r$ $\mathbf{p}_j$'s can correspond to more than one vector **w**. It would be extraordinary, however, if more than one vector **w** appeared for all the $n!/r!(n-r)!$ combinations of prices taken $r$ at a time from a set of $n$ prices if $n$ greatly exceeded $r$. We can call that set, $w$, the set of factor prices uniquely determined by the price vector, which in turn will depend on the trade policy of the country (pp. 449–50).

The last sentence is not perfectly clear, but I interpret it to mean that the set of equations $\mathbf{p} = H\mathbf{w}$ *can* in fact be solved for a unique vector **w** in terms of a given vector of product prices **p**, despite the noninvertibility of $H$. *Travis envisages trade policy as the selection of the protection that is to be given to the primary factors,* that is, a choice of **w**; this is achieved by choice of a suitable set of $r$ commodity prices; the other $n-r$ commodity prices are then found from the cost functions, and are in a sense the residuals. [Of course, we cannot guarantee that, even if the $r$ commodity prices are equal to the (exogenous) world price plus the tariff, the remaining commodity prices will bear this small country relationship, as Anderson has pointed out. Some of the goods will cease to be produced at home, and some of them will become nontraded, their prices determined by the demand.] Thus Travis writes $\mathbf{p} = H\mathbf{w}$, for which he is criticized by Balassa, Guisinger, and Schydlowsky (1970), who seem to be arguing that the small country assumption is the only condition needed for factor prices to be determined by product prices. Considering the inclusive definition of primary factors (noncompeting imported intermediates in addition to the usual primary factors), we may reinterpret the small country assumption to mean that the number of factors not *produced* at home (i.e., $r$) is no less than the number of products produced at home (i.e., $n$), *and* that foreign excess demands have infinite elasticity. The first requirement may be met if the country is very open to trade, but certainly the United States in this century does not meet either requirement, and probably did not in the last.

Having concluded that the system

$$\mathbf{p} = H\mathbf{w} \qquad\qquad\qquad\qquad (A.16)$$

can be solved for one and only one $\mathbf{w}$ in terms of a country's trade policy (that is, $\mathbf{w}$ is chosen, a set of $r$ $\mathbf{p}_j$'s is solved for, and the other goods prices are made to conform with these two sets), Travis then states that the correct test of the factoral protection of a tariff structure is the correlation of the direct-plus-indirect input coefficient (say for labor) with the nominal tariffs. (Presumably tariffs on noncompeting imported inputs should be eliminated, since they alter their respective $\mathbf{w}$'s directly, that is, such products are primary factors). The justification for the test is that, assuming the production functions are linear homogeneous in the relevant range, the cost functions imply that

$$\frac{\partial \mathbf{p}_j}{\partial \mathbf{w}_k} = g_{kj}(\mathbf{w}) \qquad\qquad\qquad (A.17)$$

where $g_{kj}$ are the elements of $H$, the matrix of direct-plus-indirect inputs of factor $k$ into product $j$. What is wanted, however, is the inverse relationship, $\partial \mathbf{w}_k / \partial \mathbf{p}_j$, or more strictly, $d\mathbf{w}_k / d\mathbf{p}_j$.

An argument for Travis's test can be made as follows: A rise in the prices $\mathbf{p}_j$ relative to some good's price as numeraire (say $\mathbf{p}_o$) would shift the derived demand curve for factor $k$ to the right, by an amount which depends on the total $k$-intensity of $j$ compared with $o$. Similarly, the derived demand for the factor $k$ is diminished for goods suffering a relative price decline. If products using much of factor $k$ are in general the object of larger price increases than are products relatively nonintensive in $k$, then there is a presumption that the aggregate (across products) derived demand for factor $k$ has shifted to the right, and, assuming less than infinite supply elasticity, the real wage in terms of the numeraire will rise.

The argument is incomplete, however, because the $g_{kj}$ coefficients indicate the shift in the derived demand for the labor *per unit of output*

$j$, and thus the presumption could be overturned if there is a strong negative correlation between the direct-plus-indirect coefficients $g_{kj}$, and the size of the industry, measured by the number of units of output $X_j$. This negative correlation is just what is expected to be the case under free trade, if factor $k$ is the scarce factor and the Heckscher-Ohlin theory of comparative advantage can be applied. A more secure test of the Travis model for the protective effect of a set of tariffs, one that does not require the prior identification of the scarce factor, would be a correlation of the nominal tariffs, $t_j$, with the total use of factor $k$ in the production of $j$, that is, $g_{kj}X_j$.

This refined test assumes, as does Travis implicitly, that the elasticities of output supply are not strongly inversely correlated with the nominal tariffs themselves. The nominal tariffs are to be used as indicators of the direction and size of the shifts in the demand for the primary factors of production. However, if *product-specific factors* are more likely to be able to obtain favorable tariffs than general or mobile factors, and use their monopoly or monopsony power (the basis of "tariff power") to appropriate to themselves the increase in value-added afforded by the tariff, rather than allow it to be dissipated by output increases, then this would weaken the relationship between $t_j$ and the increase in the demand for primary factors, and weaken the modified Travis test of factoral protection.

Finally, notice that if the Travis test is to be used to estimate the change in the factor prices, we need to know elasticities of factor supply. As it stands, Travis's method is confined to qualitative statements such as "Labor was more protected than capital by the United States tariffs of 1960." For empirical estimation of tariff-induced redistribution, Travis's method seems less useful than the net tariff approach.

## EFFECTIVE PROTECTION AND NOMINAL
## AD VALOREM RATES

It might be argued that legislatures or tariff-making bodies have attempted to generate a set of net tariffs or effective rates, but still issue a list of nominal rates designed to accomplish that end.[10] The next part

[10] The contemporary Australian Industries Assistance Commission is making such an attempt.

of the appendix explores, in a fixed coefficients model, the relationship between a set of nominal rates and a set of effective rates, and the circumstance under which one can be solved for in terms of the other. There may be no unique way to generate a set of effective rates from nominal rates, that is, there may be a number of different sets of nominal rates all of which yield the same set of effective rates. (A similar statement can be made about the set of net tariffs.)

Let the transposed vector of nominal ad valorem tariffs be $\mathbf{t}'$ where

$$\mathbf{t}' = (t_1, \ \ldots \ , t_K)$$

The transposed vector of proportionate value-added changes, or effective protection rates is $\hat{\mathbf{V}}'$:

$$\hat{\mathbf{V}}' = (\hat{V}_1, \ \ldots \ , \hat{V}_N)$$

By the definition of effective protection, we have

$$\hat{\mathbf{V}} = \Theta \cdot \mathbf{t} \qquad\qquad (A.18)$$

$$\text{where} \quad \Theta = \begin{bmatrix} \dfrac{1}{\Theta_{v1}} - \dfrac{\Theta_{21}}{\Theta_{v1}} & \cdots & -\dfrac{\Theta_{K1}}{\Theta_{v1}} \\[2ex] -\dfrac{\Theta_{12}}{\Theta_{v2}} & \dfrac{1}{\Theta_{v2}} & \cdots \\ \vdots \\ -\dfrac{\Theta_{1N}}{\Theta_{vN}} & \cdots & -\dfrac{\Theta_{KN}}{\Theta_{vN}} \end{bmatrix}$$

$\Theta_{ij}$ is the share of factor $i$ in the unit cost of output $j$

$i = 1, \ \ldots \ , K$   being the intermediate inputs

$i = v$   for the value-added input

$j = 1, \ \ldots \ , N$   the outputs

Wherever they agree, the subscripts on $t_i$ and $\hat{V}_j$ refer to the same product; however, if we take the actual tariffs (i.e., list of duties on importables) then there will be some tariffs for which there are no corresponding domestic industries, no $V_j$ ($\Theta_{vj}$ equals zero), and there will be some outputs for which there are no tariffs. The former means that the importable good is "noncompeting" with domestic industries, and it may be desirable to remove the good from the vector $\mathbf{t}'$, and treat the import when used as an input, as a part of value-added. There is some excuse for this. Effective protection measures the maximum increase in the pool of income (quasi-rent) available for the value-added factors as a result of the imposition of the set of tariffs. The increase is available to value-added factors, but not intermediate factors, under the assumption that foreign excess supply equations are perfectly elastic; the same assumption must be made for the "noncompeting" importables. Yet, from the viewpoint of the domestic economy, these noncompeting goods are "primary," since they are not produced at home, and thus have the same status in the input-output structure as the primary factors, ordinarily defined. Tariffs on these noncompeting goods can be regarded as representing the Treasury's share of the increased pool of quasi-rents that the set of tariffs has caased. The tariffs on noncompeting imports would be revenue tariffs only; however, they do affect the net tariff and *EP* available to the using industries, so it seems desirable to leave them in the vector of tariffs to be explained.

It would be desirable to have the matrix $\Theta$ invertible, which requires that the number of nonredundant tariffs be equal to the number of domestic industries. Clearly, this could be achieved by removing all noncompeting tariffs, and adding to $t'$ a zero tariff for all import-competing industries that did not otherwise have a tariff and for all exportables and nontraded goods that are produced at home. To some extent, the latter has already been done through the inclusion by the legislature of some duties that are there either as a show of legislative favor or because some industry feared future foreign competition (maybe because of actual past competition). But there are some industries with no tariff. The disadvantage of assigning a zero tariff to them is that the model of tariff formation then becomes partly a model to explain which goods are traded; in other words, a lot of noise is introduced into the system. The advantage of having $K$ equal $N$ and the modified matrix of the cost-shares square, is that we can write

$$t = \Theta^{-1}\hat{V} \qquad\qquad (A.19)$$

where $t$ is now a vector of $N$ elements, and $\Theta$ an $N \times N$ matrix. The theory of tariff formation could have two stages: explain the $\hat{V}_k$, then explain the tariffs $t_i$. If $N$ equals $K$, then the two stages become one.

*If K is greater than N*, that is, if there are more tariffs than domestic industries, then there can be at most one set of nominal tariffs to generate a given set of (linearly independent) effective rates. Any $K$ effective rates can be solved for the required set of $K$ nominal tariffs.

*If N is greater than K*, that is, if the number of effective rates is greater than the number of tariffs, there will be no unique set of tariffs for a given effective protection structure $\hat{V}_k$. There are two choices: either be content to explain the effective rates only, or try to explain the nominal tariffs in addition. The reason for spelling out these two obvious alternatives is that the second approach implies that not all effective rates can be explained. Thus, we either try to explain some effective rates and (all) the nominal tariffs, or to explain all the effective rates and none of the nominal tariffs. I will show why this choice arises.

Travis was trying to test whether the modern United States tariffs protect "labor" or "capital"; that is, he was concerned with the Leontief "paradox." The difficulty was that the unit cost equations,

$$\mathbf{p} = H\mathbf{w} \tag{A.20}$$

which give unit costs (the vector $\mathbf{p}$) in terms of the direct-plus-indirect primary input coefficients (the matrix $H$) and the primary input prices (the vector $\mathbf{w}$) are not invertible, because there are more products than primary inputs. Similarly, in trying to explain the tariffs from a model which in fact explains the effective rates (the $\hat{V}_i$) we have

$$\hat{\mathbf{V}} = \Theta \cdot \mathbf{t} \tag{A.18}$$

which is not invertible. On analogy with Travis's argument, we could assume that there are $K$ "dominant" industries—the nominal tariffs are set so as to achieve some desired values for $K$ of the $N$ effective rates, and the other $N - K$ effective rates are then residuals in the system. This can be written as follows:

$$
\begin{bmatrix} \hat{V}_1 \\ \vdots \\ \hat{V}_K \\ \cdots \\ \hat{V}_{K+1} \\ \vdots \\ \hat{V}_N \end{bmatrix}
=
\begin{bmatrix} \Theta_K \\ \cdots \\ \Theta_{N-K} \end{bmatrix}
\begin{bmatrix} t_1 \\ \vdots \\ \vdots \end{bmatrix}
\tag{A.21}
$$

where $\Theta_K$ is the square partitioning of $\Theta$ which corresponds to the dominant $K$ industries; note that the subscripts given the tariffs have to be altered, since there is no restriction requiring the $K$ dominant industries to be the industries with tariffs.

The empirical difficulty is to identify successfully the $K$ dominant industries; in Travis's work either labor or capital was dominant, whereas here there are $K$ industries, where $K$ is equal to the number of competing importables.

Completing this appendix is a result on the aggregate change in value-added due to a single duty, using partial rates of effective protection.

## THE AGGREGATE CHANGE IN VALUE ADDED

The effective rate of protection $\hat{V}_i$ can be written as the sum of the partial rates $\tau_{..}$ as

$$\hat{V}_i = \tau_{ii} + \sum_{j \neq i} \tau_{ji} \tag{A.22}$$

where

$$\tau_{ii} = t_i / \Theta_{vi}$$

$$\tau_{ji} = -t_j \Theta_{ji} / \Theta_{vi}$$

$\tau_{ji}$ is the proportional change in the value-added in industry $i$ due to the tariff $t_j$.

Consider the effect on value-added of a duty $t_i$; industry $i$ will receive an increase of $\tau_{ii}$ and any industry $j$ using good $i$ as an input will suffer a decrease of $\tau_{ij}$ in proportionate terms. In money terms, the aggregate change in value-added is

$$\tau_{ii} V_i + \sum_{j \neq i} \tau_{ij} V_j$$

$$= t_i \left[ \frac{V_i}{\Theta_{vi}} - \sum_{j \neq i} \frac{V_j \Theta_{ij}}{\Theta_{vj}} \right]$$

$$= t_i [S_i - \sum_{j \neq i} S_{ij}]$$

$$= t_i S_i' \tag{A.23}$$

where $S_i$ is the initial money value of (gross) output from industry $i$; $S_{ij}$ is the money value of good $i$ which is used as an input of good $j$; $S_i'$ is the "net" output of good $i$, that is, gross output minus what is used in intermediate production. If $S'_i$ is negative, then good $i$ must have been imported (neglect changes in stocks); if $S'_i$ is positive, then good $i$ was "exported" from the input-output structure, that is, industry $i$ made available a positive contribution of good $i$ to final demand. The word "exported" is in quotes to signal that a positive $S'_i$ does not necessarily imply that good $i$ was in aggregate excess domestic supply and that the economy had an export surplus in good $i$. In fact, even if $S'_i$ were positive, there could have been such a large domestic final demand that good $i$ had an import surplus.

It is clear from the derivation above that the gains (increases in value-added) and the losses (decreases in value-added) due to tariff $t_i$ are on net equal to zero only if $t_i$ is equal to zero, except if good $i$ has a zero "net" output, that is, a zero import or export balance with foreign economies. Except by chance, we would expect that good $i$ must then be a wholly intermediate good which is not traded internationally. For example, $t_i$ might be a prohibitive tariff, or good $i$ a very perishable or bulky item. In general, however, we would not expect that $t_i S'_i$ should be zero, or could become zero.

The result, that the net, aggregate contribution of $t_i$ to money value-added is equal to $t_i S'_i$ and is nonzero unless $t_i$ is either zero, prohibitive, or redundant, is important because it eliminates from consideration otherwise appealing (i.e., simple) economic theories of tariff formation.[11] In money terms, it is possible for every industry with a tariff on competing imports to enjoy positive increases in value-added. All that is required is that all import-competing industries have positive effective protection—for example, any set of uniform ad valorem nominal rates gives every import-competing industry a positive effective protection equal to the uniform nominal rate. This complicates the models: everything is linear in tariffs, and gains and losses have to be restrained from going to infinity in money terms. This suggests that attention be confined to the *structure* of nominal or effective rates, that is, to relative rates.

[11] Namely: that the legislature maximizes the value $t_i S'_i$; or maximizes the increase in value-added of those industries that gain, subject to the aggregate change being nonnegative.

# *Data*

T H E methods used to calculate the data are described in chapter 6. This appendix lists in table B.1 the data used in the regression analysis, and in table B.2 the actual prices and the price sources for the conversion of specific into the ad valorem equivalents, and also the wage and materials cost-shares (both the total materials cost-share and the shares of separate inputs). Table B.3 has the ad valorem equivalents and price sources for other items.

# TABLE B.1

## Data Base for Chapters Four and Six

| 1 | | 2 | 3 | 4 | 5 | 6 | 7 | 8 | 9 | 10 | 11 | 12 | 13 | 14 | 15 | 16 | 17 |
|---|---|---|---|---|---|---|---|---|---|---|---|---|---|---|---|---|---|
| 2082 | Ales, etc. | 11.7 | 17.6 | -9.7 | 7.3 | 7.3 | 20.9 | 22.5 | 59.7 | 36.4 | 11.17 | 2 | 57 | 7 | 2.79 | 1.39 | .43 |
| 34235 | Augers | 20.0 | 25.0 | -2.4 | 2.9 | 3.2 | 15.8 | 16.3 | .8 | 16.6 | 2.13 | 2 | 4 | 2 | 1.10 | .55 | .00 |
| 3423 | Axes | 20.0 | 25.0 | -2.6 | 3.0 | 3.5 | 5.7 | 114.9 | 15.6 | 51.6 | 4.17 | 2 | 76 | 4 | 3.01 | 1.38 | .05 |
| 23512 | Bonnets | 30.0 | 50.0 | 18.7 | .0 | .0 | .0 | 107.4 | 3.2 | 44.2 | 4.47 | 0 | 11 | 6 | 1.59 | 1.22 | .11 |
| 2732 | Books | 15.0 | 35.0 | -3.6 | 6.7 | 8.2 | 11.7 | 261.0 | 20.8 | 59.8 | 1.22 | 2 | 8 | 6 | 1.18 | 1.09 | .11 |
| 3141 | Boots & shoes | 87.8 | 28.8 | -8.2 | 14.6 | 14.6 | 35.8 | 94.8 | 76.7 | 25.8 | 1.68 | 1 | 142 | 11 | 3.76 | 2.22 | .52 |
| 3362 | Brass manufs. | 20.0 | 25.0 | .2 | .0 | .0 | .0 | 49.1 | 53.4 | 34.7 | 4.50 | 1 | 25 | 10 | 1.57 | 1.47 | .34 |
| 2050 | Bread, etc. | 15.0 | 15.0 | -25.9 | 11.0 | 12.2 | 76.8 | 101.8 | 13.6 | 14.3 | 1.18 | 1 | 8 | 5 | 1.50 | 1.47 | .06 |
| 3991 | Brushes | 30.0 | 30.0 | .7 | 4.0 | 4.0 | 11.4 | 56.7 | 12.1 | 27.0 | 3.97 | 1 | 6 | 4 | 1.25 | 1.07 | .06 |
| 3963 | Buttons | 20.0 | 20.0 | -9.2 | 1.4 | 1.5 | 5.6 | 43.9 | 4.8 | 16.5 | 2.98 | 3 | 4 | 1 | 1.37 | .00 | .00 |
| 2260 | Cloth, dressed | 25.0 | 30.0 | -3.8 | 14.4 | 17.3 | 40.4 | 82.3 | 20.4 | 35.6 | 6.41 | 1 | 33 | 6 | 2.47 | 1.59 | .30 |
| 39993 | Combs | 15.0 | 15.0 | -12.4 | 5.8 | 5.8 | 26.3 | 248.7 | 16.1 | 22.2 | .90 | 1 | 14 | 5 | 1.21 | .36 | .26 |
| 22981 | Cord, tarred | 60.4 | 80.5 | 13.2 | 16.3 | 16.3 | 159.6 | 16.6 | 61.4 | -17.0 | 3.47 | 2 | 32 | 6 | 1.61 | .97 | .12 |
| 2298 | Cord, white | 40.4 | 50.6 | 1.0 | 13.0 | 13.0 | 68.7 | 23.3 | 31.3 | 5.4 | 5.35 | 2 | 42 | 10 | 2.22 | 1.77 | .28 |
| 2299 | Cotton bagging | 15.0 | 26.3 | 2.3 | 8.0 | 8.0 | 25.3 | 47.4 | 3.2 | 32.3 | 3.49 | 1 | 5 | 2 | 1.35 | .62 | .19 |
| 2211 | Cotton cloth | 45.4 | 54.6 | -2.8 | 13.2 | 37.6 | 63.0 | 12.5 | 341.5 | 13.5 | 4.97 | 1 | 175 | 11 | 4.20 | 1.90 | .25 |
| 2281 | Cotton yarn | 25.0 | 71.3 | 22.9 | .7 | 1.0 | 2.9 | 10.7 | 183.7 | 13.2 | 9.46 | 2 | 139 | 15 | 3.89 | 2.26 | .27 |
| 2815 | Drugs | 7.5 | 12.5 | -21.2 | 3.1 | 4.0 | 10.0 | 30.8 | 6.0 | 33.6 | 7.14 | 6 | 6 | 3 | 1.46 | .44 | .06 |
| 34234 | Edge tools | 20.0 | 25.0 | -12.8 | 7.6 | 9.1 | 16.6 | 195.4 | 4.5 | 45.2 | 1.88 | 2 | 24 | 7 | 2.09 | 1.85 | .05 |
| 2511 | Furniture | 30.0 | 30.0 | 7.3 | 8.2 | 8.2 | 16.4 | 44.7 | 54.6 | 49.7 | 4.80 | 1 | 142 | 11 | 4.10 | 2.32 | .41 |
| 2310 | Garments | 30.0 | 30.0 | -3.6 | 9.2 | 11.0 | 15.9 | 280.5 | 8.8 | 59.9 | 1.03 | 1 | 5 | 4 | .76 | .66 | .06 |
| 3221 | Glass, bottles | 26.2 | 36.4 | 10.2 | .6 | .6 | 1.5 | 28.0 | 6.2 | 42.0 | 3.63 | 2 | 6 | 3 | 1.48 | 1.25 | .04 |
| 3229 | Glass, N.E.S. | 20.0 | 31.8 | -2.0 | 1.2 | 1.2 | 5.8 | 17.3 | 13.7 | 18.8 | 2.73 | 2 | 7 | 5 | 1.50 | 1.19 | .06 |
| 3211 | Glass, window | 29.6 | 35.5 | -5.5 | 2.3 | 2.3 | 6.4 | 14.7 | 61.0 | 32.6 | 7.14 | 3 | 21 | 7 | 2.24 | 1.75 | .08 |
| 3151 | Gloves | 30.0 | 30.0 | -1.3 | 8.7 | 8.7 | 14.6 | 148.4 | 1.1 | 59.3 | 3.40 | 1 | 4 | 3 | .18 | .00 | .00 |
| 3497 | Gold leaf | 15.0 | 15.0 | -5.9 | .0 | .0 | .0 | 120.0 | 3.7 | 20.6 | 3.33 | 1 | 2 | 1 | .52 | .52 | .00 |
| 2892 | Gunpowder | 37.6 | 37.6 | 8.2 | 2.5 | 17.0 | 4.8 | 44.8 | 49.5 | 40.8 | 17.63 | 2 | 33 | 9 | 1.94 | 1.37 | .28 |
| 19511 | Guns | 20.0 | 30.0 | 7.3 | 1.3 | 1.6 | 3.6 | 25.5 | 8.3 | 36.6 | 3.31 | 3 | 43 | 7 | 2.29 | 1.52 | .42 |

TABLE B.1 continued

| 1 | | 2 | 3 | 4 | 5 | 6 | 7 | 8 | 9 | 10 | 11 | 12 | 13 | 14 | 15 | 16 | 17 |
|---|---|---|---|---|---|---|---|---|---|---|---|---|---|---|---|---|---|
| 34296 | Hardware | 20.0 | 25.0 | -1.1 | 1.0 | 1.2 | 2.7 | 77.0 | 1.0 | 35.2 | 1.25 | 2 | 1 | 1 | .00 | .00 | .00 |
| 23519 | Hats, wool | 30.0 | 30.0 | .1 | 7.4 | 9.9 | 19.0 | 63.9 | 120.2 | 33.4 | 3.56 | 1 | 261 | 15 | 4.25 | 2.36 | .43 |
| 33122 | Iron, bar | 18.8 | 22.6 | -3.2 | 6.1 | 6.1 | 22.5 | 8.0 | 256.3 | 27.3 | 11.53 | 1 | 144 | 13 | 3.96 | 1.86 | .29 |
| 3321 | Iron, cast | 20.0 | 24.1 | 9.1 | 1.0 | 1.0 | 2.4 | 22.3 | 156.4 | 41.7 | 7.99 | 1 | 59 | 12 | 3.51 | 2.19 | .27 |
| 33127 | Iron, pig | 20.8 | 20.8 | -16.3 | .0 | .0 | .0 | 14.3 | 71.5 | 29.2 | 5.88 | 0 | 30 | 5 | 2.57 | 1.57 | .16 |
| 33322 | Iron, plow | 20.0 | 25.0 | .7 | 1.8 | 2.1 | 4.7 | 20.1 | 11.0 | 37.4 | 9.01 | 2 | 23 | 2 | 2.69 | 1.13 | .06 |
| 33123 | Iron, rolled | 56.8 | 56.8 | 15.1 | 14.4 | 17.3 | 52.5 | 40.4 | 15.2 | 8.3 | 5.22 | 1 | 6 | 4 | 1.69 | 1.19 | .14 |
| 33126 | Iron, sheet | 53.4 | 71.7 | 18.1 | 16.1 | 19.3 | 98.7 | 36.9 | 37.2 | -5.6 | 4.62 | 1 | 10 | 2 | 1.96 | 1.58 | .06 |
| 3332 | Lead | 20.0 | 39.9 | 17.0 | 3.1 | 3.1 | 6.2 | 22.7 | 3.7 | 48.6 | 7.03 | 1 | 5 | 2 | 1.07 | .91 | .00 |
| 3494 | Lead manufs. | 20.0 | 25.0 | -11.8 | 13.1 | 26.3 | 53.0 | 17.7 | 1.5 | 24.7 | 17.41 | 1 | 1 | 1 | .00 | .00 | .00 |
| 1961 | Lead shot | 33.7 | 54.7 | 12.5 | 15.8 | 31.6 | 72.1 | 15.6 | 2.9 | 13.4 | 31.97 | 1 | 1 | 1 | .00 | .00 | .00 |
| 3111 | Leather | 30.0 | 30.0 | -2.3 | .0 | .0 | .0 | 44.7 | 347.2 | 22.5 | 7.98 | 1 | 646 | 18 | 4.97 | 2.47 | .49 |
| 3274 | Lime | 44.4 | 44.4 | 5.7 | .0 | .0 | .0 | 144.6 | 11.8 | 45.0 | 2.85 | 0 | 4 | 5 | .85 | .85 | .00 |
| 2421 | Lumber | 30.0 | 30.0 | .6 | .0 | .0 | .0 | 52.9 | 80.6 | 41.0 | 5.57 | 0 | 290 | 10 | 3.79 | 1.74 | .40 |
| 3511 | Machinery | 20.0 | 25.0 | -4.2 | 3.6 | 3.8 | 10.1 | 30.0 | 36.2 | 35.4 | 3.92 | 2 | 23 | 6 | 1.88 | 1.04 | .31 |
| 32811 | Marble manufs. | 15.0 | 30.0 | 4.8 | 4.8 | 9.6 | 15.4 | 62.5 | 7.3 | 31.1 | 1.35 | 1 | 9 | 3 | 1.86 | .46 | .06 |
| 2834 | Medicines | 15.0 | 15.0 | -16.2 | .0 | .0 | .0 | 56.7 | 1.6 | 32.1 | 6.92 | 0 | 2 | 2 | .66 | .66 | .00 |
| 1497 | Millstones | 15.0 | 15.0 | -5.1 | .0 | .0 | .0 | 6.2 | 1.7 | -0.9 | 6.11 | 1 | 3 | 3 | 1.08 | 1.08 | .00 |
| 19516 | Muskets | 20.0 | 45.9 | 10.1 | 2.9 | 3.4 | 14.6 | 10.1 | 8.2 | 18.8 | 3.67 | 2 | 5 | 5 | 1.35 | 1.35 | .00 |
| 33157 | Nails | 37.5 | 46.9 | -8.6 | 12.2 | 15.0 | 58.2 | 35.9 | 95.0 | 12.5 | 3.05 | 2 | 50 | 14 | 3.09 | 2.05 | .45 |
| 26213 | Paper | 30.0 | 40.0 | 13.0 | .0 | .0 | .0 | 26.2 | 147.6 | 22.9 | 4.11 | 1 | 115 | 14 | 4.00 | 2.46 | .34 |
| 3522 | Plows | 20.0 | 25.0 | 2.9 | 3.1 | 3.7 | 4.6 | 70.8 | 5.6 | 67.4 | 8.72 | 1 | 8 | 5 | 1.61 | 1.26 | .12 |
| 3262 | Pottery | 20.0 | 20.0 | -2.1 | 1.7 | 2.2 | 3.3 | 64.1 | 19.3 | 51.4 | 2.85 | 3 | 70 | 13 | 3.35 | 2.25 | .63 |
| 2711 | Printing | 15.0 | 15.0 | -12.8 | 6.8 | 9.1 | 12.6 | 46.7 | 3.6 | 56.9 | 5.66 | 1 | 8 | 5 | 1.58 | 1.26 | .09 |
| 28167 | Prussian blue | 20.0 | 20.0 | -9.8 | .0 | .0 | .0 | 98.2 | .5 | 52.7 | 3.09 | 0 | 1 | 1 | .00 | .00 | .00 |
| 28163 | Red lead | 38.7 | 51.6 | 6.4 | 10.8 | 21.9 | 34.4 | 18.6 | 10.6 | 20.5 | 22.50 | 2 | 4 | 3 | 1.30 | .94 | .00 |
| 2062 | Refined sugar | 107.5 | 107.5 | 27.8 | 29.6 | 29.6 | 139.5 | 31.7 | 54.7 | -27.9 | 12.11 | 1 | 16 | 4 | .86 | .86 | .00 |
| 19513 | Rifles | 20.0 | 20.0 | -12.9 | 2.5 | 3.0 | 7.5 | 29.1 | 3.4 | 32.9 | 2.57 | 3 | 15 | 7 | 1.80 | 1.50 | .07 |
| 20843 | Rum | 90.5 | 90.5 | -4.3 | 31.9 | 31.9 | 316.4 | 12.9 | 87.6 | -35.7 | 19.36 | 1 | 23 | 8 | 2.49 | 1.86 | .19 |
| 2499 | Saddle trees | 30.0 | 30.0 | 7.6 | 2.6 | 3.1 | 10.1 | 40.4 | 1.3 | 21.6 | 1.44 | 1 | 2 | 2 | .53 | .00 | .00 |
| 34298 | Saddlery | 25.0 | 25.0 | -7.6 | 1.6 | 2.0 | 2.9 | 33.7 | 10.9 | 49.5 | 17.18 | 4 | 4 | 4 | 1.08 | 1.08 | .14 |
| 31998 | Saddles | 30.0 | 30.0 | -3.5 | 12.5 | 12.5 | 28.1 | 74.6 | 82.2 | 44.1 | 4.83 | 2 | 164 | 10 | 4.01 | 2.28 | .35 |

| Product | 1 | 2 | 3 | 4 | 5 | 6 | 7 | 8 | 9 | 10 | 11 | 12 | 13 | 14 | 15 | 16 | 17 |
|---|---|---|---|---|---|---|---|---|---|---|---|---|---|---|---|---|---|
| Salt | 28998 | 15.5 | 15.5 | 12.3 | .0 | .0 | .0 | 26.8 | 179.6 | 50.3 | 8.98 | 0 | 181 | 10 | 2.48 | 1.62 | .18 |
| Saltpeter | 28192 | 7.5 | 56.2 | 26.0 | .0 | .0 | .0 | 1019.2 | .6 | 45.0 | .21 | 0 | 2 | 2 | .66 | .66 | .00 |
| Satinet | 2239 | 25.0 | 30.0 | −17.7 | 8.3 | 14.3 | 34.5 | 21.8 | 129.0 | 20.7 | 3.68 | 2 | 93 | 12 | 3.25 | 2.06 | .24 |
| Saws | 3425 | 20.0 | 25.0 | −8.9 | 10.1 | 12.2 | 61.5 | 85.0 | 2.1 | 15.8 | .77 | 1 | 1 | 1 | .00 | .00 | .00 |
| Scythes | 34231 | 20.0 | 30.0 | 11.8 | 4.4 | 5.2 | 10.1 | 56.3 | 6.2 | 43.2 | 3.23 | 2 | 17 | 5 | 2.56 | 1.15 | .52 |
| Seed oils | 2093 | 15.0 | 43.8 | 10.5 | .0 | .0 | .0 | 28.6 | 20.3 | 33.3 | 12.66 | 0 | 86 | 11 | 3.53 | 2.01 | .29 |
| Segars | 2110 | 26.2 | 26.2 | −11.8 | 7.7 | 7.7 | 20.9 | 89.1 | 105.1 | 32.4 | 2.58 | 1 | 46 | 8 | 1.85 | .97 | .09 |
| Sickles | 34233 | 20.0 | 30.0 | 3.5 | 2.9 | 3.4 | 7.3 | 49.7 | 1.1 | 37.9 | 2.79 | 2 | 4 | 1 | .92 | .00 | .00 |
| Sieves | 3481 | 20.0 | 25.0 | 4.0 | 1.5 | 2.9 | 2.3 | 92.0 | 1.0 | 63.7 | 5.71 | 1 | 6 | 5 | 1.65 | 1.36 | .05 |
| Silver plate | 3914 | 20.0 | 25.0 | 7.1 | .0 | .0 | .0 | 90.8 | 17.6 | 52.6 | 6.85 | 1 | 14 | 6 | 1.46 | 1.06 | .23 |
| Spades | 34232 | 20.0 | 30.0 | 3.0 | 6.4 | 7.7 | 20.0 | 36.5 | 2.4 | 31.1 | 3.78 | 2 | 11 | 2 | 2.03 | .64 | .16 |
| Spirits | 20848 | 97.7 | 97.7 | −0.4 | .0 | .0 | .0 | 85.6 | 298.5 | 11.5 | 4.34 | 0 | 1145 | 15 | 4.70 | 2.26 | .40 |
| Tallow manufs. | 28411 | 44.8 | 59.7 | −7.0 | 14.1 | 14.1 | 66.0 | 39.1 | 78.5 | 5.3 | 6.58 | 5 | 31 | 10 | 2.70 | 1.97 | .24 |
| Tinware | 3461 | 20.0 | 25.0 | −7.3 | 5.0 | 5.2 | 10.4 | 100.0 | 31.2 | 47.2 | 4.09 | 5 | 51 | 9 | 3.31 | 2.06 | .26 |
| Turpentine | 2861 | 15.0 | 15.0 | −15.2 | 6.6 | 6.6 | 13.8 | 88.0 | 7.3 | 47.5 | 6.12 | 1 | 7 | 5 | 1.55 | .98 | .05 |
| Wagons | 3799 | 30.0 | 30.0 | 5.6 | .5 | .5 | .7 | 181.5 | 17.3 | 63.7 | 2.30 | 2 | 82 | 12 | 3.33 | 2.13 | .35 |
| Watches, etc. | 38715 | 7.5 | 12.5 | −4.9 | .0 | .0 | .0 | 277.2 | .7 | 61.0 | 1.81 | 1 | 5 | 3 | 1.13 | .68 | .04 |
| Wheels, etc. | 2491 | 30.0 | 30.0 | 4.4 | .0 | .0 | .0 | 225.6 | 4.6 | 68.2 | 2.58 | 0 | 37 | 7 | 2.95 | 1.69 | .31 |
| Whips | 31999 | 30.0 | 30.0 | 10.1 | .3 | .7 | .6 | 294.4 | 5.3 | 59.1 | .86 | 1 | 3 | 1 | .69 | .00 | .00 |
| Wicks | 2241 | 25.0 | 25.0 | −3.2 | 7.6 | 21.7 | 39.0 | 34.5 | .7 | 19.5 | 1.13 | 1 | 2 | 2 | .65 | .65 | .00 |
| Wool cloth | 2231 | 25.0 | 30.0 | −8.9 | 7.5 | 10.0 | 28.4 | 16.4 | 108.7 | 22.4 | 5.82 | 1 | 172 | 12 | 4.28 | 2.21 | .18 |
| Wool, carded | 2297 | 15.0 | 20.0 | −2.1 | 9.4 | 12.5 | 30.1 | 57.4 | 76.5 | 31.2 | 8.69 | 1 | 179 | 10 | 3.70 | 1.61 | .68 |

*Sources:* See chapters 4 and 6.

*Note:* The variables $Z1$ to $Z11$, $X1$ to $X6$ are defined in the legend to table 6.1 and table 4.3 respectively.

*Column Headings:*

| | | | |
|---|---|---|---|
| 1 | Modified Standard Industrial Classification number | 9 | Output/$10^4$ ($Z1 \cdot 10^2 = X1 \cdot 10$) |
| 2 | 1820 nominal duty (%) | 10 | Proprietorial share ($Z6 \cdot 10^2/Z1$) |
| 3 | 1824 nominal duty (%) | 11 | Capital/labor ($X6/10^3$) |
| 4 | Residuals from equation R3, Table 5.1 (%) | 12 | Input Number ($(Z5)^{-1}$) |
| 5 | 1820 net tariff (Col. 2 − $Z4$, %) | 13 | Establishments ($Z7$) |
| 6 | 1824 net tariff (%) | 14 | Senate ($Z11$) |
| 7 | Effective rate to 1820 surplus (%) | 15 | Industrial concentration ($Z8 = X3$) |
| 8 | Surplus/capital, 1820 (dependent variable, Table 4.1, %) | 16 | Sales dispersion ($Z9$) |
| | | 17 | County dispersion ($Z10$) |

*Prices and Price Sources;*[1] *Wage and Material Cost-Shares*

| PRODUCT | PRICE DATA [2] | WAGE SHARE | MATERIAL SHARES | | |
|---|---|---|---|---|---|
| | | | TOTAL | COSTED SEPARATELY | |
| Ales, etc. | 93.4¢ (CN) | .1390 | .5117 | Barley | .4632 |
| | | | | Hops | .0387 |
| Augers | ad val. | .5222 | .2964 | Bar iron | .0978 |
| | | | | Steel | .1033 |
| Axes | ad val. | .1105 | .3604 | Bar iron | .1394 |
| | | | | Steel | .0351 |
| Bonnets | ad val. | .1032 | .4019 | | |
| Books | See note 3 | .1783 | .2528 | Paper | .1676 |
| | | | | Leather | .0840 |
| Boots and shoes | 86.9¢ (CN) | .2558 | .3364 | Leather | .3364 |
| Brass mfres. | ad val. | .1921 | .3837 | Brass | .3837 |
| Bread, etc. | ad val. | .1198 | .7368 | Flour | .7340 |
| Brushes | ad val. | .1577 | .4874 | Bristles | .3652 |
| Buttons | ad val. | .1979 | .5429 | Ivory | .0850 |
| | | | | Brass wire | .0062 |
| | | | | Brass | .4497 |
| Cloth, dressed | ad val. | .0676 | .5759 | Wool cloth | .5759 |
| Combs | ad val. | .0992 | .6790 | Ivory | .3891 |
| Cord, tarred | 4.97¢ (CN) | .1775 | .7203 | Hemp | .7040 |
| | | | | Tar | .0163 |
| Cord, white | 9.89¢ (CN) | .1526 | .6576 | Hemp | .6576 |
| Cotton, bagging | 14.2¢ (CN) | .1915 | .4918 | Hemp | .4918 |
| Cotton cloth | 20¢, duty paid [4] | .3372 | .4535 | Yarn | .4535 |
| Cotton yarn | 21.05¢ (Digest) [5] | .2514 | .4941 | Cotton | .4896 |
| Drugs | ad val. | .1389 | .5556 | Saltpeter | .0887 |
| | | | | Brimstone | .0590 |
| | | | | Salt | .0417 |
| | | | | Potash | .0392 |
| Edge tools | ad val. | .1249 | .4162 | Bar iron | .3876 |
| | | | | Steel | .0284 |
| Furniture | ad val. | .2314 | .2716 | Wood | .2716 |
| Garments | ad val. | .1994 | .2253 | Cotton cloth | .2253 |
| Glass bottles | $5.50 (R609) [6] | .4279 | .1383 | Salt | .0046 |
| | | | | Potash | .0344 |
| Glass n.e.s. | 16.9¢ (R554) [7] | .4313 | .3650 | Salt | .0125 |
| | | | | Potash | .0622 |
| Glass, window | $11 (R609) [8] | .3441 | .2936 | Salt | .0137 |
| | | | | Lime | .0041 |
| | | | | Potash | .1142 |
| Gloves | ad val. | .1178 | .2888 | Leather | .2888 |
| Gold leaf | ad val. | .0750 | .6250 | Bullion | .6250 |
| Gunpowder | 21.3¢ (CN) | .0646 | .4247 | Salt | .2325 |
| | | | | Brimstone | .0129 |

| PRODUCT | PRICE DATA [2] | WAGE SHARE | MATERIAL SHARES | | |
|---|---|---|---|---|---|
| | | | TOTAL | COSTED SEPARATELY | |
| Guns | ad val. | .4416 | .1853 | Bar iron | .0671 |
| | | | | Steel | .0058 |
| | | | | Brass | .0055 |
| Hardware | ad val. | .4000 | .2150 | Brass | .1600 |
| | | | | Bar iron | .0550 |
| Hats, wool | ad val. | .1717 | .4375 | Wool | .4375 |
| Iron, bar | $3.17 (CN) | .2950 | .4323 | Pig iron | .2999 |
| Iron, cast | 4.16¢ (CN) | .2411 | .3296 | Pig iron | .0491 |
| Iron, pig | $2.24 (CN) | .3667 | .3252 | | |
| Iron, plow | ad val. | .2152 | .3948 | Bar iron | .0852 |
| | | | | Steel | .0206 |
| Iron, rolled | $2.64 (CN) | .1303 | .5952 | Bar iron | .5801 |
| Iron, sheet | 4.18¢ (CN) | .0957 | .7412 | Bar iron | .6627 |
| Lead | $5 (CN) | .3091 | .1964 | Ore | .1964 |
| Lead manufactures | ad val. | .0806 | .6715 | Pig lead | .6585 |
| Lead shot | 5.94¢ (CN) | .0439 | .7368 | Pig lead | .7105 |
| Leather | ad val. | .1063 | .5144 | Hides | .5144 |
| Lime | $2.25 (D308) | .1301 | .3340 | | |
| Lumber | ad val. | .1560 | .3841 | | |
| Machinery | ad val. | .3059 | .3343 | Bar iron | .0352 |
| | | | | Pig iron | .1439 |
| Marble mfres. | ad val. | .3690 | .3198 | Marble | .3198 |
| Medicines | ad val. | .0818 | .5975 | | |
| Millstones | ad val. | .2421 | .6667 | Burrstones | .6667 |
| Muskets | $3.27 (CN) | .5276 | .2761 | Bar iron | .1402 |
| | | | | Steel | .0214 |
| Nails | 10.65¢ (CN) | .1907 | .6004 | Bar iron | .4307 |
| | | | | Hoop iron | .0581 |
| Paper | ad val. | .3119 | .3531 | Rags | .3531 |
| Plows | ad val. | .1098 | .2120 | Bar iron | .1630 |
| Pottery | ad val. | .2824 | .2013 | | |
| Printing | ad val. | .2040 | .2562 | Paper | .2562 |
| Prussian blue | ad val. | .1778 | .2827 | | |
| Red lead | $7.76 (CN) | .0750 | .6108 | Bar lead | .3331 |
| | | | | Vinegar | .1725 |
| Refined sugar | 12.9¢ (R609)[9] | .0554 | .7322 | Sugar | .7322 |
| Rifles | ad val. | .4496 | .2135 | Bar iron | .1286 |
| | | | | Steel | .0078 |
| | | | | Brass | .0149 |
| Rum | 80¢ (R609) [10] | .0404 | .8588 | Molasses | .8585 |
| Saddle trees | ad val. | .4339 | .3137 | Bar iron | .1245 |
| Saddlery | ad val. | .0972 | .3396 | Bar iron | .0776 |
| | | | | Copper | .0368 |

TABLE B.2 *continued*

| PRODUCT | PRICE DATA [2] | WAGE SHARE | MATERIAL SHARES | | |
|---|---|---|---|---|---|
| | | | TOTAL | COSTED SEPARATELY | |
| Saddles | ad val. | .1237 | .4308 | Bar lead | .0041 |
| | | | | Silver | .2211 |
| | | | | Saddlery | .1000 |
| | | | | Leather | .3308 |
| Salt | 12.9¢ (CN) | .2096 | .2858 | | |
| Saltpeter | 5.34¢ (CN) | .2006 | .4350 | | |
| Satinet | ad val. | .2992 | .4614 | Wool | .3754 |
| Saws | ad val. | .2524 | .5825 | Bar iron | .5340 |
| Scythes | ad val. | .2438 | .3136 | Bar iron | .1991 |
| | | | | Steel | .0683 |
| Seed oils | 80¢ (R609) | .0921 | .5746 | | |
| Segars | $9.56 (CN) | .1607 | .4698 | Tobacco | .4698 |
| Sickles | ad val. | .2817 | .3273 | Bar iron | .1354 |
| | | | | Steel | .0308 |
| Sieves | ad val. | .1226 | .2333 | Iron wire | .0746 |
| Silver plate | ad val. | .0948 | .3160 | Bullion | .3160 |
| Spades | ad val. | .2333 | .4452 | Bar iron | .3220 |
| | | | | Steel | .0319 |
| Spirits | 43¢ (CN) | .1173 | .4667 | | |
| Tallow mfres. | 6.7¢ (CN) [11] | .0831 | .7032 | Tallow | .5950 |
| | | | | Potash | .0060 |
| | | | | Lime | .0160 |
| | | | | Salt | .0110 |
| | | | | Wicks | .0067 |
| Tinware | ad val. | .1175 | .4015 | Tin plate | .1812 |
| | | | | Block tin | .0017 |
| | | | | Copper sheet | .0706 |
| | | | | Sheet iron | .0101 |
| | | | | Iron wire | .0021 |
| Turpentine | ad val. | .0882 | .4366 | Gum | .4366 |
| Wagons | ad val. | .1581 | .1826 | | |
| Watches, etc. | ad val. | .1250 | .2467 | Bullion | .2467 |
| Wheels, etc. | ad val. | .1211 | .1744 | | |
| Whips | ad val. | .2400 | .1500 | Lead | .0163 |
| Wicks | ad val. | .4998 | .3048 | Yarn | .3048 |
| Wool cloth | ad val. | .2967 | .4593 | Wool | .4593 |
| Wool, carded | ad val. | .0625 | .6258 | Wool | .6258 |

[1] Deflation of prices was generally on the basis of appropriate products in Bezanson et al. (1937).

[2] The abbreviations are

CN: *Commerce and Navigation Report* (1825)  R554: Report 554, *ASP, Finance* (1819)
Digest: *Digest of Manufactures* (1820)  R609: Report 609, *ASP, Finance* (1821)
D308: House Exec. Document 308 (1833)

[3] The duty is the average of the various duties on books, weighted by shares in value of imports, 1824–25

[4] The figure of 20¢ duty paid. The McLane report gives the following prices for "brown shirting": 13¢, 1820–22; 12.5¢, 1823–24 (House Exec. Doc. 308 (1833), I, 173). The *Digest* has five quotations for shirting and sheeting between 12 and 20¢, and two of a range 10 to 30¢. Most imports in 1824 were over 33.33¢ in value, an indication that the cheaper fabrics were effectively excluded.

[5] The *Digest* gave a number of prices (34¢, 36¢, 40¢, 50¢). I took 40¢.

[6] Black bottles less than 1 quart.

[7] Plain glass. *Note:* n.e.s. = not elsewhere specified.

[8] The 8 × 10 size. The ad valorem equivalents for the other sizes are similar but a little lower.

[9] Price for loaf sugar.

[10] The prices varied according to proof, but the ad valorem equivalents in R609 for the three grades were equal. The *Digest* has the following prices (in cents per gallon): 35, 37–45, 42, 36, 37. The unit import value in 1824 of spirits not from grain was 44¢.

[11] The import unit values in 1824 were 6.7¢ for soaps, 6.0¢ for candles. The products (soap and candles) were equally weighted to arrive at the 1824 rate of duty.

Prices, Price Sources, and Ad Valorem Equivalent Tariff Rates,
1816 and 1824

| NUMBER [1] | PRODUCT | PRICE DATA [2] | 1816 DUTY (%) | 1824 DUTY (%) |
|---|---|---|---|---|
| 10 | Acid, sulfuric | 4.2¢ (CN) | 15 | 71 |
| 16 | Ale, etc., in bottles | 85.3¢ (CN 21–23) | 18 | 23 |
| 17 | Ale, etc., in other | 85.3¢ (CN 21–23) | 18 | 23 |
| 20 | Alum | $3.1 (CN 21–23) | 64 | 80 |
| 25 | Anchors | 6.2¢ (CN) | 32 | 32 |
| 32 | Anvils | 5.8¢ (CN) | 20 | 35 |
| 61 | Blacksmith's hammers | 6.1¢ (CN) | 20 | 41 |
| 117 | Bristles | 32.3¢ (CN) | 9 | 9 |
| 136 | Camphor, crude | 31.5¢ (CN) | 15 | 25 |
| 137 | Camphor, refined | 63.8¢ (CN) | 15 | 19 |
| 140 | Candles, tallow | 6.7¢ (CN) | 45 | 75 |
| 141 | Candles, wax | 6.7¢ (CN) | 90 | 90 |
| 142 | Candles, sperm | 45.0¢ (CN) | 13 | 18 |
| 152 | Cards, playing | 9.7¢ (CN 21–23) | 309 | 309 |
| 154 | Carpets, Brussels | Note 3 | 25 | 52 |
| 155 | Carpets, Venetian | Note 3 | 25 | 31 |
| 161 | Cassia | Note 4 | 17 | 17 |
| 163 | Castor oil | $1.5 (CN) | 15 | 26 |
| 172 | Chocolate | 20¢ (R609) | 15 | 20 |
| 181 | Cloves | $1 (R609) | 25 | 25 |
| 183 | Coal | 14.3¢ (CN 21–23) | 35 | 42 |
| 185 | Cocoa | 17.1¢ (CN 21–23) | 12 | 12 |
| 189 | Coffee | 20.2¢ (CN 21–23) | 25 | 25 |
| 200 | Copper rods | 25.7¢ (CN) | 16 | 16 |
| 206 | Copperas | $1.06 (CN 21–23) | 94 | 190 |
| 214 | Corks | 26.0¢ (CN) | 15 | 46 |
| 219 | Cotton, raw | 15.8¢ (CN) | 19 | 19 |
| 220 | Cotton bagging | 14.2¢ (CN) | 15 | 26 |
| 228 | Currants | 13¢ (R609) | 23 | 23 |
| 241 | Duck, Russia | 8.7¢ (Bezanson) | 27 | 27 |
| 242 | Duck, Ravens | $10 (R609) | 13 | 13 |
| 243 | Duck, Holland | $26 (R609) | 10 | 10 |
| 260 | Figs | 10¢ (R609) | 30 | 30 |
| 263 | Fish, other | $1.50 (R609) | 40 | 40 |
| 264 | Fish, salmon | $2 (R609) | 20 | 20 |
| 291 | Ginger, ground | Note 4 | 15 | 69 |
| 293 | Glass, 8 × 10 | Note 5 | 30 | 35 |
| 294 | Glass, 10 × 15 | Note 6 | 25 | 27 |
| 295 | Glass, > 10 × 15 | Note 7 | 26 | 32 |
| 307 | Glass, black bottle | Note 8 | 26 | 36 |
| 310 | Glass, demijohns | 41¢ (R609) | 20 | 61 |

| NUMBER [1] | PRODUCT | PRICE DATA [2] | 1816 DUTY (%) | 1824 DUTY (%) |
|---|---|---|---|---|
| 331 | Glue | 19¢ (CN) | 26 | 26 |
| 370 | Hemp, raw | $115 (CN 21–23) | 16 | 16 |
| 384 | Indigo | $1.7 (CN 21–23) | 9 | 9 |
| 393 | Iron band | 10¢ (CN) | 20 | 30 |
| 394 | Iron rods | 5.6¢ (CN) | 20 | 53 |
| 395 | Iron rods | 3.3¢ (CN) | 20 | 92 |
| 397 | Iron scroll | 10¢ (CN) | 20 | 30 |
| 398 | Iron bar, rolled | $2.6 (CN) | 57 | 57 |
| 400 | Iron cables | 7.9¢ (CN) | 20 | 38 |
| 459 | Mace | $2.4 (R609) | 42 | 42 |
| 480 | Molasses | 20.6¢ (CN 21–23) | 24 | 24 |
| 485 | Muskets | $3.3 (CN) | 20 | 46 |
| 494 | Nutmeg | $1.9 (R609) | 32 | 32 |
| 499 | Ocher, dry | 1.4¢ (CN) | 71 | 71 |
| 499 | Ochers, in oil | 5.3¢ (CN) | 28 | 28 |
| 507 | Olive oil, in cask | 51.7¢ (CN) | 48 | 48 |
| 535 | Paper, writing | $16 (R609) | 30 | 36 |
| 540 | Paper, folio | $4 (R609) | 30 | 70 |
| 541 | Paper, foolscap | $3.5 (R609) | 30 | 63 |
| 543 | Paper, drawing | $4.5 (R609) | 30 | 40 |
| 544 | Paper, wrapping | 8¢ (R609) | 30 | 50 |
| 545 | Paper, boards | 5¢ (R609) | 30 | 75 |
| 556 | Pepper | 23¢ (R609) | 35 | 35 |
| 563 | Pimento | 23¢ (R609) | 26 | 26 |
| 587 | Raisins, boxes | 10¢ (R609) | 30 | 40 |
| 588 | Raisins, other | 2¢ (R609) | 53 | 80 |
| 597 | Rifles | $17 (CN) | 20 | 15 |
| 607 | Salt | 12.9¢ (CN) | 15 | 15 |
| 610 | Saltpeter, refined | 5.3¢ (CN) | 8 | 56 |
| 612 | Salts, Epson | 4.5¢ (CN) | 15 | 87 |
| 613 | Salts, Gauber | 2.3¢ (CN) | 15 | 85 |
| 617 | Saws | $3.9 (CN) | 20 | 26 |
| 629 | Seines | 42¢ (R609) | 10 | 12 |
| 634 | Sheeting, Russ., brown | $18 (R609) | 17 | 17 |
| 635 | Sheeting, Russ., white | $16 (R609) | 12 | 12 |
| 638–640 | Slippers, etc. | Note 10 | 44 | 44 |
| 682 | Spikes | 4.7¢ (CN) | 64 | 85 |
| 685 | Spirits (brandy) | 44¢ (CN) | 59 | 59 |
| 694 | Steel | $11.2 (CN 21–23) | 9 | 9 |
| 704 | Sugar, brown | 5.6¢ (CN) | 51 | 51 |
| 706 | Sugar, lump | 14.7¢ (R609) | 68 | 68 |

| NUMBER [1] | PRODUCT | PRICE DATA [2] | 1816 DUTY (%) | 1824 DUTY (%) |
|---|---|---|---|---|
| 707 | Sugar, white | 8.2¢ (CN) | 49 | 49 |
| 717 | Tallow | 5.7¢ (CN) | 18 | 18 |
| 723–729 | Teas | Note 11 | | |
| 739 | Tobacco, mfd. | 44¢ (CN) | 23 | 23 |
| 746 | Twine | 40¢ (CN) | 10 | 12 |
| 753 | Vinegar | 25¢ (CN) | 15 | 31 |
| 754 | Vitriol, oil | 4.2¢ (CN) | 15 | 71 |
| 764 | Wheat | 95.3¢ (CN) | 15 | 20 |
| 765 | Wheat flour | $2.25 (CN) | 15 | 22 |
| 766 | Whiting | 10.7¢ (CN) | 9 | 9 |
| 767–791 | Wines | Note 12 | | |

[1] Numbers from Senate Report 2130 (1890).

[2] Abbreviations as in table B.2, except (CN 21–23): *Commerce and Navigation Reports,* 1821–23.

[3] Price from R470, deflated by Warren-Pearson.

[4] R609 deflated by the average price relative of spices in Bezanson (chocolate, cloves, cocoa, coffee, nutmeg, pepper, pimento).

[5] $10 (R609) deflated by Bezanson.

[6] $13 (R609) deflated by Bezanson.

[7] $15 (R609) deflated by Bezanson.

[8] $6.50 (R609) deflated by Bezanson.

[9] A much lower rate (47%) is implied by Bezanson's data.

[10] CN quantities × duties/values.

[11] The rates on teas implied by R609 are 723: 60%; 724: 125%; 725–726: 67%; 728: 84%; 729: 100%.

[12] The rates on wines implied by R609 are 767: 66%; 768: 55%; 770: 57%; 771: 50%.

# Bibliography

Anderson, A. R. 1975. "Review of Tom E. Terrill, *The Tariff, Politics and American Foreign Policy, 1874–1901*," *Journal of Economic History* 35(3):683–84.

Anderson, J. E. 1970. "General Equilibrium and the Effective Rate of Protection," *Journal of Political Economy* 78.4(1):717–24.

Armitage-Smith, G. 1903. *The Free-Trade Movement and Its Results*, 2d ed. London: Blackie.

Arrow, K. J. 1970. "Political and Economic Evaluation of Social Effects and Externalities," in J. Margolis, ed., *The Analysis of Public Output*. Conference of the Universities, National Bureau of Economic Research. New York: Columbia University Press.

—— 1974. "Limited Knowledge and Economic Analysis," *American Economic Review* 64(1):1–10.

Ashley, P. 1920. *Modern Tariff History: Germany–United States–France*. 3d ed., reprinted. New York: Howard Fertig, 1970.

Australia. Tariff Board. 1973. *Tariff Revision: Domestic Appliances, Heating and Cooling Equipment*. Canberra: Government Printer.

Baack, B. D., and E. J. Ray. 1974. "Tariff Policy and Income Redistribution: The Case of the U.S. in 1830–1860," *Explorations in Economic History* 11(2):103–22.

Balassa, B., S. Guisinger, and D. Schydlowsky. 1970. "The Effective Rates of Protection and the Question of Labor Protection in the United States: A Comment," *Journal of Political Economy* 78:1150–62.

Balinky, A. 1958. *Albert Gallatin: Fiscal Theories and Policies*. New Brunswick, N.J.: Rutgers University Press.

Bateman, F., and T. Weiss. 1975. "Comparative Regional Development in Antebellum Manufacturing," *Journal of Economic History* 35(1):182–208.

Bauer, R. A., I. de Sola Pool, and L. A. Dexter. 1963. *American Business and Public Policy: The Politics of Foreign Trade*. New York: Atherton.

Beales, H. L. 1958. *The Industrial Revolution 1750–1850: An Introductory Essay*. London: Frank Cass.

Berglund, A. and P. G. Wright. 1929. *The Tariff on Iron and Steel*. Washington: Brookings Institution.

Bergson, A. 1973. "On Monopoly Welfare Losses," *American Economic Review* 63(5):853–70.

Bergstrom, T. C., and R. R. Goodman. 1973. "Private Demand for Public Goods," *American Economic Review* 63(3):280–96.

Bezanson, A., R. D. Gray, and M. Hussey. 1937. *Wholesale Prices in Philadelphia 1784–1861.* Part II, *Series of Relative Monthly Prices.* Research Studies 30, Industrial Research Department, Wharton School of Finance and Commerce. Philadelphia: University of Pennsylvania Press.

Birch, A. H. 1971. *Representation.* London: Macmillan.

Black, D. 1958. *The Theory of Committees and Elections.* Cambridge: Cambridge University Press.

Breton, A. 1974. *The Economic Theory of Representative Democracy.* Chicago: Aldine.

Brigden, J. B. et al. 1929. *The Australian Tariff: An Economic Enquiry.* Melbourne: Melbourne University Press.

Bruchey, S. 1965. *The Roots of American Economic Growth.* London: Hutchinson.

Buchanan, J. M. 1965. "An Economic Theory of Clubs," *Economica* N.S. 32:1–14.

—— 1968. *The Demand and Supply of Public Goods.* Chicago: Rand McNally.

—— and G. Tullock. 1967. *The Calculus of Consent: Logical Foundations of Constitutional Democracy.* 2d printing. Ann Arbor: University of Michigan Press.

Clark, V. S. 1929. *History of Manufactures in the United States,* vol. 1: *1607–1860.* Reprinted. New York: Peter Smith, 1949.

Coase, R. 1960. "The Problem of Social Cost," *Journal of Law and Economics* 3:1–44.

Coben, S. 1959. "Northeastern Business and Radical Reconstruction: A Re-Examination," *Mississippi Valley Historical Review* 46:67–90.

Cohen, B. I. 1971. "The Use of Effective Tariffs," *Journal of Political Economy* 79:128–41.

Cole, A. H. 1926. *The American Wool Manufacture,* 2 vols. Cambridge: Harvard University Press.

Cole, A. H. 1938. *Wholesale Commodity Prices in the United States 1700–1861. Statistical Supplement: Actual Wholesale Prices of Various Commodities.* Cambridge: Harvard University Press.

—— and H. F. Williamson, 1941. *The American Carpet Manufacture: A History and an Analysis.* Cambridge: Harvard University Press.

Coleman, J. S. 1973. *The Mathematics of Collective Action.* Chicago: Aldine.

Coleman, R. J. 1963. *The Transformation of Rhode Island, 1790–1860.* Providence: Brown University Press.

Coppa, F. J. 1970. "The Italian Tariff and the Conflict Between Agriculture and Industry: The Commercial Policy of Liberal Italy, 1866–1922," *Journal of Economic History* 30(4):742–69.

Corden, M. W. 1966. " 'Protection.' The Vernon Report. Reviews of the Report of The Committee of Economic Enquiry," *Economic Record* 42(97):129–48.

—— 1971. *The Theory of Protection.* Oxford: Clarendon Press.

Crawford, J. G., assisted by N. Anderson and M. G. N. Morris. 1968. *Austra-*

*lian Trade Policy 1942–1966: A Documentary History.* Canberra: Australian National University Press.

Dales, J. H. 1966. *The Protective Tariff in Canada's Development: Eight Essays on Trade and Tariffs when Factors Move with Special Reference to Canadian Protectionism, 1870–1955.* Toronto: University of Toronto Press.

Danhof, C. 1969. *Change in Agriculture: The Northern United States, 1820–1870.* Cambridge: Harvard University Press.

David, P. 1970. "Learning by Doing and Tariff Protection: A Reconsideration of the Case of the Ante-Bellum United States Cotton Textile Industry," *Journal of Economic History* 30(3):521–601.

—— 1975. *Technical Choice, Innovation, and Economic Growth: Essays on American and British Experience in the Nineteenth Century.* London: Cambridge University Press.

Davis, L. E. et al. 1972. *American Economic Growth: An Economist's History of the United States.* New York: Harper & Row.

Davis, L., and D. North. 1970. "Institutional Change and American Economic Growth: A First Step Towards a Theory of Institutional Innovation," *Journal of Economic History* 30(1):131–49.

—— 1971. *Institutional Change and American Economic Growth.* Cambridge: Cambridge University Press.

Depew, C. M., ed. 1895. *One Hundred Years of American Commerce: A History of American Commerce by One Hundred Americans, with a Chronological Table of the Important Events of American Commerce Within the Past One Hundred Years.* New York: D. O. Haynes.

Desai, P. 1970. *Tariff Protection and Industrialization: A Study of the Indian Tariff Commission at Work.* New Delhi: Center for Advanced Studies, Delhi School of Economics.

Dewey, D. R. 1903. *Financial History of the United States.* New York: Longman, Green.

Dorfman, J. 1947. *The Economic Mind in American History,* vol. 1: *1606–1865.* London: George Harrap.

Downs, A. 1957. *The Economic Theory of Democracy.* New York: Harper & Row.

Edwards, R. C. 1970. "Economic Sophistication in Nineteenth Century Congressional Tariff Debates," *Journal of Economic History* 30(4):802–38.

Ehrmann, H. W. 1958. "The Comparative Study of Interest Groups," in H. W. Ehrmann, ed., *Interest Groups on Four Continents.* Pittsburgh: University of Pittsburgh Press for the International Political Science Association.

Evans, H. David. 1971. "Effects of Protection in a General Equilibrium Framework," *Review of Economics and Statistics* 52(2):147–56.

Fainsod, M., L. Gordon, and J. C. Palamountain, Jr. 1959. *Government and the American Economy.* New York: W. W. Norton.

Faulkner, H. U. 1951. *American Economic History.* New York: Harper & Row.

Fay, C. R. 1932. *The Corn Laws and Social England.* Cambridge: Cambridge University Press.

Fishlow, A., and P. David. 1961. "Optimal Resource Allocation in an Imperfect Market Setting," *Journal of Political Economy* 69:529–46.

Fogel, R. W., and S. L. Engerman. 1971. "A Model for the Explanation of Industrial Expansion During the Nineteenth Century: With an application to the American Iron Industry," chapter 11 in R. W. Fogel and S. L. Engerman, eds., *Reinterpretations of American Economic History*. New York: Harper & Row.

Gerschenkron, A. 1943. *Bread and Democracy in Germany*. New ed. New York: Howard Fertig.

Goldberger, A. S. 1964. *Econometric Theory*. New York: John Wiley.

Golob, E. O. 1944. *The Meline Tariff: French Agriculture and Nationalist Economic Policy*. New York: Columbia University Press.

Goss, J. D. 1897. *The History of Tariff Administration in the United States from Colonial Times to the McKinley Administrative Bill*, 2d. ed. Studies in History, Economics and Public Law, no. 2. New York: Columbia University Press. Rpt., New York: AMS Press, 1968.

Green, G. 1975. "Discussion" (of Bateman and Weiss, 1975), *Journal of Economic History* 35(1):212–15.

Grubel, H. G., and P. J. Lloyd. 1970. "Substitution and Two Concepts of Effective Rate of Protection: Comment," *American Economic Review* 60(5):1003–04.

Halévy, E. 1961. *A History of the English People in the Nineteenth Century*, vol. 3: *The Triumph of Reform 1830–1841*. Transl. E. I. Watkin. New York: Barnes and Noble.

Handlin, O., and M. F. Handlin. 1947. *Commonwealth: A Study of the Role of Government in the American Economy: Massachusetts, 1774–1861*. New York: New York University Press.

Hartz, L. B. 1948. *Economic Policy and Democratic Thought: Pennsylvania, 1776–1860*. Cambridge: Harvard University Press.

Hawke, G. L. 1975. "The United States Tariff and Industrial Protection in the Late Nineteenth Century," *Economic History Review* 27(1):84–99.

Hazard, B. E. 1921. *The Organization of the Boots and Shoe Industry in Massachusetts before 1875*. Reprint. New York: Johnson Reprint, 1968.

Heath, M. S. 1954. *Constructive Liberalism: The Role of the State in Economic Development in Georgia to 1860*. Cambridge: Harvard University Press.

Herring, E. Pendleton. 1929. *Group Representation Before Congress*. Baltimore: Johns Hopkins Press for The Brookings Institution.

Hoffman, R. F. 1969. "A Note on Demand for Public Goods," *Canadian Journal of Economics* 2(1):125–38.

Johnson, E. R. et al. 1915. *History of Domestic and Foreign Commerce in the United States*. 2 vols. Washington: Carnegie Institution.

Johnson, H. G. 1965. "The Costs of Protection and Self-Sufficiency," *Quarterly Journal of Economics* 79:356–72.

Johnson, H. G. 1970. "A New View of the Infant Industry Argument," in I. A.

McDougall and R. H. Snape, eds., *Studies in International Economics*. Amsterdam and London: North Holland.

Jones, F. M. 1937. *Middlemen in the Domestic Trade of the United States, 1800–1860*. Urbana: University of Illinois Press.

Jones, R. W. 1969. "Tariffs and Trade in General Equilibrium: Comment," *American Economic Review* 59(3):418–24.

Kindleberger, C. P. 1951. "Group Behavior and International Trade," *Journal of Political Economy* 59:30–46.

—— 1968. *International Economics*, 4th ed. Homewood, Ill.: R. D. Irwin.

—— 1975. "The Rise of Free Trade in Western Europe, 1820–1875," *Journal of Economic History* 35(1):20–55.

Kingaman, D., R. Vedder, and L. Galloway. 1974. "The Ames-Rosenberg Hypothesis Revisited," *Explorations in Economic History* 11(3):311–14.

Lebergott, S. 1964. *Manpower in Economic Growth: The American Record Since 1800*. New York: McGraw-Hill.

—— 1966. "Labor Force and Employment, 1800–1960," in National Bureau of Economic Research, Conference on Income and Wealth, *Studies in Income and Wealth*, vol. 30: *Output, Employment and Productivity in the United States after 1800*. New York: Columbia University Press.

Little, I., T. Scitovsky, and M. Scott. 1970. *Industry and Trade in Some Developing Countries. A Comparative Study*. Organization for Economic Co-Operation and Development. London, New York: Oxford University Press.

Lowi, T. J. 1964. "American Business, Public Policy, Case-Studies, and Political Theory" (Review of Bauer et al., 1963), *World Politics* 41(4):677–715.

Luxon, N. N. 1947. *Niles' Weekly Register, News Magazine of the Nineteenth Century*. Baton Rouge: Louisiana State University Press.

McCloskey, D. N. 1972. "The Enclosure of Open Fields: Preface to a Study of its Impact on the Efficiency of English Agriculture in the Eighteenth Century," *Journal of Economic History* 32(1):15–35.

McCormick, R. P. 1966. *The Second American Party System: Party Formation in the Jacksonian Era*. Chapel Hill: University of North Carolina Press.

McGouldrick, P. F. 1968. *New England Textiles in the Nineteenth Century: Profits and Investment*. Cambridge: Harvard University Press.

McGuire, M. 1974. "Group Size, Group Homogeneity, and the Aggregate Provision of a Pure Public God under Cournot Behavior," *Public Choice* 43:107–26.

McPherson, C. P. 1972. "Tariff Structures and Political Exchange," Ph.D. dissertation, University of Chicago.

Mikesell, R. F. 1952. *United States Economic Policy and International Relations*. New York: McGraw-Hill.

Mishan, E. J. 1971. "The Postwar Literature on Externalities: An Interpretative Essay," *Journal of Economic Literature* 9(1):1–28.

Moore, B., Jr. 1967. *Social Origins of Dictatorship and Democracy: Lord and Peasant in the Making of the Modern World*. Boston: Beacon Press.

Mussa, M. 1974. "Tariffs and the Distribuion of Income: The Importance of Specificity, Substitutability, and Intensity in the Short and Long Run," *Journal of Political Economy* 82(6):1191–204.

Nettels, C. P. 1962. *The Emergence of a National Economy, 1775–1815.* Vol. 2 of H. David et al., eds., *The Economic History of the United States.* New York: Harper & Row.

*Niles' Weekly Register.* 1811–1826. American Periodical Series, nos. 484–85 (vols. 1–29). Ann Arbor: University Microfilm.

Norman, N. 1974. "Effects of a Tariff Policy on Manufacturing Industries: A New Theoretical Approach," Paper delivered to the 1974 Meeting of Economists, Canberra, Australia.

North, D. C. 1960. "The United States Balance of Payments, 1790–1860," in National Bureau of Economic Research, *Studies in Income and Wealth,* vol. 24: *Trends in the American Economy in the Nineteenth Century.* Princeton: Princeton University Press.

——— 1966. *The Economic Growth of the United States 1790–1860.* New York: W. W. Norton.

——— 1971. "Institutional Change and Economic Growth," *Journal of Economic History* 31(1):118–25.

North, D. C., and P. R. Thomas, eds. 1968. *The Growth of the American Economy to 1860.* New York: Harper & Row.

Olmstead, A. L., and V. P. Goldberg. 1975. "Institutional Change and American Economic Growth: A Critique of Davis and North," *Explorations in Economic History* 12:193–210.

Olson, M., Jr. 1968. *The Logic of Collective Action: Public Goods and the Theory of Groups.* New York: Schocken Books.

Passell, P., and M. Schmundt. 1971. "Pre–Civil War Land Policy and the Growth of Manufacturing," *Explorations in Economic History* 9:35–48.

——— and G. Wright. 1972. "The Effects of Pre–Civil War Territorial Expansion on the Price of Slaves," *Journal of Political Economy* 80(6):1188–202.

Philip, P. 1969. "Differential Tariffs, Resource Allocation and Income Distribution," Ph.D. dissertation, Stanford University.

Pigou, A. G. 1906. *Protective and Preferential Import Duties.* Reprint. Series of Reprints of Scarce Works of Political Economy, no. 2. London: London School of Economics and Political Science.

Pincus, J. J. 1972. "A Positive Theory of Tariff Formation Applied to Nineteenth Century United States," Ph.D. dissertation, Stanford University.

——— 1975. "Pressure Groups and the Pattern of Tariffs," *Journal of Political Economy* 83(4):757–78.

Pitkin, T. 1835. *Statistical View of the Commerce of the United States of America.* Reprint. New York: Johnson Reprint, 1967.

Pope, C. 1971. Summary of Doctoral Dissertation. "The Impact of the Ante-Bellum Tariff on Income Distribution," *Journal of Economic History* 30(1):776–78.

—— 1972. "The Impact of the Ante-Bellum Tariff on Income Distributions," *Explorations in Economic History* 4:375–421.

Porter, G., and H. C. Livesay. 1971. *Merchants and Manufacturers: Studies in the Changing Structure of Nineteenth Century Marketing.* Baltimore and London: Johns Hopkins Press.

Post, J. D. 1974. "A Study in Meteorological and Trade Cycle History: The Economic Crisis Following the Napoleonic Wars," *Journal of Economic History* 34(2):315–49.

Poulson, B. W. 1969. "Estimate of the Value of Manufacturing Output in the Early Nineteenth Century," *Journal of Economic History* 29(3):521–25.

Pred. A. R. 1966. *The Spatial Dynamics of United States Urban-Industrial Growth, 1800–1914.* Cambridge: M.I.T. Press.

—— 1973. *Urban Growth and the Circulation of Information: The United States System of Cities, 1790–1840.* Cambridge: Harvard University Press.

Ransom, R. L. 1968. "British Policy and Colonial Growth: Some Implications of the Burden of the Navigation Acts," *Journal of Economic History* 28(3):427–35.

Rapoport, A. 1970. *N-Person Game Theory: Concepts and Applications.* Ann Arbor: University of Michigan Press.

Ratner, S. 1972. *The Tariff in American History.* New York: D. Van Nostrand.

Ray, E. J. 1974. "The Optimum Commodity Tariff and Tariff Rates in Developed and Less Developed Countries," *Review of Economics and Statistics* 56(3):369–7.

Riker, W. H. 1962. *The Theory of Political Coalitions.* New Haven and London: Yale University Press.

—— and P. C. Ordeshook. 1973. *An Introduction to Positive Political Theory.* Englewood Cliffs, N.J.: Prentice Hall.

Salisbury, R. H., ed. 1970. *Interest Group Politics in America.* Englewood Cliffs, N.J.: Prentice Hall.

Salisbury, R. H. and J. P. Heinz. 1970. "A Theory of Policy Analysis and Some Preliminary Applications," in Ira Sharkansky, ed., *Policy Analysis in Political Science,* Chicago: Markham.

Samuelson, P. A. 1954. "The Pure Theory of Public Expenditures," *Review of Economics and Statistics* 36:387–89.

Schattschneider, E. E. 1935. *Politics, Pressures and the Tariff: A Study in Free Private Enterprise in Pressure Politics, as shown in the 1929–1930 Revision of the Tariff.* Reprint. Hamden, Conn.: Archon Books, 1963.

Scheiber, H. N. 1969. *Ohio Canal Era: A Case Study of Government and the Economy, 1820–1861.* Athens, Ohio: Ohio University Press.

Schumpeter, J. A. 1951. "The Influence of Protective Tariffs on the Industrial Development of the United States," in R. V. Clemence, ed., *Essays of J. A. Schumpeter.* Cambridge: Addison-Wesley Press.

Sharkey, R. P. 1967. *Money, Class, and Party: An Economic Study of Civil War and Reconstruction.* Baltimore: Johns Hopkins University Press.

Shubik, M. 1971. "Pecuniary Externalities: A Game Theoretic Analysis," *American Economic Review*, 61(4):713–18.

Soligo, R., and J. J. Stern. 1965. "Tariff Protection, Import Substitution and Investment Efficiency," *Pakistan Development Review* 5:249–69.

Stanwood, E. 1903. *American Tariff Controversies in the Nineteenth Century*. 2 vols. Boston and New York: Houghton Mifflin.

Stigler, G. J. 1970. "The Theory of Economic Regulation," *Bell Journal of Economics and Management Science* 1(3):3–21.

—— 1974. "Free Riders and Collective Action: An Appendix to Theories of Economic Regulation," *Bell Journal of Economics and Management Science* 5(2):359–65.

Taussig, F. W. 1931. *The Tariff History of the United States*, 8th rev. ed. with Introduction by David M. Chalmers. New York: Capricorn Books, 1964.

Taylor, G. R. 1951. *The Transportation Revolution 1815–1860*. Vol. 4 of H. David et al., eds., *The Economic History of the United States*. New York: Harper & Row.

Temin, P. 1964. *Iron and Steel in Nineteenth Century America*. Cambridge: M.I.T Press.

Terrill, T. E. 1973. *The Tariff, Politics, and American Foreign Policy, 1874–1901*. Westport, Conn. and London: Greenwood Press.

Theil, H. 1967. *Economics and Information Theory*. Amsterdam: North Holland; Chicago: Rand McNally.

Thomas, R. P. 1965. "A Quantitative Approach to the Study of the Effects of British Imperial Policy Upon Colonial Welfare," *Journal of Economic History* 25:615–38.

—— 1968. "British Imperial Policy and the Economic Interpretation of the American Revolution," *Journal of Economic History* 28(3):436–40.

Thorp, W. L. 1926. *Business Annals: United States, England, France, Germany, Austria, Russia, Sweden, Netherlands, Italy, Argentina, Brazil, Canada, South Africa, Australia, India, Japan, China*. New York: Columbia University Press for National Bureau of Economic Research.

Tirrell, S. R. 1951. *German Agrarian Politics After Bismarck's Fall: The Formation of the Farmer's League*. New York: Columbia University Press.

Travis, W. P. 1968. "The Effective Rate of Protection and the Question of Labor Protection in the United States," *Journal of Political Economy* 76(3):443–61.

—— 1971. "A Critical Rehabilitation of Effective Protection Theory," in H. G. Grubel and H. G. Johnson, eds., *Effective Tariff Protection*. Proceedings of a Conference Sponsored by the General Agreement on Tariffs and Trade and the Graduate Institute of International Studies. Geneva.

Tryon, R. M. 1917. *Household Manufactures in the United States 1640–1860*. Reprint. New York: A. M. Kelley, 1966.

Truman, D. 1951. *The Governmental Process: Political Interests and Public Opinion*. New York: Alfred A. Knopf.

Tullock, G. 1959. "Some Problems of Majority Voting," *Journal of Political Economy* 67:571–79.

U.S. Congress. 1854. *Public Statutes At Large*, vol. 1. Boston: Little and Brown.

—— 1854. *Annals of Congress of the United States*. Washington: Gales & Seaton.

—— 76th Cong., 3d Sess. 1940. Temporary National Economic Committee. *Industrial Concentration and Tariffs*, by C. L. James, assisted by E. C. Welch and G. Arneson. Monograph 10: *Investigation of Concentration of Economic Power*. Washington: GPO.

U.S. House of Representatives. 16th Cong., 2d Sess. 1821. Committee on Manufactures. *Protection to Manufactures*. Report 609: *American State Papers, Finance*, vol. 3. Washington: Gales & Seaton, 1834.

—— 17th Cong., 1st Sess. 1822. *Duties–Ad Valorem and Specific*. Report 643: *American State Papers, Finance*, vol. 3. Washington: Gales & Seaton, 1834.

—— 17th Cong., 2d Sess. 1823. *Digest of Manufactures, Supplementary Return*. Report 675: *American State Papers, Finance*, vol. 4. Washington: Gales & Seaton, 1858.

—— 18th Cong., 1st Sess. 1824. *List of Factories in Each State*. Report 691: *American State Papers, Finance*, vol. 4. Washington: Gales & Seaton, 1858.

——20th Cong., 1st Sess. 1828. Mallary for the Committee on Manufactures. *On the Subject of the Tariff, or Regulating Duties on Imports*. Report 843: *American State Papers, Finance*, vol. 5. Washington: Gales & Seaton, 1858.

—— 42d Cong., 2d Sess. 1872. *Special Report on the Customs-Tariff Legislation of the United States* (with appendices), by E. Young. Ex. Doc. 109, Serial 1512. Washington: GPO.

U. S. Senate. 17th Cong., 1st Sess. 1823. *Digest of Manufactures*. Report 662: *American State Papers, Finance*, vol. 4. Wshington: Gales & Seaton, 1858.

—— 51st Cong., 2d. Sess. 1891. *Rates of Duties on Imports into the United States from 1789 to 1890, Inclusive, Together With Statistics Relating Thereto*. Report 2130, Serial 2827. Washington: GPO.

U.S. Treasury. 1816. Secy. Dallas to House, 14th Cong., 1st Sess. *Tariff of Duties on Imports*. Report 470: *American State Papers, Finance*, vol. 3. Washington: Gales & Seaton, 1834.

—— 1819. To House, 16th Cong., 2d Sess. *Imports for the Year Ending September 30, 1819*. Report 238: *American State Papers, Commerce and Navigation*, vol. 2. Washington: Gales & Seaton, 1834.

—— 1821. To Senate, 17th Cong., 2d Sess. *Commerce and Navigation for the Year Ending September 30, 1821*. Report 246: *American State Papers, Commerce and Navigation*, vol. 2. Washington: Gales & Seaton, 1834.

—— 1825. To Senate, 18th Cong., 2d Sess. *Letter from Secretary of Treasury Transmitting Statement of the Commerce and Navigation of the U.S. During the Year Ending on the 30th of September, 1824*. Senate Doc. 23, Serial 110. Washington: Gales & Seaton.

U.S. Treasury. 1826. To House, 19th Cong., 1st Sess. *Commerce and Naviga-tion of the United States, for the Year Ending on 30 September, 1825.* H. R. Doc. 148, Serial 139. Washington: Gales & Seaton.

—— 1833. Secy. McLane to House, 22d Cong., 1st Sess. *Documents Relative to the Manufactures in the United States.* H.R. Doc. 308, Serials 222–23. Washington: Duff Green.

—— 1846. Secy. Walker to House, 29th Cong., 2d Sess. *Weighers, Gaugers and Measurers.* Ex. Doc. 25, Serial 499. Washington.

Vernon, R. 1966. "International Investment and International Trade in the Product Cycle," *Quaterly Journal of Economics* 80(2):190–207.

Vidal, G. 1974. *Burr: A Novel.* New York: Random House.

Ware, C. 1931. *Early New England Cotton Manufacture: A Study in Industrial Beginnings.* Reprint. New York: Johnson Reprint, 1966.

Warren, G. F., and F. A. Pearson. 1932. *Wholesale Prices for 213 Years, 1720–1932.* Memoir 142. Ithaca, N.Y.: Cornell University Agricultural Ex-perimental Station.

Weitzman, M. L. 1974. "Free Access vs. Private Ownership as Alternative Sys-tems for Managing Common Property," *Journal of Economic Theory* 8:225–34.

Wilkinson, J. R. 1960. *Politics and Trade Policy.* Washington: Public Affairs Press.

Williamson, J. G. 1974. *Late Nineteenth-Century American Development: A General Equilibrium History.* Cambridge: Cambridge University Press.

Wright, C. W. 1910. *Wool Growing and the Tariff: A Study in the Economic History of the United States.* Cambridge: Harvard University Press.

Wright, D.C. 1900. *History and Growth of the United States Census.* Reprint. New York: Johnson Reprint, 1966.

Zeigler, H. 1964. *Interest Groups in American Society.* Englewood Cliffs, N.J.: Prentice Hall.

# Author Index

# General Index

Adams, John, 52n
Adams, John Q., 10, 22, 127
Adjustment assistance, 76n, 79
Aggregate benefits and contributions, 113, 123; *see also* "Efficiency approach"
Aggregation, *see* Coase-aggregation; Groups; Product groups
Agriculture: depressed, 19, 74–77; duties, 13, 64, 70; prosperous, 18; *see also* Derived demand; Sectional interests
Ales: degree of protection, 95; exported, 30; import ratio, 32; infant industry, 38
Alexander, Adam R., 70n
Almy and Brown, 27n, 29, 97
Alum: duties, 37; imports, 31; infant manufacture, 38
Amendments, 68–71
American Medical Association, 212–22
American Society for Domestic Manufactures, 52n, 56
American System, 1, 21, 72–73, 75, 97, 180; *see also* Derived demand; Internal improvements; National Market; Revenue; Sectional interests
American valuation, 36
Apparel, *see* Garments
Asymmetry: adjustment assistance, 76n, 79; in infant protection, 176–77, 179; leverage, 154; in reactions, 148, 152, 180; in transactions costs, 105, 110n; *see also* Risk aversion; Threshold of action
Auction sales, 19, 53, 56, 58, 96; *see also* Dumping
Augers, low surplus, 94

Balance-of-trade theory, 76; *see also* Comparative advantage; Surplus population
Baldwin, Henry, 52, 64–66
Baltimore: industrial structure, 16, 24; protectionism, 53, 56, 59

Banking, 1, 19–20, 30, 79; *see also* Economic conditions
Bank of the United States II, 19–20
Barbour, Phillip P., 68n, 74n
Bargaining, *see* Logrolling
Bargaining costs: bias in, 105, 110n; by-product theory, 121–22; communications costs, 48, 58–59; revelation problem, 133, 137; *see also* Coase-aggregation; Cohesion; Committees; Communications costs; Concentration of benefits; Congress; "Efficiency approach"; Factions; Free riding; Industrial concentration; Numbers; Quasi-individuals; Sidepayments; Threshold of action; Transactions costs
Bastiat, Frederic, 129
Bedford memorials, 57
Beer, *see* Ales
Benton, Thomas H., 70n
Bills and acts: sources of, 66; *see also various tariff bills and acts*
Bismark, Otto, 129–30
Blocking, 64n, 134–36; *see also* Coase-aggregation; Sidepayments
Books: degree of protection, 95; import ratio, 38; incentive to lobby, 59; memorials, 57; not infant industry, 38; secure duty, 65; Senate amendments, 69
Boots and shoes: exports, 30; heavily protected, 95; imports, 31; location, 29; Revolutionary Army's, 32
Boston: capitalists, 29; industrial structure, 16, 24; manufactures damaged, 60; memorials, 57; tanneries, 29; tariff advocates, 59; travel to New York from, 58; woolen manufacturers meet, 59
Brass manufactures: aggregated, 140; import ratio, 32
Bread, exported, 30; heavily protected, 95

Republicans, 8, 11, 20
Retaliation, 78
Revelation problem, 133, 137; *see also* Free
  riding; Voluntary associations
Revenue: adequacy, 21, 65*n*, 66, 72, 91,
  103; duties, 12, 43–44; fluctuations,
  178–80; ignored, 146–47; maximization,
  11, 179; motive, 9–11, 20, 36–37, 110,
  149; partial equilibrium, 85; prohibitive
  duties, 146*n*; uses, 20, 72*n*; *see also*
  American System; Land, sales
Revolutionary Army, 32
Rhode Island: ginghams, 96*n*; incorporation
  laws, 26
Rifles: firearms, 31, 32; low surplus, 94
Risk aversion, 75, 148, 152; incorporation
  laws 26, 33; working proprietors, 97–98
Rum: exports, 30; heavily protected, 95;
  incentive to lobby, 59; *see also* Spirits
Russian sheeting: duty, 37; *see also* Sailduck

Saddlery, *see* Bridle bits, memorials
Sailduck: lobbying in *1828*, 50–51; *see* also
  Russian sheeting
Salt: degree of protection, 95; duties, 10;
  memorials, 53
Saltpeter: degree of protection, 95; surplus,
  95
Satinet, *see* Cotton cloth; Textiles; Wool
  cloth
Say, J. B., 53*n*, 76
Scientific tariff, 177*n*
Second-best policies, 7, 172
Sectional interests: in debates, 47, 77–79; in
  early tariffs, 9; representative democracy,
  126–27, 157; theory outlined, 4, 61–64,
  105–10; theory tested, 64*n*, 168; *see also*
  American System
Sections of United States in *1820*, 15
Senate, 69–70, 156
Seventeenth amendment, 7*n*, 128
Shipbuilding: assisted, 28; duties paid, 45;
  location, 28
Shipping, 18, 19
Sidepayments: in Coase-aggregation, 109;
  in defining groups, 105–7, 110; example,
  125; sectional interests, 107; *see also*
  Transactions costs

Sieves, degree of protection, 95; *see also*
  Iron
Silks: assisted, 33; duties, 11, 14, 65; Senate
  amendments, 69
Silver question, 13
Silverware: as infant, 38; memorials, 58
Size of an industry, *see* Establishments;
  Numbers; Output size
Slate: duty secured, 65; memorials, 53
Slater, Samuel: labor system, 24; lobbyist,
  51; on proprietors, 98, 152*n*
Slavery, 11*n*, 16*n*, 78–79
Small-country assumption, 41
Smith, A., 76, 110*n*
Soap, *see* Tallow manufactures
Social contract theory, 122
Society for Encouragement of Domestic
  Manufactures, 54, 56
Society for National Industry, 51, 56
Solidarity bloc, 129–30
South: opposes tariff, 6, 50–57, 68;
  sacrificed, 78–79; *see also* Sectional in-
  terests; Slavery
South Carolina, 10
Spatial competition, 83–85, 96–103; *see*
  *also* Natural protection
Specialization: industrial (*see* Geographical
  concentration); international (*see* Com-
  parative advantage; Surplus population)
Specie: from West, 29*n*, 97; sources, 76, 81
Specific duties, to conceal high rates, 43
Specific factors of production, 152–54;
  capital, 97; prices, 89–91; in tariff for-
  mation theory, 152–54; *see also* Concen-
  tration of benefits; Proprietorial surplus;
  Voluntary associations
Spirits: cider, 30; debated, 61; duty, 11;
  heavily protected, 95; Memorials, 58; *see*
  *also* Rum
Standard Industrial Classification, 140
Statistical illusion, 161
Steam: navigation, 29; power, 27
Steel: duties, 12, 14; lobbying, 50
Stevens, Thaddeus, 179*n*
Strategic behavior, 112–19; *see also* Free
  riding
Strong, James, 74*n*
Structural unemployment, 19, 74–77

## DATE DUE

| | | | |
|---|---|---|---|
| | | | |
| | | | |
| | | | |
| | | | |
| | | | |
| | | | |
| | | | |
| | | | |
| | | | |
| | | | |
| | | | |
| | | | |
| | | | |
| | | | |
| | | | |
| | | | |
| | | | |

HIGHSMITH 45-220